Sierra Nevada

The Sierra Nevada in
Its Geographical Setting
(map by Bill Nelson)

VERNA R. JOHNSTON

Sierra Nevada

The Naturalist's Companion

Revised Edition

Photographs by the Author
Drawings by Carla J. Simmons

UNIVERSITY OF CALIFORNIA PRESS
BERKELEY   LOS ANGELES   LONDON

University of California Press
Berkeley and Los Angeles, California

University of California Press, Ltd.
London, England

© 1998 by
The Regents of the University of California

Library of Congress Cataloging-in-Publication Data

Johnston, Verna R.
    Sierra Nevada: the naturalist's companion / Verna R.
Johnston.—Rev. ed.
        p.   cm.
    Includes bibliographical references and index.
    ISBN 0-520-20936-2 (cloth: alk. paper)
    1. Natural history—Sierra Nevada (Calif. and
Nev.)   I. Title.
QH104.5.S54J64   1998
508.794'4—dc 21   97-25659

Printed in the United States of America
9   8   7   6   5   4   3   2   1

The paper used in this publication meets the minimum
requirements of American National Standards for
Information Sciences—Permanence of Paper for Printed
Library Materials, ANSI Z39.48-1984.

*To Amber Ellis, my field companion
on countless Sierra Nevada expeditions,
and to all the far-sighted people
who fought through the years to preserve
the integrity of this inimitable
mountain range.*

CONTENTS

PREFACE AND ACKNOWLEDGMENTS

THE SIERRA NEVADA RANKS as one of the world's most magnificent mountain ranges. Much has happened to it in the quarter of a century since my earlier book, *Sierra Nevada,* took the reader on a slow-paced natural history trip up and over the range.

This completely new version, *Sierra Nevada: The Naturalist's Companion,* retains all the eye-opening discoveries of early naturalists in wilder times and updates thoroughly the changes of recent decades.

The material has come from many sources: my own field experiences during more than forty years in the Sierra; the field observations of others, from John Muir and zoologists in the University of California natural history surveys of the early 1900s to current ecologists, geneticists, entomologists, botanists, and foresters; and that vast body of accumulated knowledge—the literature.

The generously given ideas and suggestions of many fellow biologists have gone into both the first and current versions of this book. I am grateful to Daniel I. Axelrod, Harold H. Biswell, Wayne Harrison, Richard J. Hartesveldt, Lloyd G. Ingles, Elizabeth McClintock, G. Ledyard Stebbins, and many unnamed others.

Special thanks go to friends who made the final product possible—Jeanette Brown for word processing; Gwen Serriere for assembling the illustrations; and Anna Beck, Dolores and Vern Harley, Ann Horvath, Norm Milsner, Arlene and Roger Mueller, Jan Mullen, Betty Ann Prescott, May Waldroup, Pixie Waldroup, and other friends for their support. My editors, Doris Kretschmer and Rose Vekony, were helpful all the way. Wally McGalliard took the author's photo.

The nomenclature in this book is taken from the following authorities:

Common and Scientific Names of Fishes from the United States and Canada. 5th ed. American Fisheries Society, Special Publication 20. Bethesda, Md., 1991.

Hickman, James C., ed. *The Jepson Manual: Higher Plants of California.* Berkeley: University of California Press, 1993.

Jameson, E. W., Jr., and Hans J. Peeters. *California Mammals.* Berkeley: University of California Press, 1988.

Peterson, Roger Tory. *A Field Guide to Western Birds.* Boston: Houghton Mifflin, 1990.

Stebbins, Robert C. *A Field Guide to Western Reptiles and Amphibians.* Boston: Houghton Mifflin, 1985.

Storer, Tracy I., and Robert L. Usinger. *Sierra Nevada Natural History.* Berkeley: University of California Press, 1963.

The index includes scientific names, in parentheses, following each common name.

Sources for quotations and anecdotes in the text may be inferred from the context and easily found in the reference list, which is organized by chapter. Only when a source is not immediately inferable from the context is a note citation given.

The book aims to offer such pleasurable, informative reading that it will be hard to put down, and will bring an increased awareness of the priceless heritage of the Sierra Nevada and the urgent need to preserve its biodiversity.

Verna Johnston
Carmel, California

INTRODUCTION

ON CLEAR COLD WINTER mornings in the Central Valley of California, you can look west to the rolling outline of the Coast Ranges, east to the snow-covered crest of the Sierra Nevada. It is roughly one hundred miles from the valley floor to the closest Sierran summits; at this distance, the mighty mountains stand low against the skyline.

It was a view much like this that inspired the naming of the Sierra. The de Anza expedition of Spanish soldiers, settlers, and friars that plodded north from Mexico into the "wilds" of central California in 1776 included a Franciscan missionary, Pedro Font. While exploring a hill in the San Francisco inner bay region one April morning, Font looked off to the northeast. "We saw an immense treeless plain," he wrote in his diary; ". . . at the opposite end of this extensive plain, about forty leagues off, we saw a great snow-covered range [*una gran sierra nevada*], which seemed to me to run from south-southeast to north-northwest."[1]

On his map, in a location east of the wide plain, Font sketched in the contours of a long jagged range and drew at its crest overlapping cumulus clouds terminating in peaks. Adjacent he printed the words SIERRA NEVADA—the first named and mapped record of this singular North American range.

California Topography
(map by Carla J. Simmons, based on Jameson
and Peeters, *California Mammals*, p. 4)

The Sierra Nevada is the middle range of three nearly parallel major mountain barriers that extend roughly north-south in the western United States. A thousand miles to the east rise the Rocky Mountains, which are separated from the Sierra's eastern flanks by the Great Basin desert—an arid, desolate land whitened by salt-encrusted lakes, interspersed with sharp-peaked mountains whose lower slopes harbor spotty forests of pinyon pine and juniper. In the opposite direction, approximately 180 miles west of the Sierra Nevada summits, the Coast Ranges fringe the Pacific Ocean. Between Coast and Sierra lies the Central Valley of California, most of it less than 100 feet above sea level. Originally an arid semigrassland, the valley is today a fertile farming and fruit-growing beneficiary of Sierran waters.

To the north the Sierra Nevada merges with the Cascade Range just south of Lassen National Park, continuing the middle mountain barrier. The two ranges are similar in vegetation at their border, but show their different geological origins increasingly as they spread apart: the volcanic Cascades extend northward to form the picturesque cones of Mounts Rainier, Hood, Adams, and Jefferson in Oregon and Washington, while the predominantly granitic Sierra Nevada stretches southward along the eastern California border to culminate in one of the boldest mountain escarpments in the world. Farther to the south, the Sierra Nevada bends in to meet the Coast Ranges near Tehachapi Pass.

The Cascades and the Rockies are more extensive mountain chains, cut up into many separate ranges. The Sierra Nevada stands alone as the longest, highest single-block mountain range in the United States. It is slightly over 400 miles long and 50 to 80 miles wide. Pushed up as a single tilted block of rock from a "hinge" in the Central Valley, it slopes gently on the west, steeply on the east. From heights of 9,000 feet in the north, its peaks rise to 13,000 feet in the central region and to the 14,495-foot climax of Mount Whitney in the southern Sierra. Around Whitney, twelve peaks of more than 14,000 feet pierce the sky, some of them dropping off precipitously nearly two miles to the Great Basin desert below.

This great eastern escarpment ranks as one of the awesome geological features of its kind in the world, a two-mile-high wall formed primarily by a monumental uplift of the Sierran block along a fault in the earth's crust. Sierran geologist François Matthes has recounted that "Albrecht Penck, the dean of European geomorphologists, upon viewing this stupendous mountain front, was visibly affected by its grandeur and begged his guide to leave him for several hours that he might contemplate and study it in solitude."[2]

The Sierra Nevada in its present form is a young range. Along with the Rocky Mountains and Cascades, the Alps and Himalayas, it rose to its current heights in the Tertiary mountain building, 2 million to 25 million years ago. Its geologically new sawtoothed profiles contrast sharply with the rounded, worn-down contours of more ancient chains such as the Appalachians of the eastern United States, which are more than 250 million years old.

Many of the range's most striking features owe their character to the Pleistocene glaciers that blanketed the subalpine heights and flowed down the river canyons, sculpturing cliffs, spires, and domes, turning broad river valleys into deep-cut U-shaped valleys with leaping waterfalls, and pocketing the high country with numberless little rock-bound lakes, or tarns. The plants and animals that came to thrive in this unique complex of soil, rock, climate, and topography show a diversity unusual in temperate-zone coniferous forests. Along with the variety emerged a magnetic beauty.

Neither of these was lost on John Muir. From the day in 1868 when the young Scottish naturalist walked into the Sierra Nevada until his death in 1914, he sang the praises of the range. From its tawny foothills through its pine and fir forests to timberline, from its cone-dropping tree squirrels to black bears met as fellow berry-pickers at brambles, the Sierra was for him a radiant, unpredictable, lively world. As he swung in a Douglas fir at the height of a mountain storm, as he slid down into Yosemite Valley on a snow avalanche, as he listened to the song of the dipper on a wild winter morning, as he lay in a mountain meadow watching bees pollinate flowers, Muir felt the joyous pulse of the mountains: "And after ten years spent in the heart of it, rejoicing and wondering, bathing in its glorious floods of light, seeing the sunbursts of morning among the icy peaks, the noon-day radiance on the trees and rocks and snow, the flush of the alpen-glow, and a thousand dashing waterfalls with their marvelous abundance of irised spray, it still seems to me above all others the Range of Light, the most divinely beautiful of all the mountain-chains I have ever seen."[3]

Muir's writings unveiled the range to the world. His militant fight to preserve its natural beauty was a major influence in the critical period around the turn of the century, when national parks and forest reserves were new ideas that hung by tenuous threads. The Sierra Club, which Muir helped found in 1892, has kept a vigilant eye on trespass of the range's treasures ever since.

Today's Sierra Nevada contains three national parks (Yosemite, Sequoia, and Kings Canyon), one national monument (Devil's Postpile), nine national forests, and numerous state parks. The high southern Sierra above 8,000 feet is a vast panoramic wilderness, the roadless haven of summer backpackers and family burro parties. Lower, easier passes broach the northern and central crest, following trails earlier trod by Indians and pioneers, now crossed by highways. A trip up and over these cross-mountain roads from June through October unfolds in a succession of changing scenes, different on each pass but similar in the plant belts appearing at equivalent levels.

All high mountains of the world have plant belts, or "life zones," that vary with elevation. The zones are actually intricate communities of plants and animals that live at altitudes where temperature, moisture, soil, slope, and other environmental conditions meet their needs—and where circumstances of history and evolution have put them. In the Sierra all but the highest communities are accessible by road.

For a close look at the wildlife communities of the range, we shall climb up and over: up the western slope through foothill woodlands of gray pine and oak and thickets of chaparral, into the midmountain forests of ponderosa and sugar pine and groves of giant sequoias, higher still through red firs and lodgepole pines to subalpine forests that lead to timberline, beyond trees to alpine crests, and then down the steep east side into a land mightily different from the one where we began.

One

THE SUN SHINES THREE hundred days out of the year, on average, in the western foothills of the Sierra Nevada. In winter, when the Central Valley below lies locked in fog, sunshine is frequent above the 1,000-foot level; the remainder of the year it is practically guaranteed. Foothill plants are well adapted to their sunny habitats. From lower levels of 200 to 400 feet, where the foothills begin, to their merger with the midmountain forests several thousand feet above, they form two distinct plant communities—foothill woodland and chaparral. Through a belt of hills and ravines running the length of the range, twenty or more straight-line miles east to west, these two communities appear and disappear and intermingle as tightly packed shrub jungles of chaparral alternating irregularly with the open stands of trees and grasses that form the woodlands.

The role of grasses is a unique and historically interesting one in the foothills. In summer, grasses roll in nearly continuous golden-brown waves up the gentle lower slopes from the valley, under the oaks and pine of the woodlands, around the slanting tombstonelike rocks, past the chaparral, all the way to the denser shade of the midmountain forests at 3,000 feet or higher.

This is the hot season. The sun bears down unimpeded day after day, bringing temperatures mostly in the nineties and above. The relative humidity hovers around 20 percent. In this dry, hot atmosphere the woodland grasses and forbs (broad-leaved herbs) drop their seeds early but retain luminous stalks and empty seed cases that sway in the parching breezes all summer. To the casual eye this low growth looks like a well-adapted native ground cover. Well adapted it is; but natural as the ground cover appears, 50 to 90 percent of it is alien. From the time of the Spanish missions, California's grasslands have been prime targets of foreign invasions.

It was probably a nearly virgin flora that greeted the eyes of Fray Junípero Serra and his companions when in May 1769 they reached San Diego to begin the conquest of Alta California for Holy Church and the Spanish crown. The few previous explorers had arrived by sea and made only transient landings. "The followers of Saint Francis brought with them flocks and herds, and in the careful preparations for their expedition they had been particularly charged to provide themselves with a store of seeds of useful plants."[1]

Step by step the long chain of missions stretched northward until the last one was founded near Sonoma in the San Francisco Bay region in 1823. "Everywhere, one of the first proceedings was the planting of gardens and the sowing of fields; and the neophytes, as they gathered in, were taught to be farmers and herdsmen, so that each mission speedily became a hive of industry, based on its wide acres and countless herds." This was the beginning of the end for the native grasses that once covered California's valleys and foothills, the fields "tall in the wind" which Spanish horsemen called the finest pasture, enough for all their flocks and herds. The native grasses, both perennial and annual, along with the wildflowers that splashed yellow, purple, and orange over the hills in spring, formed a uniquely Californian range. Throughout the centuries they had evolved on western soils; they had held their own against the sharp teeth of antelope, deer, elk, and rodents; they had withstood the vagaries of the climate. They had never met the degree of grazing pressure and seed invasion that came with the advent of white men.

The invading seeds arrived in the wool of sheep, in hay carried aboard ships for cattle feed, in droppings of domestic animals, in

Foothill Woodland
(map by Carla J. Simmons)

clothing, on implements, mixed with the seeds of garden crops. Once established on the trampled ground around missions or at the edges of fields cleared for farming, the exotic grasses and weeds held on until opportunity favored their spread into the native vegetation of the open range. Nearly all of the invading plants were annuals. Each year they would bear fruit and die, leaving buried in the soil seeds that could resist extreme dryness and germinate when the rains finally came.

Most of the native perennial grasses were well adapted to withstand drought. Like the foothill pine bluegrass (*Poa scabrella*), they could remain dormant from May to November, when rains would stimulate the root clumps to sprout anew. But consecutive years of low rainfall weakened them severely. Heavy grazing reduced further their ability to tolerate drought. When excessive grazing by thousands of longhorn Spanish cattle and long-legged sheep combined with rainless years, as in the great drought of 1828–1830, the native perennials succumbed by the millions, and the great wave of invading plants began its takeover.

Developed in lands with a climate similar to that of their new home in the foothills, the immigrants thrived in competition with the natives. Some of them produced good forage; some became pests; most of them—grasses like wild oats (*Avena*), the bromes (*Bromus*), and foxtails (*Hordeum*), and legumes such as bur clover (*Medicago hispida*)—had the advantage of being self-fertilizing. Those first, well-adapted individuals that moved into available niches quickly built up large, homogeneous, highly reproductive populations. Through occasional outbreeding, they produced enough genetic variability to infiltrate a wide range of diverse habitats. During the mission period, aliens as common now as ripgut grass (*Bromus rigidus*), foxtail grass, bur clover, wild oats, star thistle (*Centaurea*), and filaree (*Erodium*) spread over the state. Gold rush days and the increasing arrival of travelers from all parts of the globe brought additional plant introductions, some deliberate, many inadvertent.

The livestock boom of 1850–1870 produced more domestic droves than had ever before descended on the burgeoning state's grasslands, peaking at 3 million head of cattle and close to 6 million sheep. They fed virtually wherever they pleased. The range country was impossible to fence in those pre–barbed wire days, and the state's publicly owned lands were wide open to whoever got there first. Sheep migrating up the foothills to the higher Sierra Nevada meadows for summer forage sometimes nibbled the ground bare en route.

All abuse seemed to aid the invading annuals at the expense of the natives. The kind of constant grazing pressure and trampling applied by large numbers of domestic animals proved entirely different from that of wild animals such as antelope and elk. The native grasses, never having been exposed to such grazing pressure, were not adapted to it. Here the introduced Mediterranean annuals, which had evolved over thousands of years in direct association with agricultural peoples' flocks and herds, held the advantage. There was soon hardly a piece of virgin grassland left in California. (In recent years a few, such as the Nature Conservancy's Jepson Prairie, have been preserved.)

Today a cosmopolitan grass and forb population from Europe, Asia, South Africa, Australia, South America, and the eastern United States dominates in foothill grasslands: nearly four hundred foreigners that have taken up apparently permanent residence in the state. The most common central foothill grasses are now annuals—the slender wild oat, soft chess (*Bromus mollis*), ripgut grass, common foxtail, red brome (*Bromus rubens*)—and they all are aliens. Among the prominent forbs, broadleaf filaree, bur clover, star thistle, annual clovers (*Trifolium*), and tarweeds predominate. Of these only the last two are native. Many native wildflowers hold their own, but new species are still arriving. Even the specialized niche of the native tarweeds may be in danger of being usurped.

The tarweeds (*Hemizonia, Holocarpha*) spread a basal rosette of leaves at the surface of the ground in early spring, at the time when the spring annuals emerge. As the neighboring plants continue through their full blooming cycle, the tarweeds lapse into dormancy. In late summer, during drought and severe heat and in fields long since brown with the dried annuals, tarweeds resume growth at a rapid pace, shooting up viscid stalks and heads of resinous flowers. A more specific adaptation to foothill habitat would be hard to find, yet the tarweed's niche is, in some places, being stolen by yellow star thistle, an introduction from Europe. In the foothills the two plants often occupy complementary niches, the tarweed on relatively sterile soils that have been grazed but not cultivated, and yellow star thistle in bottomlands that frequently have been previously cultivated.

Native or introduced, these hardy plants have made themselves at home in one of the rarer climates of the world. Hot dry summers and cool wet winters are unusual around the globe. They occur sparingly on all continents, principally in small areas between 30° and 42° latitude. Within this range lie the countries bordering the Mediterranean Sea—hence the term "Mediterranean climate."

The western foothills of the Sierra Nevada follow a Mediterranean climatic rhythm that is different from anything in North America east of the Sierra. From May to October scarcely a drop of rain touches the land. Birds finish nesting early. Streams dry up. Flowers wither. Woodland trees nod quietly above the golden grasses. Only the tarweeds break the dormancy of late summer, thrusting pungent yellow heads above the baked earth. The hills are peaceful, quiet, warm, dry.

With the approach of November, the rains come: sometimes gently, soaking in every drop, sometimes in drenching downpours, running brown in the newly awakened streams. Between November and May the land gathers all the moisture it will get to carry the plants through the long dry summer. In the foothills this amount varies from eleven inches in the lower mesas to about forty inches in the higher, more forested woodlands. Snow whitens the higher hills for a few brief days most winters, but it is copious rain that kindles the new life.

Within weeks after the first rains, green shoots sprout everywhere. In wet years a layer of green velvet covers much of the summer's old brown by Christmas. Made up of leaf rosettes of filaree, basal leaves of the soap plant (*Chlorogalum pomeridianum*), and other herbs, it is the promise of flowers to come. Growth slows during the cold of December, January, and February, when night temperatures may hover around freezing. But with the onset of warmer weather in early March everything that grows comes alive.

Native wildflowers burst through the warming earth. Goldfields (*Baeria chrysostoma*), one of the pioneers, spreads its three-inch-high heads over the slopes in a golden blanket, carrying pansy-faced Johnny-jump-ups (*Viola douglasii*) and the curious closed flowers of butter-and-eggs (*Orthocarpus*) in its mantle. Tidytips (*Layia fremontii*) wave white-tipped yellow rays among fields of popcorn flowers (*Plagiobothrys*), birds-eye gilia (*Gilia tricolor*), and the miniature magenta clovers (*Trifolium*). The first of the spring succession of brodiaeas, blue dicks (*Brodiaea pulchella*), break ground, sending up foot-high barren stalks topped by clusters of bluish purple waxy flowers.

Today California poppies (*Eschscholzia californica*) no longer flame the hills with the massive color displays that inspired the early name *tierra del fuego,* land of fire; but their brilliant orange still brightens undisturbed roadsides, open flats, and slopes. Lupines are frequent companions, unfurling symmetrical racemes of seemingly endless shades of blue, bluish purple, and ivory. (The index of *The Jepson Manual of Higher Plants of California* requires nearly three tall columns to list the state's lupines.)

Perhaps the most spectacular of the early wave of wildflowers is meadowfoam (*Limnanthes alba*), which springs out of the pools and wet meadows of the foothills, literally like a white foam. So close together do its flowers grow that at a distance they seem more like a snowdrift than thousands of white petals lined with bright pink nerves. Distinctively Californian, meadowfoam requires wet feet and fades to a rose, later a brown, as the pools dry up.

In drier meadows baby blue-eyes (*Nemophila menziesii*) spill across the grass, opening inch-wide corollas of pale blue. Tall spurred delphiniums add a royal-blue touch. As the lower meadows fade the higher ones bloom, and monkey flowers (*Mimulus*) outline the creeks in brilliant yellow. From March through May floral luxuriance can be found somewhere in the foothills.

What Sierran foothill flowers were like before the gold rush, no one knows. One of the earliest descriptions was left by John Woodhouse Audubon, son of the famous artist-naturalist John James Audubon. Young Audubon, then thirty-seven years old, journeyed overland with a party to the goldfields of California in 1849–1850. In the spring of 1850 he jogged by mule through the Sierran foothills, visiting mining camps and Indian villages. On March 28, 1850, following a trail from Wood's diggings to Hawkin's Bar, not far from the present town of Sonora at the 2,000-foot level, he encountered a foothill floral display at its zenith.

> Every turn gives some vista of beauty in this Garden of Eden; the soft southerly breeze is perfumed with the delicate odor of millions of smaller varieties of prairie flowers, in some places so abundant as to color acres, whole hillsides, so thickly as to hide the ground, and my mule had to eat flowers rather than grass. One without home

ties might well feel all his days could be passed in the beauties of these valleys, roseate yellow and blue, so soft that the purest sky cannot surpass the color for delicacy. Tangled masses of vines climb everywhere, hiding the hard surfaces of the quartz rocks, and beyond this exquisite vegetation always some view, wild and impressive, meets the eye.[2]

Foothill woodlands, in their higher isolated reaches, are still wild and impressive. The trees consist mainly of silvery gray pines and a variety of evergreen and deciduous oaks. Occasionally their crowns meet in an enclosing canopy, and the tangles of vines and shrubs can be quite dense.

The Sierran woodland's nearest counterparts occur in the inner California Coast Ranges and the mountains of southern California, Arizona, and northern Mexico. The Coast Ranges, though they adjoin the Sierra at both ends, are for the most part separated from it by the fifty-mile-wide Central Valley; southern California is cut off from the Sierra by several transverse ranges; Arizona and northern Mexico lie 600 to 1,000 miles southwest across an arid desert. How does it happen that such relatively widespread geographic regions share oak woodlands that are much alike yet recognizably different? Studies of fossil plants throughout the western United States by Daniel I. Axelrod, Ralph W. Chaney, Harry D. MacGinitie, and others have turned up some significant clues.

In early Tertiary times, 40 to 60 million years ago, the interior of western North America and of California was still inundated by an inland sea. The Sierra Nevada probably formed a low range of hills and harbored a vegetation much different from that growing there today. The forest was of subtropical broad-leaved evergreen trees like those now found in the forests of central Mexico at elevations of 5,000 to 6,000 feet. There was ample rain, chiefly in the summers.

As the Tertiary wore on, important changes occurred in the Earth's climate as the oceans cooled and inland dry land areas increased in size. In California, the combined effects of these changes led gradually to the development of a new climate. Winds blowing from a colder ocean onto an arid land were warmed and dried, with little of the former potential for rain in the warm season. By the end of the Tertiary, a Mediterranean climate of wet winters and dry summers had evolved.

Meanwhile, from at least early Tertiary times, a group of plants especially adapted to a semiarid climate had been evolving in the dry lands of Arizona and northern Mexico. These plants, mostly small-leaved, drought-resistant shrubs and small trees, thrived under limited seasonal rain, hot summers, and prolonged sun. Some of them were deciduous, dropping their leaves in the driest part of the season. As a dry climate expanded over western North America, these plants followed it—north, east, south, and west. By 10 to 15 million years ago they had invaded and come to dominate the Sierra Nevada western foothills.

Plant migrations such as these sound disarmingly rapid when viewed over a geological epoch; translated to the distance spread per year, however, the rate of travel slows to a crawl. Daniel Axelrod calculated that it took these plants approximately 16 millions years to migrate the 600 miles from southeastern California to southern Oregon—an average of 19.54 feet per century, or around 2.37 inches per year.

The flora that took over Sierran foothills and much of the semiarid West in the middle and late Tertiary period was a mixture of woodland and chaparral that included many plants adapted to the summer rain and relatively warm climate still prevalent. Paleobotanists have named this mixed plant community the Madro-Tertiary geoflora, signifying a major plant type of wide geographic extent in Tertiary times, originating in the Sierra Madre Occidental of Mexico (hence Madro). Relicts of it still survive in the Sierra Madre as well as in limited areas of California.

As the Tertiary drew to a close, tremendous regional uplifts occurred in the western half of the continent. The Sierra Nevada, Cascades, Rocky Mountains, the Basin Ranges of Nevada, and the Sierra Madre assumed their present heights. The high mountains and the continued cooling of the oceans brought about major changes in climate. Greater extremes of temperature developed throughout the region, deserts appeared, and winter rains became the pattern in the far West.

Sierran woodland and chaparral began to change, by elimination. As summer rains vanished in the Sierran foothills and the region became colder in winter, plants that required summer moisture or could not stand cold disappeared. Those that could adapt to the changes survived and became the nucleus of today's flora. Many of the warmer-weather, summer-rain species, formerly Sierran, thrive today in the woodlands and chaparral of southern California, in the thorn scrub of northern Mexico, and in the Sierra Madrean woodlands of the Southwest, where, separated from the Sierra by deserts, the environment still meets their needs.

In all of these regions the oak woodlands look much alike—a savanna-type growth of spaced trees and grass. The appearance is similar; the species of oaks are different. For in the last few million years of isolation, each region has been a proving ground for the evolution of its own species.

Unquestionably the most distinctive indicator of the modern Sierra Nevada foothill woodland is the gray pine (*Pinus sabiniana*), formerly known as digger pine. Sometimes called "the tree you can see right through," the gray pine has loose, long, pale green needles that cast a sparse shade compared to the ample shade of the tight dark green clusters of higher-mountain pines. The brownish trunk commonly forks and holds in its tops, forty to eighty feet above the ground, clusters of heavy cones six to twelve inches long and half as broad. The cones, armed with fierce upcurved spines and generous resin, are full of sweet nuts, a valuable food source for Native Americans.

In the few woodland areas where gray pine is missing, perhaps because of lower resistance to fire, oak associates persist. The blue oak (*Quercus douglasii*), a medium-sized deciduous tree of grayish trunk and bluish green leaves, can take the drier, or xerophytic, soils. Interior live oaks (*Q. wislizenii*), evergreen trees with dark green shiny leaves, grow to the ground and cast a dense shade. Valley oaks (*Q. lobata*) sometimes occur in moister sites. On steep rocky slopes, canyon oaks (*Q. chrysolepis*) and California buckeyes (*Aesculus californica*) often join the "exquisite" tangles of poison oak (*Rhus diversiloba*),

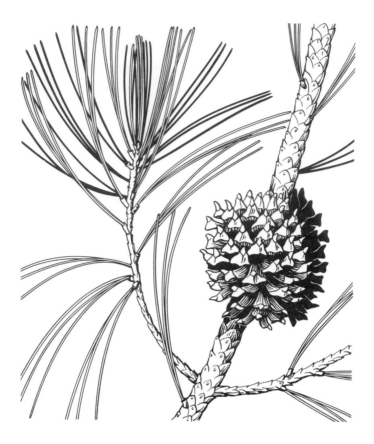

Gray pine, the foothill's chief
conifer

western clematis (*Clematis ligusticifolia*), and the blackberries (*Rubus*)
that so impressed John Woodhouse Audubon.

Woodland often occurs on the moister north-facing slopes, with
chaparral occupying the sunnier south-facing ones. But the hills are
so many and the slope exposures so varied that every sort of habitat
mixture emerges. One of the most favorable combinations for wildlife
is the marginal zone, or ecotone, between foothill woodland and the
midmountain forests above. The best of both possible worlds seems to
blend in a broad mixture of trees and shrubs, an ample ground cover,
and a rich assemblage of animal life.

Here, on an April day, the strange courtship dance of the Sierra Nevada salamander (*Ensatina eschscholtzi platensis*) takes place among the leaf litter of the moist forest floor.[3] Solitary the rest of the year, for a brief while during the spring breeding season these wide-eyed gray and orange–spotted amphibians travel in pairs and court.

The ceremony begins with the male creeping to the side of the female, his five-inch-long body and tail carried close to the ground. As he approaches her head, he reduces his pace to very slow motion, noses her neck, then rubs her face and throat with his. If she responds by tilting her head upward, he slides his body under the elevated head, keeping contact with her throat as he moves slowly past. He comes to a stop with his lower back under her chin and begins to massage her throat with a rotary movement of his hindquarters. If he has captured her interest, she leans her throat against his lower back and follows him as he creeps slowly forward, his back arched sharply upward, his tail trailing between her legs. This "tail walk" may go on for several hours over the forest floor.

Finally, in a spot of his choosing, the male stops, presses his vent against the substratum, and begins a lateral rocking on his rear legs. The female keeps time with counterswaying. When the male crawls onward, the spermatophore (mass of spermatozoa mixed with gelatin) that he has deposited stays behind. The pair tail-walks forward till the female squats above the capsule of sperm cells. She pulls it into her vent and inner cloacal chamber with her cloacal lips, the male meanwhile stroking her back with his tail.

Weeks or months later she will lay a clutch of a dozen eggs in an underground rodent burrow or in the softly crumbling interior of a rotten log, fertilizing the eggs with the stored spermatozoa before they leave her body. During the long dry summer she will stand guard over them in their moist, well-insulated nest, often curling her constricted tail around the jelly clusters, keeping them moist with her own body fluids if desiccation threatens. When the first rains of autumn seep into her hideout, she and her newly hatched young will emerge, to go their separate ways for the active season.

The same rains bring other moist-skinned relatives, the arboreal salamanders (*Aneides lugubris*), climbing down from their summer holes in interior live oaks. All sizes, ages, and numbers sometimes use the same quarters. Up to thirty-five individuals have been found sharing one tree hole, scraping off fungi inside the knothole for a dry-season diet, while their eggs hang like stalked grape clusters from the ceiling. The largest specimens reach almost eight inches in length, smooth brown-skinned amphibians with sparse yellow dots.

Aneides is the most agile climber of Sierran lungless salamanders (family Plethodontidae), using expanded toes and a prehensile tail as climbing aids. Like the Sierra Nevada salamander and other lungless types, it breathes through its skin and throat. Mucous glands scattered throughout the thin skin keep it moist; this permits oxygen from the surrounding air to pass through skin pores in a liquid film into the blood vessel network just beneath the surface. A similar vascular network lines the mouth, and air is passed over this lining and absorbed by rhythmic movements of the salamander's throat.

All this necessitates a moist environment to permit breathing. During the rainy season Aneides can choose its habitat liberally, feeding on spiders, centipedes, false scorpions, termites, flies, and other insects. The heavy jaw muscles, especially well developed in males, enable it to seize prey as large as the pencil thin California slender salamander (*Batrachoseps attenuatus*), which uses the same under-bark runways. But with the advent of the dry season Aneides, in company with other salamanders, must seek a damp retreat.

It has, on occasion, more to fear than the dehydrating air of summer. The common king snake (*Lampropeltis getulus*), which roams the foothill woodlands, is a good climber and includes amphibians in its wide-ranging diet. This handsome black-and-white-banded snake, adapted to a variety of North American habitats, is probably most famous for its ability to kill and eat rattlesnakes. In the Sierran foothills it meets them at regular intervals, since the western rattlesnake (*Crotalus viridis*) frequents wooded grassy areas with rocky outcrops, chaparral, and streamside canyons.

Rattlesnakes occur in many plant belts of the Sierra Nevada to the 8,000-foot level or even higher. Their abundance varies locally from none to plenty. Their enemies number more than might be suspected for a poisonous reptile. Many snakes besides king snakes are immune in large degree to rattlesnake venom. Striped racers (*Masticophis lateralis*) take a periodic toll of rattlesnakes in chaparral areas. Experiments indicate that a rattlesnake can sense the approach of possible enemies such as king snakes, racers, and whip snakes by detecting certain odorous substances in their skin. These cause the rattler to retreat with its head and neck held close to the ground and showing no inclination to rattle or strike.

Foothill rattlers come out of hibernation when temperatures rise above 70°F, usually in mid March, and are most abundant in the balmy months of April, May, and June. Summer heat drives them to hole up in burrows or rock crevices during the day and seek food at dusk and during the night. The temperature-sensitive structure contained in the pit below the eyes helps them locate the warm-blooded cottontail rabbits, ground squirrels, voles, and pocket mice, California quail and brown towhees, that are their chief prey. Most foothill hikers never see a rattlesnake; the snakes usually vanish silently unless caught unawares. But, like the ticks of the woodland grasses and chaparral, they are a potential hazard to respect.

Sometimes mistaken for a rattlesnake is the nonpoisonous Pacific gopher snake (*Pituophis melanoleucus catenifir*) of the foothill grasslands. The Pacific gopher snake's mottled tan-and-brown back pattern can superficially resemble a rattler's as it melts into the summer grass. And when alarmed, a gopher snake may vibrate its tail, producing in dry grass a sound much like the feared rattle. Its ability to vibrate the epiglottis, so that air can be sucked through in a loud hiss, and to spread its head adds further to the impression of a viper. These habits may be the basis of the erroneous story that rattlesnakes and gopher snakes occasionally interbreed to produce a dangerous hybrid, the "bull rattler," having the option of either poisoning or squeezing its prey to death. Actually, the Pacific gopher snake kills by constriction only. Like its eastern U.S. counterpart the bull snake, it climbs trees in search of small animals and the eggs of birds. And it is equally adept at digging, loosening dirt with its snout, then hooking the soil out in a loop of the neck. This technique gains entrance to plugged holes and the runways of gophers, mice, ground squirrels, and other rodents.

While many snakes and lizards, and some birds and mammals, move freely between the two major foothill communities—woodland and chaparral—the dominant woody plants of the two are very distinct. The densely aggregated masses of evergreen shrubs that make up chaparral form one of the unique vegetative habitats of the world. The word *chaparral* is a Spanish-Californian derivative of the Spanish *chaparro,* meaning scrub oak, an evergreen oak common in much Californian chaparral.

Sometimes known as elfin forest or Mediterranean scrub forest, chaparral grows primarily around the borders of the Mediterranean Sea, in central Chile, the southern tip of Africa, southwestern Australia, and parts of Mexico, in addition to California and Arizona in the United States. Along the Mediterranean, chaparral is known as *machis*. In South Africa it is called *macchia,* or *fynbos,* an Afrikaans word for small bushy vegetation. Australians speak of it as mallee scrub. Everywhere it presents a nearly impenetrable front of shrubbery five to eight feet high, with a few taller plants shooting up to heights of perhaps fifteen feet. The species of plants that compose it are distinct for each part of the world, but their growth aspects and their adaptations to their semiarid environments have much in common.

Sierran chaparral, though long since adapted to a dry-summer climate, still carries links to the summer-rain chaparral of Arizona, its ancestral home region. A number of shrubs are common to the two areas, among them deerbrush (*Ceanothus integerrimus*), mountain mahogany (*Cercocarpus betuloides*), hollyleaf redberry (*Rhamnus crocea ilicifolia*), and gooseberry (*Ribes quercetorum*). In addition, such California chaparral species as fremontia (*Fremontodendron*) and tree poppy (*Dendromecon rigida*) occur only as relicts in central Arizona chaparral.

In California, chaparral covers about one-twelfth of the state, spread widely over the southern mountains, in arid sections of the Coast Ranges, and as a discontinuous band throughout the length of the western Sierra Nevada foothills. Sierran foothill chaparral forms a climax plant community that will replace itself over and over again under natural conditions, which include fire.

The shrubs are adapted in every conceivable way to the rigors of long dry summers and withering heat. Their leaves are tough, waxy, and often small, reducing evaporation to a minimum. The larger leaves carry sunken stomata (pores) to further preserve moisture. The plants' roots, as in the widespread dominant chaparral species, chamise, may extend far deeper into the coarse rocky soils than the plant extends above ground.

So tight a web do the stiff branches make that a man attempting to push his way through mature chaparral will wear himself out and within a few hundred yards tear any but the toughest clothing. This is why cowboys of the early West used to wear trouserlike leggings of leather over their blue jeans. These flared breeches were called chaps, an abbreviation of the Mexican-Spanish word *chapajeros,* meaning apparel for chaparral. Chaps provide equal protection against thickets and burs and rope burns and are still a part of some brush riders' gear today.

Chaparral shrubs follow closely the seasonal pattern of their Mediterranean climate. Growth in chamise begins in January after winter rains have permeated the soils, accelerates in April and May, terminates in June. August and September are the chaparral's dormant "winter."

No plant demonstrates this seasonal adaptation more dramatically than the oddly picturesque California buckeye of the dry foothill slopes and canyons. The pale green compound leaves of this small deciduous tree unfurl in February, long before the blue oak buds show any sign of bursting. The buckeye is the first fresh green tree of spring in the foothills. By May its white flower spikes have come and gone. By late July the leaflets dangle withered and brown; their drying retains water that would otherwise be lost through their pores. Pearlike fruits appear in August on branches that remain functionally leafless and crookedly silver for six months of the year.

Chaparral reveals considerable diversity in the Sierran foothills. The dominant plants vary with the region and local conditions. One of the most common and widespread chaparral shrubs is chamise (*Adenostoma fasciculatum*), the *chamiso* of the early Spanish Californians. Pure stands of chamise cover miles of south-facing slopes with a uniform growth of woody bushes four to eight feet high, each clothed with fasciculate bunches of short green needlelike leaves. Much of the year the terminal growth carries the brown seedcases of last June's flowers, giving a characteristic green-brown tone to entire hillsides.

Mature chamise chaparral is notably meager in wildlife. Its thin leaves offer scanty shade on the bush and decompose slowly into a sparse, acidic humus that repels most plant life except fungi. Studies of the inhibiting process reveal that the leaves, flowers, litter, and roots of chamise contain water-soluble and heat-labile saponins and unsaturated lactones. These accumulate in certain soils (mostly poor noncalcic stony and sandy types and shallow lithosols) to act as inhibitors of the germination and growth of grasses. The effect is so distinct that on steeper slopes chamise sometimes separates itself from adjacent grassland by a bare strip as much as nine feet wide.

When chamise grows on calcareous soils or serpentine or on deeper, more fertile clays, its plant toxins seem to be canceled out—effectively absorbed or decomposed by a combination of microbiological and chemical activity that allows a subshrub and grass understory to appear.[4]

In addition to forming pure stands, chamise is a common member of the mixed chaparral community in the Sierran foothills. At least forty species of shrubs occur in many combinations from north to south, interlaced with vines like western clematis, wild cucumber (*Marah*), and poison oak. It is the mixed stands that support most chaparral wildlife. Here grow the ample berries of toyon (*Heteromeles arbutifolia*), California coffeeberry (*Rhamnus californica*), and the manzanitas (*Arctostaphylos*). Acorns from scrub oaks add to the insect crop and to seeds of the many species of ceanothus, mountain mahogany, flowering ash (*Fraxinus dipetala*), and others. Chaparral thus supplied with food and cover for birds and mammals, yet open enough to provide variable spaces through which small creatures can travel, contains a representative wildlife population.

One's best chance to observe the wildlife undetected comes on hikes along isolated dirt roads or the fire lanes cut through some chaparral. You never know what will cross the road just ahead of you and disappear into the sheltering brush, or what may be lying along the road's edge unmoving, like the striped racer that startled me one day. It could almost have passed for a garter snake—slim and black with an ivory stripe down each side—except for the long, tapering racer tail. I crept up on it cautiously, taking photographs at ten feet, seven, five, four. I began to wonder if it were alive; not a flicker of life showed. The body lay round and firm, its scales smooth and glistening, lacking the keels of the garter snake. The neck looked a bit flattened; the big eye stared. As I bent over the snake it rippled into the brush, out of sight in an instant. Striped racers are among the West's fastest snakes, estimated to attain speeds of up to eight miles per hour. They can glide swiftly through the interlacing branches of chaparral, at home in any height of the shrub jungle.

Chaparral birds are, by nature of the habitat, difficult to see. Occasional small trees that protrude above the shrub mass serve as singing posts, but the singers are more often heard than seen. Unquestionably the most abundant bird in mature chaparral is the wrentit. It virtually typifies chaparral, since the bird's total distribution is only slightly more extensive than that of foothill chaparral itself. Found solely on the Pacific Coast of the United States, wrentits belong to a family of their own, the Chamaeidae, and are closely related to the dippers and wrens. Some authorities, however, regard them as isolated offshoots of the large Old World family of babblers.

Brown sparrow-sized birds with a white iris and long cocky tail, wrentits behave somewhat like wrens slipping through the brush. Their strong legs and maneuverable wings enable them to hop and flit from twig to twig "as fast as a man can run with no shrubs to block his way."[5] They rarely make flights of more than thirty feet, instead staying within the brush, where they maintain year-round territories and sing throughout the year. Although it is unusual for small perching birds to mate for life, banding experiments at Strawberry Canyon, Berkeley, indicate that wrentits are an exception.

The song is the only indication of the wrentit's presence that most chaparral observers get—its secretiveness is legendary. The bird's song rings out loud and clear, unmistakable once learned. The male starts with a series of slow staccato notes all on one pitch, then speeds them into a final trill. The female omits the speeded-up trill.

Wrentits make up one-fourth to one-third of the bird population in southern and coastal California chaparral areas where census counts have been taken. They appear equally abundant in Sierran foothill chaparral. Scrub jays, although not restricted to chaparral, are prominent in it as well. They control wrentit numbers somewhat by robbing nests, and they add a touch of bright blue to a bird world dominated by browns and tans. The California thrasher, wrentit, bushtit, Bewick's wren, and brown towhee—which is partial to chaparral edges—are all drab brown in color.

The California quail blends camouflage and brightness: the male's brown back is complemented by a black-and-white face and throat pattern; the short black head plume, curving forward from the crown, bobs with each step. The quail, California's state bird, prefers somewhat broken chaparral with dense-foliaged trees nearby for night roosting and water within walking distance. It slips easily through the spaces on the elfin forest floor in its search for seeds and berries. All winter long, its three-syllable call—which translates perfectly as Chi-*ca*-go—can be heard at intervals.

At nesting time the coveys break into pairs, choosing territories that the males guard from singing perches, sometimes uttering an explosive "All's well" signal every fifteen seconds or so. When nesting is finished, the heat of summer is usually in full swing. California quail then often migrate up to the 4,000-foot level, where summer water and food are more abundant, overlapping the range of the mountain quail at this season. When the rains come, they return to the foothills.

Not all of them make it. The gray fox (*Urocyon cinereoargenteus*) keeps an eye out for quail, as well as for the mice, brush rabbits, and woodrats of the chaparral. And bobcats, coyotes, and Cooper's hawks are all known to relish a plump, juicy quail. The fox may sometimes be seen in the daytime following a trail or sniffing at a hole. Favored chaparral areas may support as many as four gray foxes per square mile. They are graceful creatures, the size of a small dog, steel-gray with reddish yellow flanks and black hairs along the top of the back and tail. Retiring in the presence of other predators such as raccoons, they are patient hunters and possess a tree-climbing agility unusual for members of the dog family. One that I watched denned in an interior live oak knothole five feet above the ground to produce its four pups. The gray fox ranges into the midmountain forests of the Sierra Nevada but not into the high-mountain realm of the red fox (*Vulpes vulpes*).

Bobcats (*Lynx rufus*) are wider travelers, living in every plant belt from valley to timberline. They sometimes crouch in the mottled shadow of chaparral edges, eyes following any movement. The timid brush rabbit (*Sylvilagus bachmani*), which generally stays within a few feet of its hiding place in a dense thicket, may venture farther afield in search of tasty grasses. The lithe bobcat, one of the major controllers of the chaparral's small-mammal population, tests the rabbit's alertness. In addition to rabbits, it crops deer mice (*Peromyscus*), pocket mice (*Perognathus*), pocket gophers (*Thomomys*), California ground squirrels (*Spermophilus beecheyi*), and woodrats (*Neotoma*).

Woodrats have many enemies. Widely distributed throughout western North America, from the Yukon to Guatemala, this rat occupies every sort of habitat from mountains to deserts. It superficially resembles the introduced Norway rat, but is a much more appealing mammal. The fur is softer, the underparts are white, and the tail is furry or hairy, not scaly as in the Norway rat.

The two Sierran species of woodrat occur in widely separated plant belts. The larger bushytail woodrat (*Neotoma cinerea*) lives in rock crevices of the high country, from 6,500 feet upward, while the dusky-footed woodrat (*N. fuscipes*) inhabits chaparral thickets and woodlands of the foothills. Both are known as "trade rats" or "pack rats" because of their habit of carrying off objects that they may then drop, or trade, for more attractive ones.

In the years before this habit was well documented, some curious incidents occurred in the wild. Walter Fry, one of the early naturalists at Sequoia National Park, tells of a camping trip he took in September 1899 with Professor W. F. Dean to the Castle Rocks area of the park, altitude 8,900 feet. They spread their blankets on the ground and, since the weather was quite cold, slept with most of their clothing on. Before retiring, Dean took from his pocket three gold pieces and a small amount of silver and placed them, along with a spectacles case holding his gold-rimmed glasses, in his hat at the side of the bed.

In the morning the money and spectacles were gone. In their place

Bushy-tailed woodrat at
its stick nest

was a round ball of horse dung slightly larger than a walnut. Dean
asked Fry what kind of trick he was playing on him. Fry was per-
plexed. Neither of them at that time knew anything about woodrats.
After breakfast they threw a canvas over their camping gear and left to
inspect the 480 acres that Dean owned nearby.

As they returned at dusk, they saw a bushytail woodrat run from
their camping supplies to a nearby rock pile, carrying a spoon in its
mouth. Hastily they dismantled the rock pile. Beneath it, beside a soft
grassy nest, they found not only the money and glasses but also their
two table knives, forks, and spoons.

"Never shall I forget the incident," wrote Fry, "which caused both of us some eleven hours of continuous worry and came mighty nigh to destroying what proved later a lifelong friendship."

Fourteen years later, Fry watched the woodrat's trading technique at even closer hand. On this trip, in August 1913, he tented with a detachment of soldiers at Alta Meadow, elevation 8,600 feet, in Sequoia National Park. As Fry and Sergeant McCall lay on their cots reading by a dim candle at about nine o'clock one evening, they noticed a bushytail woodrat slyly enter through the tent flap carrying a small bone in its mouth. It moved alongside a sack of potatoes, dropped the bone, and picked up a potato that was lying loose. Scrambling up over a pile of stove wood onto a bench, it found a small cake of soap. Dropping the potato, it took a bite of the soap, picked it up, and jumped to the tent floor near an eight-inch saw file. It examined the file thoroughly, then picked up its soap and ran to McCall's cot, where the sergeant's large corncob pipe was lying. Here it dropped the soap, sniffed into the pipe, sneezed twice, picked up the pipe, and moved over to some cavalry spurs. After scrutinizing the spurs, it picked up one of them and started dragging it toward the tent flap. With that the men drove the woodrat into the night.[6]

Foothill woodrats build bulkier nests than their high Sierran relatives. The house of the dusky-footed woodrat sometimes stands six feet high and almost as wide at the base. It is a rainproof shelter made of sticks, cow manure, tin cans, barbed wire, campers' silverware—anything the owner happens to carry home. Many other foothill animals share crevices in these quarters: fence swifts, arboreal salamanders, deer mice, triatoma bugs. A woodrat may own several houses, each containing nest chambers that connect with runways into nearby logs or ground cover to facilitate escape. The mounds frequently stand in the center of gooseberry thickets, which form an almost impregnable barrier to large predators.

The woodrat usually forages within twenty-five yards of its home, seeking berries, seeds, and grasses—or, generally, any plant materials it can carry. Slightly over a foot long, this brownish gray rodent with the clear white throat is of suitable meal size for most carnivores in the vicinity. If the striped skunk (*Mephitis mephitis*) doesn't surprise it at dusk, there is always the risk that the ringtail (*Bassariscus astutus*) will toward midnight.

The ringtail is one of the more strictly nocturnal foothill mammals. On moonlit nights it carries its long, furry, black-and-white-banded tail arched high over its back when hunting among the boulders of brushy slopes. Its slim, agile body, slightly larger than a gray squirrel's, merges into an inquiring pointed face. The large brown eyes, set off by nearly encircling white borders, peer with an acute curiosity.

In the chaparral and rocky slopes of the western and southwestern United States, where it dwells, the ringtail's distribution corresponds closely to that of its chief prey, woodrats and deer mice. In these areas it dens mainly in rock openings and the hollow limbs of trees.

But it has always been quick to take advantage of the shelter of buildings as well. During the mining boom of more than a century ago, the animal was commonly called "miner's cat" because it moved into miners' cabins and kept them free of mice and pack rats. Visitors to the old movie house in Yosemite Valley in the 1930s recall the ringtails that stole the show chasing each other over the rafters. In the Sierra Nevada the ringtail occupies favored habitats to 7,000 feet, often utilizing mountain cabins for shelter.

The largest mammals in the foothill belt, the mountain lion and the mule deer, both range to timberline. In California's untrammeled past, another powerful animal occupied the foothill scene, one that perhaps exerted more influence on the local wildlife than any species around today. The grizzly bear (*Ursus arctos*) once made most of California its domain. It wore conspicuous trails in the chaparral and sought out resting places beneath the interlocking branches. It ate the berries of manzanita, poison oak, toyon, elderberry, and coffeeberry, and acorns from nearby oaks; it dug out the rodents and brodiaea bulbs with its huge front claws, and gobbled up yellow jacket nests.

The grizzly vanished from California before its relationship to the land and wildlife could be ecologically assessed. But Tracy Storer and Lloyd Tevis Jr., who surveyed all the available historical literature in their 1955 book *California Grizzly,* expressed no doubt as to the big bear's role: "The grizzly must have been a dominant element in the original native biota of California—it was usually avoided by the Indians, and because of its size, prowess, and temperament it could preempt any available food."[7] Indeed, its adaptability in diet was exceeded by no other local mammal. The grizzly was a big, resourceful beast weighing as much as a thousand pounds or more, with tremendous daily food demands that left their mark on the coinhabitants of its home area. The only creature to whom the grizzly gave a wide berth was *el sorillo,* the skunk.

Before white men invaded California, there was space for Indians and grizzlies. When active hunting between 1849 and 1870 killed off the grizzlies in the valleys, the survivors took to the most rugged, isolated spots on the western Sierra Nevada slopes. A few scattered to the very crest of the range. The areas in which they held out longest were those where heavy and continuous chaparral kept out the sheepherder. The last California grizzly of certain record was shot in 1908, but there were fragmentary reports of the big grizzled beast with the shoulder hump in Sequoia National Park as late as 1924.

Grizzlies were common in the chaparral lands of northwestern Mexico and adjoining Arizona and New Mexico as late as 1892. By 1968 all had been extirpated except a small population in the upper Yaqui Basin of Sonora, Mexico. Grizzlies today occur primarily in the Rocky Mountains of the northern United States and Canada, and in Alaska.

Hunting in California is currently regulated by the California Fish and Game Commission. Despite some disagreement among ecologists, hunters, and ranchers as to the numbers of mountain lions, deer, and tule elk that have a right to share the land, no species of large game mammal within the state stands in obvious and imminent danger of following the grizzly's path to extinction. Rather, the future of foothill animals depends on what happens to their habitat—a habitat that is rapidly changing. The foothills today are among the most popular sites in the state for new homes and golf courses, which are springing up in one subdivision after another. Oaks and pines face destruction from chain saw and bulldozer in ever-growing numbers. State and county parks, subdivision greenbelt corridors, and private pine-oak preserves are badly needed to preserve the diversity of both woodland and chaparral.

Chaparral has long been recognized by many soil conservationists as a valuable watershed cover that absorbs heavy rains and helps prevent mudslides, erosion, and floods in the valleys below. Its usefulness as a land sponge varies tremendously with the age and shrub composition of the chaparral, the amount and type of leaf litter and humus, the soil character, and the gradient of the slope. Many ranchers, however, rate all chaparral as worthless. Mature dense chaparral affords almost no cattle feed and consequently is being bulldozed, burned, and seeded to pasture over thousands of acres throughout the foothill belt.

Eliminating chaparral is not a simple procedure, for chaparral is a rugged vegetation that evolved in the continued presence of fire long before humans' arrival on the scene. In unprotected situations few chaparral stems can be found that are more than twenty-five years old: lightning fires throughout the eons have pruned the elfin forest and kept it young.

Chaparral shrubs adapt to fire in two readily observed ways. Some sprout from buried root crowns after their tops are destroyed. Others produce heavy crops of seeds throughout their lives, seeds with hard coats that require a fire's heat to crack them for germination. Some plants use both means. During the first year after an ordinary burn, the root sprouters such as chamise, scrub oak, and mountain mahogany send up vigorous green shoots. The fire-stimulated seeds of the manzanitas, ceanothus, and other nonsprouters begin to grow more slowly. Grasses and invading herbs such as redstem filaree, miner's lettuce, and golden brodiaea, meanwhile, move in and quickly cover much of the burned ground with a profusion of seed and color. The seeds attract California quail, mourning doves, western meadowlarks, lark sparrows, and other adjacent grassland birds, and deer browse on the new green shoots. For three to five years this grassy herbaceous vegetation, with its bird and mammal life, dominates the stripped chaparral area.

By the fifth year, however, the brush sprouts shoot up, close the canopy, shade out most of the grasses, and take over. Grassland birds disappear, and chaparral birds return from adjoining areas. Resident small mammals, which survived in rock crevices and burrows, increase to normal populations. The many-faceted song of the Bewick's wren once again rings out from a shrub cover that will become increasingly dense with each year—until the next fire, or until ranchers employ techniques to keep the region permanently in grass.

Although foothill chaparral often looks monotonously alike to the cursory traveler, it holds much hidden diversity for the botanist. California is especially rich in species of plants that grow in only very limited areas. Geneticist G. Ledyard Stebbins calculated that per unit of area the state has more than sixty times as many of these localized species, known as endemics, as northeastern North America. Only Spain, the Cape region of South Africa, and the Middle East can compare with California in this regard.

The Sierra Nevada has provided, over time, the variations of topography, temperature, rainfall, and soil that foster the development of restricted species. One of the more intriguing endemics grows in the central Sierran foothills near Ione. For about two miles the landscape along Highway 88 is dominated by a low-growing, heathlike shrub, Ione manzanita (*Arctostaphylos myrtifolia*), which occurs only here and on several "islands" like it a few miles north and south. The plant's tiny, elliptic, leathery leaves are brightened in January and February by clusters of pink and white bell-like flowers. The rest of the year its gnarled stems spread a brittle semiprostrate cloak of bronzed green over the earth.

Several other rare plants grow on the same ecological island. Woolyleaf ceanothus (*Ceanothus tomentosus*), a shrub with striking leaves dark green above and matted wool below, occupies some of the depressions. Its flowers of deep blue come out in April and May. Where the spaces between the Ione manzanita are a little wider and the gradient a little steeper than usual, the shrubby rockrose (*Helianthemum suffrutescens*) spreads its low, densely hairy branches and yellow flowers. One of the Sierra's two recorded species of rockrose, this species is confined to the Ione vicinity.

The rarest plant on the island, however, is an undistinguished-looking wild buckwheat that survives on the most barren, inhospitable hillsides where nothing else can grow. This species, *Eriogonum apricum,* was first discovered and described in the mid-1950s by John Thomas Howell. The plant is a low grower, with small roundish leaves that lie flat on the ground and branching stems that support tiny whitish flowers in midsummer. In the 1970s on a field trip in the Ione hills, Stebbins could spread his arms over the only known specimens and proclaim to his colleagues, "I can cover with my arms all of the *Eriogonum apricum* in the world." Since then more patches have been found nearby.

At the periphery of the Ione manzanita island, the usual live oaks and taller gray manzanitas of the regular chaparral-woodland take over, and beyond them, the familiar blue-oak woodland. These common trees and shrubs are as completely barred from the Ione island as the islanders are from ordinary foothill terrain. The main reason seems to be the unusual soil of the Ione island. Phenomenally acid, it carries a pH rating of 3–4, ranking at the far acid end of a scale where 7 is neutral and alkaline ranges to 14. In addition, it is extremely poor in the minerals that most plants need for growth, hence in all ways a soil hostile to ordinary foothill plants. Composed of a hardpan clay of unique texture, it was deposited along the shores of the inland sea that covered the Central Valley of California some 50 million years ago. Perhaps Ione manzanitas once spread their low olive-green thickets abundantly along these same valley margins.

Fifty million years brought intensive geological and climatic changes, among them the reduction of the former seashore margins to occasional outpockets of clay. Today's Ione manzanita exists as a holdover from an environment that was once more common. Ecologically it is a relict species. Relicts usually persist as long as their habitats do. In the case of Ione manzanita, the habitat came close to being destroyed. The clay of the Ione island proved an excellent texture for ceramic products, and was commercially mined for many years. In 1980, however, the Nature Conservancy deeded an Ione Chaparral Preserve to the California Department of Fish and Game, thus protecting some of the remaining habitat and its endangered species.

Farther south, in the Sierran foothills east of Fresno, another rare plant holds out in a very limited range. This one, *Carpenteria califor-*

nica, is a good-sized bush that grows right in with mixed chaparral and scattered woodland trees on moderately steep foothill slopes. Carpenteria is thought to be a relict of former times when the climate was more moist than it is now. The gradual climatic desiccation apparently restricted the species to the few less-harsh sites it occupies today, most of them along foothill tributaries of the San Joaquin River. Its entire world distribution encompasses a longitudinal range of about twenty miles and an altitudinal range between 1,500 and 4,000 feet. Within this zone, its occurrence is sporadic; locally it may be quite abundant, nearby entirely absent. The shrub is a spreading type, many-stemmed from the ground, ranging from six to twelve feet tall; frequently four or more individuals form a huge clump. Long evergreen leaves hide a rather unusual bark, smooth and of light buckskin color and shed in paper-thin sheets. The flowers are particularly appealing, over two inches across, with usually six white petals surrounding a central core of more than one hundred rich golden stamens.

Carpenteria was for many years "the lost shrub" of California's botanical history. Originally collected by General John C. Frémont in 1846 somewhere in the Sierra Nevada of California on the San Joaquin River watershed, the plant remained undiscovered for nearly thirty years. In 1876 Gustav Eisen exhibited specimens found in the foothills east of Fresno, and the limited range of the rare shrub soon became known.

A part of Carpenteria's range lies within the Sierra National Forest. Where the plant grows thickly, its blossoms form sparkling clusters over the mountainside at the end of May. They stand apart from the white spikes of California buckeyes and the flat-topped white heads of elderberry by their brighter, cleaner look, and often bloom at the same time as golden fremontias. Around and among them grow redbuds (*Cercis occidentalis*), choke cherries (*Prunus virginiana*), bladdernut (*Staphylea bolanderi*), hoptrees (*Ptelea crenulata*), gooseberry, manzanitas, yerba santa (*Eriodictyon*), ceanothus, Sierra plum (*Prunus subcordata*), poison oak, California laurel, and others. The usually common chamise is strangely absent here.

Wild cucumbers twine the scattered live oaks. Occasional gray pines rise from a knoll. The views lead to blue mountains beyond. In the lushness of spring it would be difficult to find a more idyllic foothill setting. The chaparral is rich, some of it rare. And nearby are the moister, deeper soils where woodland trees grow in profusion; where ash-throated flycatchers and Bullock's orioles nest; where plain titmice whistle querulous tunes and acorn woodpeckers hitch up the furrowed trunks toward a foothill sky.

Two

IN THE LATE 1800S, TOURISTS and scientists traveled long distances to visit the newly publicized forests of the Sierra Nevada. Among them were such renowned botanists as the American Asa Gray and the Englishman Sir Joseph Hooker. Sitting around a mountain campfire one night with Gray and Hooker, John Muir asked Hooker, who had seen and studied most of the great forests of the world, if he knew any coniferous forest that rivaled the Sierra's. Hooker's reply was decisive. "No," he said. "In the beauty and grandeur of individual trees, and in number and variety of species, the forest of the Sierra surpasses all others."[1] More than a century later his evaluation still stands.

The midmountain forests of the Sierra Nevada's western slope begin where the foothill woodlands end. From roughly 2,500 to 6,000 feet they cover the broadest timbered segment of the range, a region of mellow summer climate, moderate winters, and varied plant and animal life. Dominating this forest belt of mixed conifers is the ponderosa pine (*Pinus ponderosa*).

Widely distributed throughout the western United States in several racial forms and subject to greater variations in temperature and precipitation than nearly any other North American tree, this versatile conifer reaches its prime growth in Sierran montane forests. Here the

Ponderosa pine

broad-plated, yellowish tan trunks of mature pines rise from sunlit forest floors brown with needles. In favored sites they attain diameters of eight feet and heights exceeding two hundred feet, soaring well above the California black oaks (*Quercus kelloggii*) and incense cedars (*Calocedrus decurrens*). The incense cedars, as well as the sugar pines (*Pinus lambertiana*), which grow in the middle and upper reaches of the zone, are almost exclusively Californian, with a slight overlap into Oregon's Cascade mountains; the white firs (*Abies concolor*), common associates, occur widely throughout much of the West. All can form, as Hooker said, specimens of "beauty and grandeur," amid forests of intriguing diversity.

Midmountain Forests
(map by Carla J. Simmons)

The broad belt of midmountain forest is dissected at frequent intervals by deep canyons. Cut by the ten master rivers and their tributaries, later plucked and quarried by glaciers, the canyons expose the
granite core of the range, particularly in the central and southern sec-
tors. Sometimes the granite forms massive monoliths, unbroken by
any stress; sometimes it rises in vertically jointed blocks hundreds of
feet high; sometimes it rounds off in domes that exfoliate loose layers

of rock much as an onion sheds its skin; sometimes it forms cliffs of small jointed blocks.

Wherever exposed rocks of the canyon walls develop cracks into which water seeps, freezes, and expands, fragments break loose and go tumbling down to join the jumble of rocks below. This sloping rock mass at the base of cliffs, known as talus, shelters many animals—from insects to lizards and small mammals. Talus slopes occur commonly in the Sierra, from middle elevations to the bases of the highest cliffs.

On the older talus slopes and in adjacent canyons of the middle elevations grow other trees of the mixed conifer community. Douglas firs (*Pseudotsuga menziesii*) send up tall spires softened with down-sweeping streamers. California bays (*Umbellularia californica*) hug the slopes, their long shiny leaves emitting a pungent aroma when bruised. The rare California nutmeg (*Torreya californica*) flanks some canyons with its small checkered trunk and dark green foliage. In summer the nutmegs dangle miniature avocado-like fruits over beds of old sharp pointed needles. It was the resemblance of their wrinkled seed coat to the true nutmeg of the Molucca Islands that gave the Sierran tree its common name. It is actually a member of the yew family.

The most abundant tree of the canyon slopes is a species with several growth forms as well as many names. The canyon live oak (*Quercus chrysolepis*) is equally known as goldencup oak for the velvety golden cups that hold its acorns; canyon live oak because of its evergreen leaves; golden oak for the golden fuzz on the leaf undersides; maul oak because of its tough wood. In canyons of the Merced, Kings, Kern, and other rivers, canyon live oak often grows straight and clean of branches for forty or more feet, sometimes reaching one hundred feet in total height—the deeper the canyon, the taller the oak. But among the huge granite boulders of Yosemite Valley's north talus slopes it becomes a different tree. From a short thick base mighty branches, successively dividing, wind into a dome-shaped crown sometimes 120 feet across, lower branches trailing to the ground or supported by gigantic rocky buttresses.

Whatever form the tree takes, tall or open growing, its acorns and abundant leaf insects attract many birds and tree-climbing mammals to the canyon live oak areas. Bandtailed pigeons swallow the acorns entire. Gray squirrels relish their nutritious meat. More than fifty kinds of fly and wasp larvae grow to adulthood in the multishaped galls on the tree's leaves and twigs.

The colorful nymphalid butterfly known as the California sister (*Limenitis bredowii*) flies regularly about canyon live oaks, host trees on which she lays eggs and where her caterpillars get their start. The sister's black wings, marked with two vertical white streamers and large orange tips, are as distinctive as her flight style. She alternates a few rapid wing beats with a glide in which the wings are held just below the horizontal. Boisduval's hairstreak (*Habrodais grunus*) is another butterfly that prefers the canyon oak domain. A one-inch brownish creature unusual for its crepuscular or dim-light habits, it sometimes flies in the semidarkness before dawn or hovers above the oaks well after the last rays of sunlight have deserted the canyon walls.

The deeper rock crevices hold ringtails and spotted skunks, which come out at night to forage. Brush heaps conceal western fence lizards (*Sceloporus*) doing their curious pushups off and on during the day and alligator lizards (*Gerrhonotus*) climbing sinuously through the thickets, purple tongues flicking, in search of crickets, spiders, termites, ground beetles.

Sometimes the secretive Gilbert's skink (*Eumeces gilberti*) moves in from the adjacent open-forest floor to hunt for insects among the surface cover in late afternoon. This colorful lizard sports a brilliant blue tail and striped back in youth; both change to an overall copper color in the adult. If attacked the skink drops its tail and often escapes while the wriggling tail holds the surprised enemy's attention. A new tail soon grows, usually not quite as smooth in its body connection as the original, often bearing a different color and of somewhat different structure, but functional in helping the lizard maintain proper balance in locomotion.

Many lizards possess this ability, known as autotomy or self-cutting, to break off a tail at zones of weakness in several specialized tail vertebrae. Immediate blood-vessel pinch-off prevents significant bleeding. The severed tail writhes for two or three minutes until the bare muscle at its base wears out and stops contracting.

Can a skink lose its tail more than once? Almost certainly yes. The regenerated tail itself can probably not break in two, since it usually grows back with a fibrocartilaginous rod and nonsegmented muscles that lack the capacity for self-cutting. But in the similarly autotomous side-blotched lizard (*Uta stansburiana*), which has been extensively studied, additional breaks always occur between the regenerated portion and the body.

The usual food of the smooth-skinned, six-to-eight-inch-long Gilbert's skink is small insects, but it will tackle readily an antagonist as formidable as a three-inch scorpion. Anne Belisle of the Yosemite Field School once watched such an encounter. The skink, jaws open wide, rushed at the scorpion, seized the middle of its long abdomen, bit down hard, and shook its prey violently. Up swung the scorpion's tail with the stinger at its tip and delivered a solid strike on the side of the skink's head. The skink dropped the scorpion like a lead weight and rubbed its head slowly in the gravel. The scorpion moved dully off.

After a minute of head rubbing, the skink charged again and was again stung and repelled, but with less effect than the first time. On the third charge, the scorpion's stings were completely ineffectual and the skink bit and shook its victim until the body grew limp. Laying down the carcass, the lizard picked off and discarded the scorpion's crusty pedipalps, which bear the pincers, bit off the foresection of the scorpion's body, and gulped it down. It then seized the front end of the abdomen and swallowed it whole by a series of muscular contractions, first shaking its reddish head from side to side. It kept on until the entire body, including the tail and stinger, was consumed. And after all was gone, the skink continued to open its mouth, contract its throat, and shut its mouth again and again, as though smacking its lips over the tasty morsel.

The talus slopes resound in spring with the songs of a variety of birds that use either the trees or the cliffs and air above them. There is the shrill chatter of white-throated swifts zigzagging high over the canyon; the slurred whistle of circling red-tailed hawks; from a rocky promontory the liquid cascade of the canyon wren "tripping down the scale." On the canyon floor, in the more open trees near water, male black-headed grosbeaks sing in mellow grosbeak style as they take their turn on the eggs. The canyon live oaks usually harbor Hutton's vireos and the natty black-throated gray warbler, whose feeding grounds are the crown and upper foliage of the oak.

Sierran wood warblers, in the course of time and evolution, have "parceled off" their scenic summer mountain land between them so that each species has a separate foraging and nesting niche and competes little with the others. The black-capped Wilson's warbler forages in creek dogwood thickets of the lodgepole fir belt. For the yellow warbler, "home" means streamside willows, alders, and cottonwoods, which it uses from nearly top to bottom. It, along with other warblers, has been facing a devastating loss of eggs to parasitic cowbirds in recent years. MacGillivray's warbler incubates her eggs in moist shady thickets of thimbleberry, bracken, or currant and forages close to the ground, slipping silently through the dense low cover. She may sometimes find a Nashville warbler as an associate ground nester in slightly drier thickets, but the Nashville's foraging territory is well up in the black oaks and maples. High in the dense canopies of Douglas fir, white and red fir, hermit warblers sing and feed, nesting slightly lower in thickly tangled branches. The more widespread yellow-rumped warbler forages and nests in nearly all of the conifers, from 3,000 to 10,000 feet, hunting small insects in outer foliage and fly catching adroitly in short flights beyond the leafage.

All of the warblers except the yellow-throat, resident locally on the lower western slope, migrate to warmer winter regions. Yellow-rumped and some orange-crowned warblers winter in the Central Valley; the others move south to southern Arizona, Mexico, or Guatemala, where they face increasing loss of winter habitat through forest destruction. By early May the survivors are back in their Sierran breeding niches. The buzzy song of the black-throated gray warbler floating out from the canyon live oaks once again seems as much a part of the talus slopes as the canyon live oaks themselves.

The other prominent oak of the montane forests is the California black oak, the only oak in the Sierra with deciduous leaves resembling those of the abundant red and black oak types of eastern North America. The California black oak is a true associate of the ponderosa pine, contrasting its shiny, sunlit foliage and broad, graceful crown with the pine's tall narrow spires on slopes and valleys throughout the mid-mountain belt. In spring its new leaves glow chartreuse and radiant; in summer they offer welcome shade; October drops them, russet and golden, onto misty meadows or crunchy forest carpet.

Like the canyon oak, the black oak forms the focal point of a whole small subcommunity of animal life. The noisiest, most gregarious component is unquestionably the acorn woodpecker, a bird closely linked to oaks in its entire Pacific Coast range from Oregon to Mexico and found abundantly in foothills and lower midmountain forests of the Sierra. Nasal, grating *yakup, yakup, yakup* calls pour out of the oaks where these flashy black-and-white woodpeckers with the harlequin head pattern are at work. The birds become so closely associated in a communal living style uncommon to most birds that they live in territorial groups the year around, breed cooperatively, and cooperate in nest excavation, incubation, and feeding of the young. Acorns are their stock food, though they occasionally vary the diet with insects seized flycatcher style. Nesting holes are usually drilled in decayed parts of living oaks or in dead trees, or, where these are missing, in telephone poles or fence posts.

The acorn-storing habits of this woodpecker never cease to amaze ornithologists. During years of plenty, the bird tucks away endless numbers of acorns in holes individually drilled for each nut, in tree trunks, poles, fence posts, or wooden buildings. The acorns are usually inserted point first into these custom-made pits, then tamped in for a tight, flush fit with the surface.

Some of the woodpecker storehouses or "cupboard trees" show riddled bark from three feet above the ground to forty feet up. Joseph Grinnell and Tracy Storer estimated 2,360 holes in one forty-five-foot dead incense cedar in Yosemite Valley, and 10,500 in a large living ponderosa pine. William Ritter, in his classic study *The California Woodpecker and I*, estimated that there were 31,800 holes in an old ponderosa pine log in the San Jacinto Mountains. Small wonder that the early Spanish Californians called the bird *el carpintero*.

The "carpenter's" apparent "foresight" in filling the granary for a rainy day takes a curious turn in its drillings in wooden cabins built of

Acorn woodpecker storing acorns

shingles. The pit in a shingle or siding is easily drilled, but when the acorn is hammered into place, it slips through the hole and drops out of sight. As long as the hole remains, the bird must fill it and so pushes through acorn after acorn. The pile on the floor inside builds higher and higher. Ritter reported finding over 62,000 acorns inside an old abandoned miner's house. Countless attics and walls of buildings hold bushels of acorns never retrieved. Further indication of the instinctive rather than reasoning nature of the acorn woodpecker's actions shows up in some of the other objects it sometimes stores—cherry pits, prune pits, bracts of pine cones, pieces of bark, pebbles, and rock fragments.

The bird's carving of nest holes produces home sites for other dwellers of the black oak subcommunity. A regular occupant of the holes is one of the Sierra Nevada's smallest owls, a round-headed, yellow-eyed hunter no bigger than a bluebird, which, unlike most owls, is active and abroad by day. The northern pygmy owl's mellow series of whistles, all on one pitch and punctuated by regular pauses, may be heard in ponderosa pine forests up and down the length of the Sierra either by day or night. The clear song is disproportionately loud for a seven-inch ball of feathers.

Pygmies usually nest near meadows, where their preferred food of mice and grasshoppers abounds. They are affectionate mates, snuggling shoulder to shoulder in courtship and greeting each other with soft fluttering trills at the nest hole. The male owl provides the lizards, snakes, voles, and other varied fare for his incubating partner and for the scraggly little owlets that appear in late May. While the owlets are growing, the male's talons often take a heavy toll of small songbirds near the nest. The small birds caught are plucked first, an unusual habit among owls, which customarily swallow feathers, hair, bones, and all and cough up the indigestible parts later as pellets. Charles Michael, who studied pygmies extensively in Yosemite in the 1920s, reported that pygmies produce no pellets. He watched plucking many times and described a male pygmy bringing a limp solitary vireo to his mate. For ten minutes there was a rain of feathers down from her perch as the female held the vireo under her feet and plucked the feathers one by one. Then off she flew in a swift undulant manner to a black oak and disappeared into an old woodpecker hole with her burden. Through the opening echoed the squeals of ravenous young birds. As the young owls mature, the male hunter reverts to the mammal-reptile diet that predominates most of the year, and the female teaches her progeny to tear off bites from chipmunks or skinks held in her talons.[2]

The western gray squirrel (*Sciurus griseus*) spends much time beneath the oaks in the autumn, bounding gracefully about, gathering and burying acorns. Two feet long, including the bushy gray tail, the squirrel pretty well confines its range to that of the oaks, leaving the higher coniferous forests to the chickaree, or Douglas squirrel (*Tami-*

asciurus douglasii). Acorns are its staff of life and old woodpecker holes in oaks its usual brood den, although it frequently builds large nests of leaves, twigs, grasses, and needles far out on branches in either oaks or pines.

Chickarees also live in the midmountain forests, but there is little apparent competition for food between them and the gray squirrels, the chickarees feeding largely on conifer cones, and the gray on acorns. The gray squirrel theoretically could survive in the next higher mountain zone above the oaks and live on the pine nuts and fungi it sometimes eats. Mammalogist Lloyd Ingles pointed out a curious behavior pattern that seems to limit the animal's effective spread. The gray buries every item of its cache singly in the ground, a nut here, a fungus there. When the winter snows come, it finds this hidden food by smell, digging a hole through the snow for each solitary tidbit. In the pine-oak belt where it lives, the snows are not too deep or persistent; in the fifteen-foot snows of the red fir forests the energy output to reach so little food would be too great.

The chickaree has a different behavior pattern. It buries its cones in large numbers at the same site, and when the snow becomes deep it has only one hole to dig to reach them all. Thus it thrives in the red fir community, moving down into the ponderosa forests, where its inherited food-storing pattern operates equally well, when vacancies occur. The presence of the agile marten in the red fir forests also militates more heavily against the slower-moving western gray squirrel than the lively chickaree.

The only nocturnal member of the squirrel tribe in the Sierra Nevada appears equally at home in the black oaks and the red firs. The versatile northern flying squirrel (*Glaucomys sabrinus*) occupies old woodpecker holes or tree cavities in both zones, sleeping during the day curled up, tail over its face. As darkness fills the forest, it sallies forth in search of food—whatever can be found in the way of berries, nuts, fruits, fungi, seeds, birds' eggs, buds, insects, flesh. More nimble in the treetops than any of the other squirrels, it is also an extremely adept glider. Leaping outward from a high fir or pine, the squirrel extends the furred membrane that connects wrists and ankles, flattens the extended tail, and volplanes swiftly and silently downward at a fairly steep angle. Gauging the distance to the target carefully, it bends its body upward just before contact and lands head up with a light plop low on the trunk of another tree. Up the trunk it races, pelting the ground with a shower of bark, and proceeds on to more glides from the heights as it scours the woods for food.

Without actually flying at all, these little glider pilots can cover distances of as much as 150 feet in a single leap; they can make sudden turns of ninety degrees, and can change either direction or landing speed by manipulation of the parachutelike membrane and rudder-like tail. They have been observed walking clotheslines like tightrope acrobats, hanging by one foot and pulling themselves erect and running in a split second. Such agility renders them immune from enemies except for large owls and barbed-wire fences.

Whether living in the lower black oaks or the higher red firs, the flying squirrel is active year round, feeding in winter on the black hair moss lichen (*Alectoria*) when it can get nothing else. Probably as abundant as the diurnal squirrels, it passes unnoticed by most campers. Occasionally, light sleepers hear curious thuds or pelting sounds during the night and discover that their butter or bacon has been nibbled by "some creature larger than a mouse." Yosemite naturalist Robert McIntyre, camping in the Ten Lakes Basin, was once awakened by the noise of a whole family of flying squirrels trying to get the trout from a creel hanging above his sleeping bag. This squirrel, more than most, has a taste for meat or flesh. Observed at close range, it is a handsome animal. The fur, buffy gray above and whitish below, is soft and silky; the eyes, dark and lustrous, are large, as in most nocturnal creatures. The squirrel's low, vibrant calling note is sometimes heard in the darkening oaks at twilight.

Yosemite Valley's black oaks, one source of this colorful oak fauna, have drawn naturalists' attention in recent decades to an ecological problem of wide-reaching implications in Sierran montane forests, a critical absence of young black oaks around many of the magnificent old ones. Fenced-in study areas, which afford protection from deer and rodents, have been established in Yosemite in an attempt at oak reforestation, but the real answers to the problem go much deeper.

Thomas Blackburn, Kat Anderson, and others have documented what the Native Americans knew and practiced for centuries: black oaks need fire. Black oak acorns were the favorites among the tribes of the central and southern Sierra; Washoe and Paiute Indians back-packed heavy loads of them from the west side of the Sierra Nevada to the east side each fall. Black oak groves were special places, marked for ownership and managed by burning the grasses and herbs under them every few years. The fires killed the filbert worm and weevil wintering in the duff, guaranteeing a worm-free acorn crop. They encouraged growth of the black morel (*Morchella elata*), a delicacy. Fire also released buds at the base of oak trunks, producing long flexible switches handy for baskets, granaries, and other uses, and reduced invasion by conifers. The parklike stands of ponderosa pine and black oaks reported by early naturalists, with magnificent broad canopies and open areas, all indicated the need of both trees for full sunlight. While lightning accounted for some of the fires, Indians planned them on a regular basis. The fire suppression policies of U.S. agencies from the turn of the century until recently have caused black oaks to be crowded out by shade-tolerant conifers. To restore and keep black oaks thriving in Sierran midmountain forests, a return to the way the Indians managed them seems essential.

The incense cedars, white firs, and sugar pines that have escaped fire over long intervals and have grown too close together for their own health often meet up with a problem of their own: a root-rot fungus (*Heterobasidion annosum*) that attacks them with deadly results. The fungus spreads along roots from one tree to the next, killing them. It can wipe out a whole section of coniferous forest within an amazingly short time. Yosemite Valley trees have been active targets, leading to the loss of more than a million board feet of infected timber in recent years.

Root rot, along with fire, drought, and bark beetles, is one of the natural agents by which mixed conifer forests reshape themselves over the centuries. Another more recent agent is white pine blister rust (*Cronartium ribicola*). Introduced into British Columbia in 1910 on infected white pine seedlings from France, blister rust moved rapidly into Washington, Oregon, and California; although it appeared to subside briefly, it has resurfaced recently in potent array. The wind-blown fungal spores of the rust spread from infected five-needled white and sugar pines to currant and gooseberry shrubs (*Ribes*), where they develop further and blow back to the pines. On the pines, they kill the needles and branches, and if they reach and encircle the main trunk, they kill the tree.

Healthy sugar pines add a special distinction to Sierran midmountain forests, often soaring two hundred feet or more, with outstretched asymmetrical limbs near the top dangling the world's longest cones—ten-to-twenty-four-inch beautiful brown pendants. The loss of this tree species would be a major one. Fortunately, some sugar pines are resistant to white pine blister rust, and the U.S. Forest Service Institute of Forest Genetics at Placerville is working with ecologists and foresters to locate such trees and grow their offspring for use in reforestation. Other means of saving this lovely tree include a moratorium on logging healthy, potentially resistant sugar pines and protecting the few old-growth mixed conifer forests left, both as a gene bank and for the biodiversity that their age and mosaic of plant life provide.

The Sierra Nevada Ecosystem Project (SNEP), funded by Congress in 1996, documented how severely Sierran old-growth forests have been impacted over time by logging, clear-cutting, and other human activities. It emphasized the richness of forest ecosystems containing trees of all ages and sizes, including snags and fallen trees, which continue to provide diverse habitats for wildlife and contribute to the nutrient cycles. For sugar pines, abolishing clear-cutting—a practice that favors currant and gooseberry growth, on which rust spores depend—would help break the rust cycle within local areas, since shrub rust spores travel only about 1,500 feet.

White fir and incense cedar fill equally prominent niches in Sierran middle-elevation forests. White fir, the traditional Christmas tree, carries tiers of flat-needled, bluish green branches and papery cones that stand erect like candles on its upper limbs before falling apart on the tree. The white fir climbs higher in the western Sierra than its companions, eventually mingling with the red firs of the next-higher belt. White fir likes moisture and prefers north-facing slopes. It is often the conifer to die first in a drought.

Sugar pine, elegant conifer of the
midmountain forests

SNEP studies have shown that droughts occurred for much longer periods in the Sierra Nevada's past than had previously been realized. Some lasted over a century, and between A.D. 900 and 1300 one went on for four hundred years. Apparently prolonged droughts are normal variations in Sierran climate, and surviving trees must adapt to them.

Incense cedars can take varying moisture as well as either sun or shade and are probably the most versatile of the midmountain conifers. Their lacy branchlets of scalelike leaves shed snow like an A-frame roof, and their vertically grooved cinnamon bark adds a rich hue to the western Sierran mixed conifer forests.

For eons, these forests have been the home of the Sierra Nevada's only species of deer, the mule deer (*Odocoileus hemionus*). It takes its name from the large mulelike ears, eight inches long and half as wide, which, as in all of its kind, flick periodically for sounds of danger. Bucks stand on average forty inches high at the shoulder and five and one-half feet long, weigh around 170 pounds, and are toned reddish brown in summer and grayish brown in winter. Does are a trifle smaller. The tail, white with varying amounts of black and usually held flat; the two-to-five-inch metatarsal glands on the hind legs; and the dichotomously branched antlers of bucks distinguish the mule deer readily from the white-tailed deer, whose nearest distribution is southern Oregon.

All the mountain deer migrate seasonally from well-defined winter feeding grounds to summer ones, returning to these same winter and summer ranges year after year. In its summer meadows the herd browses, fattens on the lush green forage, and produces fawns that increase its numbers by nearly a third. Upon returning to the restricting winter quarters it often loses excess population to starvation. This has been the pattern in much of the Sierra Nevada since the 1930s. In primitive California, deer populations were probably relatively stable, kept down to the carrying capacity of their ranges by abundant predators, which included the grizzly bear. Today Sierra Nevada predators are too scarce to remove the deer surplus that otherwise starves each winter; they take only a fraction of it.

The coyote (*Canis latrans*) is the predator that most frequently makes itself heard; its yaps and howls are regular night sounds in many parts of the range. Coyotes sometimes run down yearling or weakened deer, especially in winter. In Yosemite Valley one January day, Rangers Sedergren and Robinson noticed a small deer standing in the frigid waters of the Merced River a short distance from shore. The animal, visibly trembling, gave every evidence of fright and fatigue from a chase. On the riverbank a coyote lay in wait. Deer often try to throw off pursuit by seeking refuge in a stream, where coyotes will not follow. But this stream was too wide, deep, surging, and cold to permit a crossing, and the deer was stranded. The rangers couldn't resist driving the coyote away to give the shivering deer a second chance.[3]

Coyotes take fawns occasionally, as do black bears, golden eagles, and bobcats, but none of them regularly goes after healthy, alert adults. That role falls to the mountain lion, or cougar (*Felis concolor*), the prime natural predator of deer. Six to eight feet long including the long black-tipped tail, and standing taller than a police dog, the big reddish gray cat totals 165 pounds of sinewy power. It is a proficient hunter, with a geographical range from British Columbia to Patagonia. The bulk of the mountain lions in the Sierra roam the 2,000-to-6,500-foot western belt, although some are known to cross the crest as high as 11,500 feet.

Elusive and seldom seen until recently, when increasing numbers of people have encroached upon their foothill and midmountain range, cougars seek out brush and timber on rocky, rugged terrain—concealment that helps them approach deer undetected. During a night's hunt they often cover great distances with their easy, striding walk, muscles flowing like rippling water. On horseback, Donald McLean, of California Fish and Game, once followed fresh tracks in falling snow for five hours, until darkness turned him back. In that time the lion had covered almost twenty miles. The cougar's route meandered along the sides of a high ridge for about seven miles, turned off down a long spur ridge for another five miles, crossed a canyon to a different series of ridges, and followed these to their end. "The lion swung back and forth from one side of the ridge tops to the other exactly as would a good deer hunter working the same country," wrote McLean. "In this manner, one basin head after another could be scanned." Ridges frequently occupy a good part of a male cougar's one-hundred-mile or so circuitous beat. Females ordinarily travel in canyons and on shorter circuits, especially when the young are too small to go far.

The kittens may be born any month of the year, but in the Sierra Nevada birth most frequently occurs from April to August. The litter usually contains two or three, rarely more than four, spotted, ring-tailed babies with eyes closed and with the usual appetite for milk. After ten days the eyes open on to their nest world in a thicket or rocky cavern. Long before the spots disappear at about eight months, the mother has been leading the young to her fresh kill to feed, and she has been teaching them to hunt. They learn on rabbits, mice, squirrels—anything that moves—and later, in hungry times, they may fall back on these small mammals when no larger food is obtainable. It is a long jump from the awkward pounce of bumbling young lions to the skilled spring achieved by the maturing cougar from his second year onward.

The mule deer, the cougar's principal target, is no easy prey. In the tens of thousands of years that these two have lived in the Sierra, the long cocked ears and moist black nose of the deer have tested each breeze to detect the approach of the big cat. So effective is their defense that former state lion hunter Jay Bruce claimed two out of three deer escape a mountain lion's charge. A successful stalk must be a work of art, a masterpiece of perfection, or the tawny cat with the flowing rhythm will go hungry.

When well done, it is a remarkable performance. At Pigeon Flat in the western foothills, a large cougar crawled on its belly for about two hundred yards, stalking a lone doe that was browsing on buckbrush. The last shielding rock between them stood no higher than a large sombrero, yet the lion crawled thirty feet from a small ditch with this single rock as his sole cover. Behind it he crouched, still seventy-five feet from his prey, until the deer was off guard for an instant. Then the charge! In three and one-half bounds he closed the distance and struck the deer as she started her second jump, killing her quickly with a bite through the base of the skull. Don McLean read this story in the snow after coming onto the doe's still-warm body and interrupting the cougar's siesta.

In their book *The Puma,* Stanley Young and Edward Goldman quote biologist Daniel Singer, who watched a cougar stalk a doe through frost-tipped foot-high grass that harmonized perfectly with the cat's coat: "So light, silent and cautious was his every move that he might be said to drift light as a wisp of smoke toward his prey before making the death dealing spring."

In today's world, as people move into cougar territory they need to be aware of the big cat's silent ways and to keep an observant eye on their surroundings, from foothills through midmountain forests to the high Sierra.

Three

WHEN HUNTER A. T. DOWD, chasing a wounded grizzly bear, stumbled on to the huge trees of the North Calaveras Grove in 1852, he forgot all about the bear in his astonishment. He wondered if he were suffering from hallucinations; there couldn't be trees that big! The men back at camp ridiculed his "big trees" story. Only by the ruse of needing their backs to haul out a monstrous bear that he had shot did Dowd get them to the grove to prove his find.

There the trees stood, mostly in groups, immense brownish red trunks rising with a clean nobility to rounded green crowns two hundred feet or more overhead. It took twenty men standing with outstretched arms barely touching to circle one. Word of the "mammoth trees" in Sierran midmountain forests spread quickly to the nearby gold camps of Murphys and Angels and to the outside world. Murphys Camp immediately became famous as the nearest stopping place to the grove of big trees and saw a steady stream of tourists and scientists. One of them, William Lobb, a British botanical collector, took seeds and specimens back to England in late 1853. From these botanist John Lindley named the tree in honor of the hero of Waterloo. Wrote Lindley, "We think that no one will differ from us in feeling that the most appropriate name to be proposed for the most gigantic tree which has been revealed to us by modern discovery is that of the greatest of modern heroes. Wellington stands as high above his contemporaries as the Californian tree above all the surrounding foresters. Let it then bear henceforward the name of *Wellingtonia gigantea.*"[1]

But *Wellingtonia* met an abrupt taxonomic wall the very next year. Belgian botanist Joseph Decaisne pointed out that the genus *Sequoia* had been described seven years earlier by Hungarian Stephan Endlicher when he christened the coast redwood of the northern California Coast Ranges with the scientific name of *Sequoia sempervirens.* By nomenclature's sacred international rule of priority, if the big tree was a sufficiently close cousin of the coast redwood, its genus already had been determined as *Sequoia;* only its species was new to science.

So, to many botanists convinced of the close generic kinship, it was as *Sequoia gigantea* that the massive trees of the Sierra became known. And so they remained by long usage, including that of the National Park Service, until 1939, when a new name, *Sequoiadendron giganteum,* attained general acceptance. Research indicated clear distinctions between *Sequoia sempervirens,* the coastal redwood, and *Sequoiadendron giganteum,* the Sierran big tree. Chromosome numbers differ; the formation and development of the embryo is different; and the two appear to have no immediate common ancestors.

To the tourist of the 1850s, "big tree" was the only name that was needed for the "biggest-around tree on earth." "Sierran redwood," "sequoia," and "giant sequoia" were other naturals. Endlicher's source of the name sequoia is not known; but since he was a linguist as well as a botanist, it is generally supposed that he gave the name in tribute to the Indian chief Sequoyah. This remarkable Cherokee invented an alphabet so simple and so effective that anyone in his tribe could become literate in Cherokee within a short time—one of the significant cultural achievements of the nineteenth century.

Dowd's discovery, which led to scientific recognition of the big trees, was not the first sight record—the Joseph Reddeford Walker party apparently saw them in 1833 in the Yosemite region—but Dowd was the first to publicize the tree's existence. During the thirty years

Giant Sequoia Groves
(map by Carla J. Simmons)

after Dowd's find, one grove of giant sequoia after another was discovered in the isolated mountain forests between the deep river
canyons of the central and southern Sierra. All were on the western
slope in scattered locations from 4,500 to 7,500 feet. A total of seventy-
five groves grew in a narrow broken band 260 miles long, from the
middle fork of the American River south to Deer Creek. The largest
groves and biggest trees were in the south. Within this Sierran

province, in protected spots where the soil was deep, rich, and moist, where winter snows built ten-to-fourteen-foot anklets around the broad tree bases, where temperatures sometimes fell to zero, lived the surviving giants of a once widespread tribe.

As the trees became known to admirers, they were eyed equally by exploiters. The 1880s rang with the crackling thunder of falling sequoias. In sharp response boomed back the battle cries of Visalia news editor George W. Stewart, John Muir, and the California Academy of Sciences' Gustav Eisen. They wrote, talked, and fought to preserve the trees and get them into safe hands. But protection took time.

Meanwhile, loggers felled hundreds of the giants in accessible areas, despite the difficulty of the operation. A six-foot platform had to be erected to clear the flying buttresses. Standing on it, two men chopped out chips, so large that a boy could hardly hold one, until a ten-foot notch was cut. The fellers then carried a twenty-foot saw around to the opposite side of the tree and for days ground it in and out, greasing it to make it slip, and inserting huge wedges to prevent settling. At last the ponderous trunk leaned and pitched to earth with a roar that shook the forest. The trunk usually broke into transverse chunks on falling, making it an exceedingly wasteful lumber tree; but the great durability of the brittle wood promised long-lasting shingles, fence stakes, posts, and flumes.

Western Mono Indians, to whom the sequoia was sacred, tried to persuade lumbermen to spare the *wawona,* their name for "big tree," and warned them that wawona destroyers would be visited by bad luck. But the loggers steamed on, blasting down by dynamite the trees that were impossible to saw. In Converse Basin only a single sequoia, the Boole tree, was left standing in what had been one of the finer southern groves. The ground beneath it lay strewn with thousands of logs never utilized because they proved too big or too costly to handle or had smashed to bits in the fall. Mill crews invaded Big Stump Basin, Redwood Mountain Grove, and others.

It was probably the Kaweah Cooperative Colony, a group of about fifty-five socialists who set up a utopia near the Giant Forest in 1885–86, that ignited the fuse of events leading to federal action on the southern big trees. The colonists, some half of them from San Francisco, planned an economy based on lumber sales. After applying for quarter-sections of timberland in the area surrounding the Giant Forest, they built an eighteen-mile road into their timber stands. They renamed the largest local sequoia (General Sherman) the Karl Marx tree and other big trees for their various heroes. In the office of the *Visalia Weekly Delta,* thirty miles away, George W. Stewart and Frank Walker shifted into high gear to get the trees into a national park. Said Stewart later: "We wrote letters to every person in the United States, in and out of Congress, whom we knew to be in favor of forest conservation and to every magazine and newspaper we knew to favor the idea. Their name was not legion in those days. The response, with few exceptions, was cordial."[2]

The movement to save the big trees spread across the country. Washington was listening. In 1890, in two bills, Congress created Sequoia National Park to preserve thirty-two groves of big trees and General Grant National Park to save the General Grant Grove. (General Grant National Park was incorporated within Kings Canyon National Park in 1940.) The Giant Forest became a part of the park, along with extensive high-Sierran wilderness. A year later the Giant Forest's socialist colony crumbled in dissension.

The Mariposa Grove of big trees had come under state protection along with Yosemite Valley in 1864; both became part of Yosemite National Park in 1906. The North Calaveras Grove was acquired by the state in 1931 with the help of the Save-the-Redwoods League and the Calaveras Grove Association, among others. In the early 1950s these same two groups, aided by John D. Rockefeller Jr., the California War Memorial Park Association, the Sierra Club, and others, raised matching funds to add the South Calaveras Grove of big trees and prime sugar pines to the state park system.

For nearly a century, from 1864 to 1954, every grove had to be fought for, wrested from the ever-threatening saw. Gradually the better-known giant sequoia groves gained protection in national or state parks and in national forests. In the 1980s and 1990s, however, it took other conservation battles to prevent giant sequoia habitat destruction by the U.S. Forest Service in Sequoia National Forest. And the threat of ozone damage from air pollution generated in the San Joaquin Valley remains ominous. From Moro Rock in Sequoia National Park, on countless days, a brown layer can be seen hanging over the valley. When afternoon breezes blow it into the park, it kills pines and young sequoias. Preserving what has already been saved still requires constant vigilance. Today numerous locales in Sequoia National Park have been dedicated as memorials to those who made the park a reality, including Mount Stewart and Mount Eisen, two towering peaks of the Great Western Divide in the southern Sierra; Zumwalt Meadow; Muir Grove; and the Founders Group in the Giant Forest.

Every sequoia grove diffuses a mood of its own, distinct from the others. In sheer forest depth and diversity, none exceeds Sequoia National Park's Giant Forest. Here the groves go on for miles; hikers may wander, as Muir did, for days among the cinnamon columns, crunching the egg-shaped cones into the soft duff, shaking out the tiny seeds, tracing the reddish trunks up and up.

Reaching out at the base for a firm though shallow grip on the mountainside, the big trees climb with hardly a taper to the first clumps of green foliage 100 feet up. Above these, muscular branches push out and turn abruptly upward, hiding the burnished boles with scalelike leaf tufts until they emerge 200 to 275 feet high in round green crowns against the sky.

The size of the trees is incomprehensible at first view. People who live among sequoias say that they never really get used to them; photographers reach quickly for a wide-angle lens. The immensity is concealed by the harmonic proportions. From buttressed base to superstructure they look so perfectly proportioned that you hardly notice the twenty-foot width of the trunks or reflect that if one fluted base were moved into a city street it would block it from curb to curb. The neighboring conifers offer little help in eye comparison; sugar pines, magnificent large trees in their own right, seem moderate-sized alongside sequoias.

Which is the largest giant sequoia? There is no one answer. The greatest in girth is not the tallest, and exact dimensions are not always agreed upon. The three most voluminous individual specimens are Sequoia National Park's General Sherman tree (275 feet high; 36 feet maximum basal diameter), Kings Canyon National Park's General Grant tree (267 feet high; 40 feet maximum basal diameter), and Sequoia National Forest's Boole tree (268 feet high; 35 feet maximum basal diameter).

The National Park Service considers General Sherman "the largest living thing in the world" based on estimated total volume in the trunk. In 1978, the General shed a branch, growing out of the trunk 130 feet above the ground, that was itself larger and longer than most forest trees of the eastern United States, measuring 7 feet across and 150 feet long. Yet General Sherman is only a nod bigger than three others less than a mile from it in the Giant Forest, one of which, the McKinley tree, is taller, 291 feet high. Some big trees have exceeded 300 feet in height, but 220 to 275 feet is a more common attainment. Several thousand of them have basal diameters greater than 15 feet, and a good many range from 20 to 30 feet. No living giant sequoia comes close to the record heights of 368 feet or more held by the coast redwood; and no coast redwood approaches the girth of the biggest giant sequoias.[3]

It was once thought that size and age were correlated directly, that you could judge the age of a living tree by counting the growth rings of a fallen tree of equal size. Studies reveal that it doesn't work this way. Environment is more important than age. A young sequoia that sprouts in a sunny area where there is plenty of soil moisture will quickly outgrow an older sequoia struggling in the shade with less favorable water supply.

The story of the famous Stump tree in the North Calaveras Grove shows how misleading size can be. In 1853, five men decided to cut down the largest standing big tree in the grove, partly to see how old it was. They had no saws large enough, and it was impossible to chop it down, so they hit on the idea of boring the tree down with two-inch augurs. There were no augurs long enough to reach through the trunk, but by welding iron bars to the augurs to extend their length they managed to bore completely through in one direction again and again, and to cross-bore in the same painstaking way. It took twenty days to sever completely the trunk from the stump; but still the tree stood. They inserted large wedges; the giant refused to fall. On the twenty-second day after work began, while the men were away at lunch, a sudden wind toppled the tree. (Another version says that two pine trees were felled against the sequoia finally to push it down.)

The tree measured 24 feet across at stump level, 30 feet across at the ground. In spite of its enormous size, one of the largest on record, and a height of 302 feet, its growth rings showed only around 1,200 years of age. Situated in a moist, favorable site in the grove, it had simply shot up in a hurry. The stump was smoothed and became famous as a dance floor accommodating thirty two couples; it was later roofed over to become at different intervals a theater, a small hotel, and a newspaper office. Today it stands open to the sky.

One thousand two hundred years represent adulthood for the big tree, but they are a long step from old age. Longevities of 1,500, 2,000, and 2,500 years appear common. Experts of the past century have estimated that the age of patriarchs like General Grant and General Sherman is between 3,000 and 4,000 years, and the Grizzly Giant in Yosemite's Mariposa Grove is perhaps the oldest of them all. But the detailed research of the San Jose State University team of Richard Hartesveldt, Thomas Harvey, and Howard Shellhammer in the 1960s and early 1970s led them to suspect that these three trees, like the Stump tree, grew very rapidly because they were in especially good sites, with ample soil moisture during the entire growing season, and that they might be quite a bit younger than the earlier estimates.[4]

The usually helpful increment borer offers no certain solution to the age puzzle in living sequoias. The borer proved invaluable in determining the age of the more ancient but much smaller trunked bristlecone pines by removing a core of countable tree rings from bark to center. But such instruments will penetrate only the outer two feet of a big tree, a rather inadequate sample of a fifteen-foot trunk. At present, the only authentic records come from logged trees, and ring counts of these verify the oldest known giant sequoias as about 3,200 years old.

Is it possible for human beings who live seventy-year cycles to comprehend such life spans? That fire-scarred giant at the meadow's edge was a sprouting seed on the moist bare earth when Rome was founded. In the first two hundred years of its youth, it sprang steadily upward, a conical shape clothed to the base in blue-green leaves. Beneath the ground its roots spread laterally at a six-foot depth, beginning the horizontal network that would reach out ultimately to two-thirds of the tree's height.

By the birth of Christ seven centuries later, the rich red bark and upbending arms gleamed high above the meadow. Inside the trunk, rose-colored heartwood deeply impregnated with tannin was forming, increasing as a thousand years passed so that by the time of the discovery of America it filled most of the vast interior with a rot-resisting durable wood. Outside, the bark thickened to a two-foot blanket of asbestoslike cinnamon fibers.

Throughout the fires and storms of centuries, through the rise and fall of Rome, the Mayan empire, Spain, through Magna Carta, the Renaissance, 1776, the birth of the United Nations, this statesman has heralded each sunrise anew for nearly three millennia.

Dawn is a magical time in the groves. As the first rays of sun strike the big-tree tops and lance down from one ruddy limb to another, the birds take over the forest. From still dim recesses ring out the robins' morning carols. The three-part song of the western tanager lends a strident base to the rapid bubbling warbles of California purple finches. Wood-pewees dart about, snapping mandibles on tardy moths. A burst of melody hovers over the meadow—the black-headed grosbeak's morning flight song. On upturned fingerlike roots of fallen sequoias, dark-sided juncos pipe out a dry trill. The day's foodlift recommences in the red-breasted nuthatch nesting hole in a white fir stump. The *yank-yank-yank* notes of busy parents rebound from insect-collecting forays up the higher trunks and branches of all the taller trees that furnish a foraging niche.

Sometimes the deep *kuk kuk kuk* of the West's largest woodpecker resounds throughout the forest, as the big black bird, nearly the size of a crow, wings its way to a favorite snag. Landing with flaming topknot erect, the male pileated woodpecker turns his striped red, black, and white head to right and left and goes to work. Tilting back his

Pileated woodpecker

body, leaning on stiff tail, gripping tightly with the claws, he throws his heavy head and long sharp beak through an arc of eight to ten inches. As he bombards the trunk, striking first where wood is more decayed, his bill's hard glancing blows split off slivers a quarter-inch wide. Chips and flakes fly as the woods ring with the pummeling. The pileated woodpecker's Sierran niche includes dead trees of midmountain forests, where for rapid woodcutting it is unexcelled; it has been known to dig out a hole large enough for concealment within thirty minutes in a dead but still firm sugar pine.

All woodpeckers possess extrapowerful neck muscles; the pileated can render a whack nearly equal to that of a person with an ordinary hammer. Its holes often measure six inches long, three inches wide, and three inches deep in trees or logs, where it drills to reach the boring beetle larvae and carpenter ants that form its major diet.

Occasionally it eats wild berries. This can be awkward for such a heavy bird. Ranger-naturalist Allen Waldo observed a pileated feeding on ripe blue elderberries, bending the branches over in so great an arc that the bird hung upside down as it cleaned off a berry clump at top speed. When eating was nearly finished, its feet suddenly slipped from the stem, and the woodpecker dropped to the ground flat on its back. It recovered immediately and flew off.

In spite of its size and power, the bird has enemies. Among avian predators, both goshawks and Cooper's hawks inhabit its range. Lowell Sumner and Joseph Dixon tell the story of a family of pileateds that suffered a tragic loss at the Parker Group of big trees in Sequoia National Park. A pair of these woodpeckers chiseled out a nest chamber at a height of twenty-four feet in a large fir stump above the camp kitchen of a troop of soldiers. The birds, wary at first, grew used to the men's presence and became quite tame. The soldiers, in turn, became greatly attached to the birds, naming them Cap and Phoebe.

Phoebe laid an egg a day from May 7 to May 10. The parents shared daytime incubation, "but at night Phoebe always occupied the nest, while Cap roosted in the doorway with his head outward." After the eggs hatched, both parents went far afield seeking food for their young. On the evening of June 16, as Phoebe was flying toward the nest, a Cooper's hawk struck and killed her and carried her to a nearby tree. Cap, who witnessed his mate's death, appeared to lapse into a state of shock. For a day and two nights he just sat in the door of his nest. On the morning of the eighteenth the continuous chirping of his extremely hungry brood seemed to rouse him, and he flew into the forest to quiet their appetites. From then on he was a diligent provider.

The task became more and more strenuous as the fuzzy fledglings grew large and waited, clamoring, at the nest door. On July 19, as Cap left the nest, "they all sailed out after him . . . and soon hit the ground with a thud." Cap collected them as best he could and led out into the forest, feeding on nearby stumps and logs, his brood scrambling and flapping along after him. For several days the procession remained around the camp, but finally the birds drifted away.

A companion woodpecker with feeding habits different from those of the pileated is the smaller white-headed woodpecker. Hopping up the trunks of conifers, it pries off thick bark scales to obtain insects living in the crevices. Its bill serves as a crowbar more than a hammer.

Whiteheads sometimes tunnel nesting holes in spongy sequoia bark, which is thickest at the lower trunk levels that the birds prefer.

Midday hours in the groves are a mingling of hot sun in the clearings, cool shade under the trees. The lupines, the crimson snow plants, the dogwoods of the forest understory pass from dazzling radiance to somber eclipse as the shadows come and go.

In depressions in some of the sequoia buttresses where bits of bark have accumulated, chipmunks, juncos, and robins take "bark baths," wallowing in the fine cinnamon dust, flipping it over their fur and feathers. Dust baths of any sort are thought to help animals clean their skin of oil, to discourage parasites, and to yield a pleasant sensation. Sequoia bark dust, impregnated with tannin, probably acts very much like insect powder. Tannin's astringency renders it unpalatable to most insects and antiseptic to most fungus diseases. In the huge sawdust piles along the Big Stump Trail, tannin is believed to be the ingredient that has inhibited plant growth on the piles for more than a century.

In July and August that lively little harvester of big-tree cones, the chickaree, goes into action, and any time of day a shower of two-inch bombs may thud to earth. This small, impish tree squirrel, also called the Douglas squirrel, is the Pacific Coast relative of the North American red squirrel. It frolics up and down sequoia trunks, peels off soft spongy bark strips for its nest, leaps from the high swaying branches of one tree to the next, explodes spontaneously in high-pitched squeals and scolds, and pops around trunks totally unexpectedly, its bushy short tail jerking and bright eyes bulging.

When it decides to harvest cones, several hundred feet up and out on the tip of a branch, the chickaree does it as though winter were closing in the next day. Its ivory incisors often snip off more than twenty cones a minute. Working at peak activity, it can drop a fusillade of thirteen green sequoia "grenades" in ten seconds. When enough have accumulated on the ground, it descends and stores them away, carrying one at a time to great caches in hollow logs, under prostrate trunks, in crevices or creeks. These moist, cool, and shady spots keep cones from opening for at least three years.

California ground squirrels and golden-mantled ground squirrels frequently run off with a share of the fallen harvest, but the chickaree manages to tuck away most of it. Naturalist Walter Fry watched one energetic chickaree cache more than thirty-eight barley sackfuls of cones in twelve days. From these, Fry extracted over twenty-six pounds of seeds.

With pine cones, chickarees discard the woody scales and eat the seeds. But the seeds of sequoia average 91,000 to the pound; the seeds of a single cone weigh less than .06 ounce altogether, only a fraction of which is embryo food. What chickarees eat is the fleshy sequoia cone bract, which they strip while the cones are green and soft. Not all of the hidden cones are eaten during winter's scantier times. The chickaree's habit of storing big-tree cones alongside decaying logs at meadow edges has allowed many trees to sprout and grow over the centuries.

Chickarees favor sequoia cones that are two to five years old, and dislodge many seeds in their harvest. Older sequoia cones, aged four to nine, form a favorite egg-laying repository for the tiny, long-horned beetle (*Phymatodes nitidus*). As it tunnels into the cones, it often severs the water pipeline, creating cracks through which sequoia seeds can tumble out. Updrafts from fires also cause cones to pop open and release seeds.

Sunset in the groves intensifies the burnt umber of the big-tree pillars, setting them off in bold relief against the lengthening shadows. This is the time when deer seek the meadows, when the last bird calls rend the stillness. As night's cool air rises into a darkening forest, chipmunks retire to their burrows and the nocturnal mammals emerge.

The coyote trots out on its beat. Raccoons (*Procyon lotor*) amble along the creeks and through the campgrounds. The black bear (*Ursus americanus*) prowls looking for promising morsels, rising on hind legs at certain preferred trees to reach high up and sharpen its claws on the bark. The bear manicure tree in Sequoia National Park is one of its favorites. Naturalist Ernest Thompson Seton believed that such trees were used as bear signboards, conveying through the bear's acute sense of smell pertinent facts about the tree's previous user—much the same as the urinary signal posts of dogs, wolves, and coyotes. The trees may

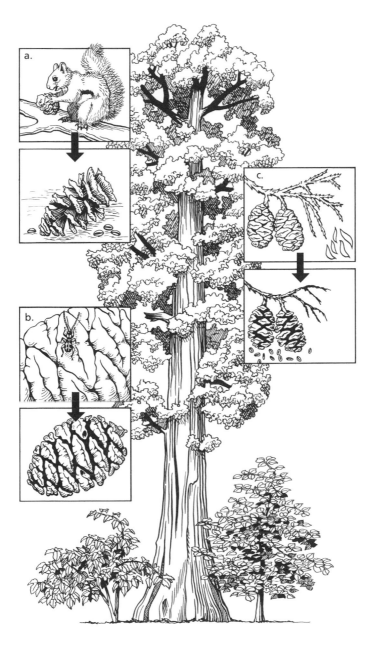

Giant sequoia seed dissemination. (a) Chickaree eats fleshy green cone, releasing seeds. (b) Cone beetle lays eggs in cone. Beetle larvae cut water line, causing cones to open and release seeds. Adult beetle escapes through hole. (c) Fire updrafts dry and open cones, releasing seeds.

be a kind of social register, telling a newcomer that his claw marks are the highest on the trunk or that a larger bear is boss of this domain.

All through the underbrush, in hollow logs, among rocks, in the myriad openings that tiny animals make use of, the most abundant mammals of the groves, the deer mice (*Peromyscus maniculatus*), scamper on their nightly hunt for seeds and berries. Almost every bird and mammal predator feeds on these little mice, yet they are one of the most successful animals in the Sierra—indeed, in North America, if judged by numbers and wide range. Joseph Grinnell and Tracy Storer estimated that in Yosemite they nearly equaled in numbers all the other mammals of the area. Sumner and Dixon considered them the most widely distributed mammals in Sequoia and Kings Canyon National Park in the early 1950s. George Lawrence's live-trapping census of the mammals of Whitaker's Forest, in the same region, found them extremely abundant but cyclic. In many places where mammal surveys are made, deer mice are so numerous that it is necessary to trap them out before other species can be captured.

This elegant native is far different from the drab-colored, musky-smelling city-dwelling house mouse. The soft brownish gray fur and pure white underparts of the deer mouse contrast cleanly. Its tail is well furred with dark hair above and white below. The large delicate ears and wide eyes surmount an inquiring face.

Deer mice in some forested regions of the United States perform a real service by feeding on larvae and pupae of insects detrimental to the trees. Whether similar ecological relationships exist in Sierran forests is yet to be determined, but the rodents are known to eat heavily of insects in the spring. In the summer and fall they turn to buds, nuts, berries, and seeds or, when within reach of cabins or campsites, meat, butter, and cheese. Throughout the long cold winters of the groves, the mice remain active underneath and above the snow, weaving a tracery of tiny footprints, living on large caches.

They climb trees readily, if slowly, and in emergencies jump into space from any height without hesitation. Sumner and Dixon watched deer mice fall thirty-eight feet and run away with no noticeable distress. "Since they are so light in relation to their surface, a fall usually has no serious consequences for them."

All their defenses cannot, of course, ward off the long-tailed weasel, striped skunk, and innumerable other enemies. Among the crawling predators is a native member of the boa family, the "two-headed snake," with a blunt tail that closely resembles the head and sometimes even moves and strikes like a head. Known as the rubber boa (*Charina bottae*), it both looks and feels to the touch like brown rubber, and is, like all Sierran snakes save the rattlesnake, harmless to humans. Sheltering by day in damp places under logs or rocks, often near streams, it produces in season up to eight young, born alive. Nightly at dusk its search for small mammals and lizards begins, a hunt that may require burrowing, swimming, or climbing to appease its hunger. A visitor who reported seeing "an eel" climbing a giant sequoia at twilight was among the few fortunate enough to watch a rubber boa in action. Although rated the most common snake in Yosemite's Mariposa Grove in a summer vertebrate survey, the boa, like most nocturnal creatures, is seldom seen by humans.

Nocturnal life has its sway in the groves; again comes the dawn. Over the centuries the wheel goes round and round. Individual chipmunks tumbling in their bark dust baths are here probably three years at most and gone; the woodpeckers, four years; mule deer, five years; humans, perhaps six decades. A three-thousand-year-old sequoia, the same solitary individual, lives on and on—through 1,000 generations of chipmunks, 750 generations of woodpeckers, 600 generations of deer, and 50 generations of humans.

Four

FIRE ECOLOGY

IN THE FORMER AFRICAN states of Rwanda and Urundi there was a legend of Batutsi tribal origin. The first Batutsi came from the sky. His father was Imana, God the Powerful. His mother was called Gasani. Though life in the sky was beautiful, Gasani had not been happy. She wanted children and begged Imana to help her.

So Imana took a piece of clay, moistened it with his tongue, and shaped it to form a child. "Hide this in a pot of fresh milk for nine months," he told Gasani, "and promise to tell no one."

Gasani promised, nine months passed, and the clay child awakened and began to cry. It was a handsome boy. Then Imana made a brother and sister so the little boy wouldn't be lonely.

When Gasani's sister saw the beautiful children, she coaxed Gasani incessantly, trying to discover her secret. One day she tricked Gasani into drinking too much beer, and Gasani whispered the story. Imana heard at once. Very angry, he seized the children of Gasani and dropped them through a big hole in the floor of Heaven onto the inhospitable earth.

For ten days they suffered, cold and hungry, until Imana relented. He shot a streak of lightning to start a fire in the grass. The next day seeds and plants rained down—peas, corn, beans, sorghum, bananas—

and began to sprout and grow in the fertile ash. Imana had helped his children.[1]

In legend and actuality nearly all primitive peoples have been associated with fire from their earliest days. Carbonized artifacts are linked with the oldest human remains. Australian aborigines still burn the isolated outback on animal hunts perfected in age-old tradition.

Humans have probably used and "kept" fire for more than 500,000 years, though they seem to have learned to produce it only during the last 20,000. In the beginning their constant concern must have been to keep alight flames secured from lightning fires. Their methods of fire "storage," the inevitable escape of sparks to the surrounding wilderness, and the use of fire in the hunt for plants and animals marked the initial stamp of their influence on the earth's landscape. Curiously, that long walk with fire now seems to be circling back toward its starting place, for different reasons.

The American Indians probably knew how to make fire when they crossed the Bering Strait land bridge from Asia to Alaska some 15,000 years ago. From the California Indians to the Incas of Peru, they used the fire drill for producing fire.

Ishi, the last California Yahi Indian to emerge from the Stone Age culture of the northern Sierra–Mount Lassen border, lived as a modern for nearly five years. He had always carried his fire drill with him on wilderness travel, protecting the drill and tinder in rainy weather with a buckskin covering. Ishi demonstrated its use to many avid Sunday crowds at the University of California Museum of Anthropology in San Francisco, where he lived the final years of his life, from 1911 to 1915.

Ishi's fire drill was typical of those used by other California Indians. It consisted of two pieces, an upper and a lower. The lower, called the hearth, was a flat slab of wood (usually willow or cedar) with one or more sockets gouged a quarter of an inch deep, notched on one side and with a shallow groove leading from each notch to the edge. The upper piece, the drill itself, was an ordinary round stick of a size that would fit the hearth socket; the length of an arrow, it was larger in diameter at one end, and preferably made of buckeye.

Before drilling, Ishi spread dried moss, thistledown, or shreds of inner willow bark along the channel of the hearth and on the ground beside it. Then, squatting and pushing the hearth firmly against the ground with his toes, he placed the larger end of the drill in the socket and, holding the other end between the palms of his open hands, began to rub back and forth. Applying downward pressure, he pushed the rotating stick into the socket, grinding off sawdust on the inner edges. As he twirled faster and faster, this fine wood powder began to pile up, turn black, and smoke; as the smoking pile grew, it moved out into the notch and down the channel. When a spark finally twinkled, it was in the notch, whence it spread down the channel to the tinder on the ground, where Ishi fanned it gently into "his fire."[2]

Producing fire with a fire drill takes much skill, strength tempered with delicate control, and perseverance. So laborious and time-consuming a job was it that American Indians, as well as ancient cultures all over the world, went to considerable trouble to preserve fire rather than manufacture it. This was done by allowing fire to burn into a large log or into the roots of a bush, where it would stay kindled, or by banking a fire with ashes, so that a spark would be available upon the group's return from a hunting or food-gathering trip. Some tribes, such as the eastern, northern, and southern Sierran nations, carried a "slow match," a tightly rolled rope of bark that would stay alight by burning very slowly at one end.

Early trappers and explorers in the American West were amazed to discover that most Indians did not extinguish their campfires. There were good Amerindian reasons for this. It gave the Indians a chance to get fire easily if their slow match went out, and they recognized no harm in igniting, whether by accident or on purpose, any vegetation that would burn. The burning of vegetation has long been recognized by anthropologists as a nearly universal custom among early humans. Omer Stewart, a University of Colorado anthropologist, claims to have "evidence of almost every tribe in the western United States using fire to modify its vegetational environment." He is convinced "that primitive man, with fire as a tool, has been the deciding factor in determining the types of vegetation covering about a fourth of the globe."[3]

There seems little question that Indians across the United States used fire as a land management tool. Cabeza de Vaca, the Spanish soldier who survived shipwreck near Galveston Island in 1528 and lived for eight years among the natives of the Gulf Coast, told of the Indians firing the plains to destroy mosquitoes and to compel deer and other animals to go for food where they wished them to go. Fire was also used to encircle game and stampede it within range of hunters. In New England of the 1620s, Thomas Morton noted in his *New English Canaan* (1637), "the savages are accustomed to set fire to the country in all places where they are and to burn it twice a year. . . . The reason that moves them to do this is because it would otherwise be so overgrown with underweeds."[4]

Explorers of the American prairie in the early 1800s reported that Indians set grassland and forests on fire to aid traveling and hunting and to improve pasture for wild game. One observer, a man named Wells, concluded that the tallgrass prairies between the Mississippi River and the Appalachians were caused by repeated intentional burning by Native Americans.

Carl Sauer, a University of California geographer, pointed out that much of the primeval scene discovered by European invaders of the New World had indeed been "painted by primitive man," using fire over thousands of years to modify vegetation in various ways. Grasslands the world over exist largely because of fire. Remove fire, and woody shrubs or trees quickly take over, as grass-woodland managers in Texas, Arizona, California, and Africa have found to their dismay in recent decades.

Were the forests of the Sierra Nevada likewise so "painted"? Anthropologist Alfred L. Kroeber gave a clear-cut answer in his classic *Handbook of the Indians of California*. The Maidu of the northern Sierra, he indicated, burned over the country frequently, often annually. The Indians were not attempting to protect the stands of large timber; they merely preferred an open country. They also burned unforested tracts. Travel was better, views farther, ambushes more difficult, hunting more remunerative, and a crop of grasses and herbs was of more food value than most brush.

Galen Clark, who came to Yosemite in 1854 and served for many years as official guardian of Yosemite Valley and the Big Tree Grove, wrote of those early years:

The Valley had then been exclusively under the care and management of the Indians, probably for many centuries. Their policy of management for their own protection and self-interests, as told by some of the survivors who were boys when the Valley was first visited by whites in 1851, was to annually start fires in the dry season of the year and let them spread over the whole valley to kill young trees just sprouted and keep the forest groves open and clear of all underbrush, so as to have no obscure thickets for a hiding place, or an ambush for any invading hostile foes, and to have clear grounds for hunting and gathering acorns. When the fires did not thoroughly burn over the moist meadows, all the young willows and cottonwoods were pulled by hand.[5]

Miwok Indians in ponderosa and foothill sections of the central Sierra burned off dry brush in August, both to get a better growth the following year and to prevent fires hot enough to ignite the acorn oaks on which they depended for food. They set meadow fires that attracted deer, and then shot the curious animals with arrows from ambush. Miwoks also collected grasshoppers by building a large circular fire in a flat grassy spot and letting it burn slowly toward the center where a hole had been dug. "This took care of everything except ladling the hoppers out after they had been roasted."[6]

The California Indians probably molded the Sierra landscape with fire for more than three thousand years. For much, much longer, jagged forks of lightning have struck dry tinder ablaze and sent flames licking through the pine and fir forests. The Mediterranean climate of the Sierra Nevada's middle and lower western slopes and the arid climate of the eastern slope provide just the long, hot, dry summers that make the land extremely vulnerable to fire. Despite the lack of rain, thunderstorms build up at regular intervals to spark the earth.

Meteorological figures from the California Forest and Range Experiment Station show that in the area from Yosemite Park north to the Feather River, lightning caused well over one hundred fires a year in the 1960s. Some seasons saw up to three hundred such fires, with at times as many as three hundred lightning strikes bombarding the dry timber during a single storm. Lightning fires are thus a natural climatic feature of the Sierran environmental scene, and rate as an important landscape architect of the past—as far back as similar climate prevailed, throughout the eons of time when fire suppression and control measures of today were totally lacking in the summer-dry forests.

Lightning starts forest fires in one of two ways. A direct, intense hit will split most conifers wide open, blow them apart, and set the remnants ablaze. More often, a strike will run down the trunk, imposing lesser damage on the tree itself, and light fine fuels, dry needles, leaves, and brush near its base. Giant sequoias, extraordinary trees in most ways, show a unique response to lightning. John Muir described it vividly in "Hunting Big Redwoods":

> No ordinary bolt ever seriously hurts sequoias. In all my walks I have seen only one that was thus killed outright. . . . I have seen silver firs, 200 feet high, split into long peeled rails and slivers down to the roots, leaving not even a stump. . . . But the sequoia, instead of being split and slivered, usually has 40 or so feet of its brash knotty top smashed off in short chunks about the size of cord wood, the beautiful rosy-red ruins covering the ground in a circle a hundred feet wide or more. . . . All the very old sequoias have lost their heads by lightning. All things come to him who waits; of all living things sequoia is perhaps the only one able to wait long enough to make sure of being struck by lightning.

Individual sequoia strikes have occasionally been observed by rangers. In a 1942 storm, lightning struck the Grizzly Giant in Yosemite's Mariposa Grove six times, wreaking great havoc and piling branches many feet deep on the ground beneath. Near the Telescope tree of the same grove could be read, decades after it happened, the story of one of the most titanic dramas that ever took place in these giant forests. Some eighty years ago, a low-hanging thunderhead moved up the east side of the basin that shelters the grove, churning, swirling, and massing so low as to swallow the treetops. Suddenly a blinding flash lit the forest. Spears of flame simultaneously struck each of a group of three big trees about one hundred feet above their bases, blasting twelve feet out of the center of their trunks and hurling huge pieces fifty feet away. The first tree, fourteen feet in diameter, was struck just beneath its lowest limb; the remaining snag was pushed twenty feet forward against the second tree, its trunk seared to the ground by the bolt, which ripped out huge slabs of bark and left a fire to crater its dead crown. The upper half of each of the three trees, suspended in midair for the microseconds of the flash, crashed to earth, smashing smaller trees. True to the species' durability, the second and third sequoias sprouted new luxuriant foliage from their fragmented tops 150 feet up.[7]

To the lightning fires and Indian fires of the past that helped shape Sierran forests must be added three more potent fire influences: miners, stockmen, and loggers. Before 1849, the ridges, canyons, meadows, and slopes of the Sierra were Indian country, with each tribe having a well-defined territory. The discovery of gold in the western foothills changed all of this forever. The inrush of immigrant miners precipitated one of the most frenzied digging sprees in human history, accompanied by the cutting of timber for houses, stores, flumes, mining props, and fuel and the burning of slash and brush to bring gold-bearing rocks into better view and give easier access to working and living areas. With these changes came the quick demise of the Indian and the advent of the cow and sheep.

In the 1850s, 550,000 sheep plodded the trails to mine diggings throughout the foothills' Mother Lode belt. As a standard food item for work and exploring parties, they were highly popular, "furnishing their own transportation and needing no refrigeration."[8] When the first gold bloom had faded, men began eyeing more thoughtfully those lush green mountain pastures and these baaing dollars on the hoof.

In 1860, the Civil War cut off the supply of cotton from the South and spurred a boom in wool and sheep prices. Sheep in California increased in number from one million in 1860 to six million by 1876, and there were equally impressive numbers of cattle and horses. From 1860 to nearly 1900, the Sierra Nevada became a "shepherd's empire," with cattlemen not far behind. The mountains were free for the taking—and the stockmen took them.

It was in the 1860s that the first great trail herds began their circular sweeps through the mountains. Starting in Kern County in the southwestern Sierra in the spring of the year, thousands upon thousands of sheep moved through Walker Pass to Inyo County, northward up the east side of the range, crossed back via Sonora Pass, and nibbled their way southward down the west slope of the mountains to winter lambing grounds back in Kern County.

Up every thoroughfare into the mountain's heart moved imported Basque, French, and Portuguese herders with flocks of up to two thousand sheep apiece. Shrouded under a cloud of dust, the flocks came on "like a plague," cropping every green thing in their path. The tinkling of bells, the bleating of ewes, the barking of dogs, the bleating of lambs, the calls of herders became unwelcome familiar nightmares to ranchers along the way, many of whom guarded their own green holdings with shotguns.[9]

For the first few years the formerly unexploited middle and higher mountain meadows and forest undercover could take it, but by the 1870s ranges everywhere were overgrazed dustbowls, prompting Muir to write in 1873, "It is impossible to conceive of a devastation more universal than is produced among the plants of the Sierra by sheep. . . . The grass is eaten close and trodden until it resembles a corral. . . . Where the soil is not preserved by a strong, elastic sod, it is cut up and beaten to loose dust and every herbaceous plant is killed."[10] After a hike through the Tule River sequoia forests two years later, he wrote in "Hunting Big Redwoods": "All the basin was swept by swarms of hoofed locusts . . . until not a leaf within reach was left on the thorniest chaparral beds, or even on the young conifers, which unless under stress of dire famine sheep never touch."

Along with the sheep came the sheepmen's fires. In place of a corral, many shepherds hemmed in their flocks for the night by setting fires in fallen timber or living trees, at points that would keep "wild beasts" off. At their camps one could hear burned-through pines fall in the night. The fires burned for days, sometimes spreading over large areas.

It was the habit of many herders to set fire to the undergrowth as they passed out of the mountain forests in the autumn en route to the valleys below, in order to ensure an abundant growth of tender sprouts on their return the following spring. The next spring, however, when flocks five times the size that the range could support came eating their way back up the mountain, they followed close behind the melting snow; reaching the fire-stimulated newly sprouting shoots before the plants had time to mature, they quickly cut the soil, exposed the plant roots, and nullified the effects that the autumn fire might have brought.

Muir pressed home a sizzling indictment of the incendiary shepherds in a *Sacramento Record-Union* article of February 5, 1876. "Indians burn off underbrush to facilitate deer-hunting. Campers of all kinds often permit fires to run, so also the millmen, but the fires of 'sheepmen' probably form more than 90 percent of all destructive fires that sweep the woods. . . . Incredible numbers of sheep are driven to the mountains every summer . . . and fires are set everywhere to burn off old logs and under brush. These fires are far more universal and destructive than would be guessed. They sweep through nearly the entire forest belt from one extremity to the other."

Two decades later Stanford botanist William Dudley echoed Muir's sentiments on fire-and-sheep damage after a horseback survey of the southern Sierra. Marsden Manson, an explorer of the sheep-denuded Pyrenees, Caucasus, and Atlas Mountains, was appalled to find the same sort of bare-earth erosion on northern and central Sierran slopes, fires that followed shepherds like a rash, and, in what had by then become Yosemite National Park, sheepmen openly threatening to burn the government out.

For over forty years sheepmen thought they owned the Sierra Nevada on a no-rent, free-feed, burn-as-you-please ticket. The fortunes that some of them reaped were immense, and their "rights" to the land were relinquished under the new park and forest reserve laws of 1890 and 1893 only when enforced by United States cavalry troops.

Compared to "mutton-chasing firebugs," as the shepherds were sometimes dubbed, loggers ran a scorching second. The prevalence of logging fires made the early lumbering period of 1850–1890 the most destructive to the forest cover ever recorded. By 1893, when the Sierra

Forest Preserve was set aside by President Harrison to protect timber and watershed lands, tremendous wooded areas of the Sierra had been slashed and burned.

The Lake Tahoe region, the largest lumber-producing center in the state in 1875, was the scene of much flaming carnage, including a forest fire accidentally set by neophyte claim-staker Mark Twain and graphically described in *Roughing It:* "Within half an hour all before us was a tossing blinding tempest of flame. It went surging up adjacent ridges, surmounted them and disappeared in the canyons beyond . . . flamed out again directly, higher and still higher up the mountainside—threw out skirmishing parties of fire here and there, and sent them trailing their crimson spirals away among remote ramparts and ribs and gorges, till as far as the eye could reach the lofty mountainfronts were webbed . . . with a tangled network of red lava streams."[11]

Thus, by the time that the three national parks, one national monument, and nine national forests in the Sierra Nevada were set aside as protected areas in the 1890s and early 1900s, large sections of all of them (probably close to 100 percent) had gone through a bath of fire innumerable times.

The midmountain forests were "fire-type" forests, mixed stands of ponderosa pine, sugar pine, incense cedar, white fir, California black oak—species able to maintain themselves in the face of recurrent fires so long as the fires were not of too great intensity at any one time. Recurrent fires had been a part of their normal environmental fluctuation for millennia.

What were these fire-pruned forests like in the 1800s? No one knew them more extensively or intensively than John Muir. "The inviting openness of the Sierra woods is one of their most distinguishing characteristics. The trees of all of the species stand more or less apart in groves, or in small irregular groups, enabling one to find a way nearly everywhere, along sunny colonnades and through openings that have a smooth, park-like surface, strewn with brown needles and burrs. . . . One would experience but little difficulty in riding on horseback through the successive belts all the way up to the storm-beaten fringes of the icy peaks."[12] Clarence King, a member of the first party to make a geological survey in California, wrote of the openness of the forests, of woods through which his horse could gallop freely.

With the institution of fire protection and suppression at the turn of the century, a new element quickly made itself apparent in the forest scene. It had already been evident in Yosemite Valley, which gained protection in 1864, where naturalists and residents noticed decided changes in the forest cover. A manuscript of Galen Clark's, written about 1907, described the evolution in detail:

> A great change has taken place in Yosemite Valley since it was taken from the control of the native Indians who formerly lived there. In the early years, when first visited by white people, three-fourths of the valley was open ground—meadows with grasses waist high and flowering plants. On the dryer parts were scattered forest trees—pines, cedars, and oaks—too widely separated to be called groves of underbrush, leaving clear, open, extensive vision up and down and across the valley from wall to wall on either side. The Indians kept the valley clear of thickets of young trees and brushwood shrubbery, so they could not be waylaid, ambushed, or surprised by enemies from outside, and to not afford hiding places for bears (grizzlies then inhabited the valley) or undesirable predatory animals, and also to have clear ground for gathering acorns, which constituted one of their main articles of food. At the present time there is not more than one-fourth of the floor of the valley clear, open ground, as there was fifty years ago. Nearly all the open ground between the large scattering trees is now covered with a dense growth of young trees, which also extend out over hundreds of acres of the driest portion of meadow land.[13]

The usual fate of mountain meadows that once were lakes and would eventually become forest unless deterred was overtaking the Incomparable Valley.

John Muir had spotted the trend and the accompanying dangers back in 1896:

Since the fires that formerly swept through the valley have been prevented, the underbrush requires much expensive attention. . . . The underbrush and young trees will grow up as they are growing in Yosemite, and unless they are kept under control the danger from some chance fire, from lightning, if from no other source, will become greater from year to year. The larger trees will then be in danger. Forest management must be put on a rational, permanent scientific basis, as in every other civilized country.

But for more than seventy years following Muir's comment, the problems of young-tree congestion and fire hazard mounted ever more critically throughout the forests of the montane Sierra Nevada. As the Leopold Committee report to the secretary of the interior summed it up in 1963,

Much of the west slope is a dog-hair thicket of young pines, white fir, incense cedar and mature brush—a direct function of overprotection from natural ground fires. Within the . . . national parks . . . Yosemite, Sequoia, and Kings Canyon—the thickets are even more impenetrable than elsewhere. Not only is this accumulation of fuel dangerous to the giant sequoias and other mature trees but the animal life is meager, wildflowers are sparse, and the vegetative tangle is depressing, not uplifting. Is it possible that the primitive open forest could be restored, at least on a local scale?

Attempts to do just that had gotten under way in the 1950s to early 1960s in several parts of the Sierra by pioneer prescribed burners Harold Biswell and Richard Hartesveldt. Biswell worked first in privately owned Teaford Forest, dominated by ponderosa and sugar pines.

Prescribed burning removed the fuel buildup of thickets and some of the forest floor litter that had been smothering ground vegetation. It was done when the trees were dormant and the soil was still moist soon after a rain. The top pine needles dried quickly and would soon carry a surface ground fire along paths carefully fire-laned beforehand by the operators. Such fires usually removed about 75 percent of the needles and about 23 percent of the duff underneath, leaving sufficient soil protection against runoff and erosion and a layer of ash that acted as a fertilizer on some plants.

Prescribed burning ignited the dead brush after the forest area around it had been safely burned. Its heat cracked the hard seed coats of manzanita, deerbrush, and buckbrush, fire-type shrubs that reacted by germinating. Burning stimulated the black oaks to sprout and prepared a receptive seedbed for their acorns.

The result of this burning/thinning treatment over fifteen years was an open, sun-dotted forest in which the fire hazard lay at a minimum and the ground cover comprised ample grasses, legumes, bracken, and wildflowers. New green shrubs replaced old dried ones in the clearings, offering more and better forage for deer. There was more air space, and more berries and seeds for forest-edge wildlife. The project was paid what might be termed the supreme compliment of our times when the owner announced that the forest was now so appealing a piece of real estate that he was going to subdivide it.

Teaford Forest did not have to stand the test of a wildfire, but other prescribe-burned ponderosa pine forests have. On the Fort Apache Indian Reservation, Arizona, in June 1963, the Penrod Mountain fire, driven by thirty-to-forty-mile-per-hour winds, swept northward along both sides of a road. The ponderosa forest on the left side of the road, a forty-year-old stand, had been prescribe-burned in 1956 and again in 1961. The fire crept through it on the ground, causing only minor hot spots. Over 90 percent of the dominant and co-dominant trees survived. On the right side of the road, the ponderosa forest had not been prescribe-burned. When the fire reached this self-made fuel depot, it leaped for the tree crowns immediately and continuously, destroying the forest almost completely. According to Harold Weaver, veteran of nearly thirty years of prescribed burning in ponderosa pine forests of Arizona and Washington, a single prescribed burn can reduce fuel by 50 percent and damage done by wildfires by 90 percent.[14]

Harold Biswell's fire-conditioned eye, meanwhile, had settled on another trouble spot in the southern Sierra: University of California–owned Whitaker's Forest. Across Redwood Mountain from Whitaker's, a team led by Richard Hartesveldt of San Jose State University was investigating the same problem for the National Park Service. Both involved sequoias. Both studies began around 1964 or 1965. Hartesveldt slid into his project more or less by accident. His doctoral dissertation on the effects of human impact on sequoias in Yosemite's Mariposa Grove had found some indication of compacted or eroded soils around certain big-tree bases but little evidence of tree impairment. Staring him in the face everywhere he turned, however, were blatant symptoms of other more critical problems.

For one thing, the big trees were being engulfed by a forest of white fir! In some places firs surrounded the big cinnamon trunks like bodyguards, shielding them completely from view. Elsewhere fir canopies cast deep shade over countless dead young sequoias that had lost the race for sun and soil moisture. One foot high to sixty feet high, in all sizes and ages, white firs were taking over. Beneath their dense stands lay a thick litter that sequoia seeds could not penetrate to reach soil. Sequoia reproduction had come to a virtual halt.

Equally serious, the accumulation of dead, combustible branches, brush, and debris of many years—along with resinous fir thickets of all heights—set up a fuel supply that could trigger a holocaust. How had this tinderbox situation, and others like it throughout the sequoia groves, come about? The answer began to sound monotonously familiar: overprotection from fire—seventy-plus years of it. The last good crop of young sequoias dated back seventy or eighty years to a sudden opening of the forest by fire. In the absence of fire since, forest succession had favored white fir, which could reproduce in its own shade. Sequoias could not. The big trees needed a forest-opening disturbance every now and then for survival. Strong evidence indicated that throughout the centuries this disturbance had been fire.

Fire scars occur on virtually all sequoias exceeding five feet in diameter. In the process of healing, fire wounds become covered with a layer of woody growth that forms a permanent record of the fire. Correlating these healed "scars" with tree rings, it has been possible to date fires in the Mariposa Grove back to A.D. 450, and to show that between 1760 and 1900 the grove averaged one fire every seven or eight years.

Anyone walking through sequoia groves cannot avoid noticing the frequent char marks on the tree boles, occasional blackened snags and crowns, and the cavernous burns of individuals like Mariposa's Telescope and Haverford trees, which have been gutted by fires and burned through in several directions, left with only a few narrow strands of trunk to support several hundred tons of stem in midair, but very much alive and flourishing.

Mature intact sequoias probably share few rivals as the most fire-resistant species on the Earth today. It takes weeks for a fire, fed by fallen branches or trees next to the trunk, to penetrate the thick unbroken bark. Even when this happens and its armor is pierced, the tree often meets future fires with a wood that chars more than it burns. However, the tree is far from fireproof. Loosened sequoia bark, when dry and flaky, burns rather well; sequoia wood exposed in a fire scar also burns well when dry; and the dead branches in the upper part of the tree burn readily.

Sequoias of the past lived with recurrent fires—fires that "cleaned up" the groves at chance intervals so that disastrous accumulations of debris never had time to pile up. John Muir spent several days in close quarters with a sequoia fire near the Kaweah River's middle fork in 1875, watching the flames creep and spread beneath the trees, with no danger of his being hemmed in. "In the main forest belt of the Sierra," he wrote, "even when swift winds are blowing, fires seldom or never sweep over the trees in broad all-embracing sheets as they do in the dense Rocky Mountain woods and in those of the Cascade Mountains of Oregon and Washington. Here they creep from tree to tree with tranquil deliberation."[15]

Today prescribed burns are the policy, to try to keep fires controllable. California spends millions of dollars a year on fire prevention and suppression, utilizing the finest skills of the craft and doing a superb job, but major fires still pose a critical annual threat.

Since Muir's day fire ecology has done a complete about-face. Now recognized as a part of the natural cycle, fire is prevented, where possible, near forest dwellings but often allowed to run its course in wilderness. Prescribed burns are a regular feature in national and state parks and many national forests. They prevent the fuel buildup that could lead to a holocaust.

Big fires in national parks such as Yellowstone and Yosemite have educated millions of tourists about how quickly fresh green vegetation replaces the charred stumps left by a fire and how essential the new sunny forested openings are for the natural succession of plant life. Nature and Native Americans both offer us workable management tools for living with fire. We are finally coming to recognize their value as role models.

Five

RED FIRS AND LODGEPOLES

THE GLACIERS THAT CAPPED the Sierra Nevada during Pleistocene times gouged out many U-shaped valleys on their downward flow, leaving piles of soil and rock along their sides and at their termini as they melted. On these lateral and terminal moraines, and in unglaciated deep soils throughout the 6,000-to-9,000-foot elevations of the Sierra, grow today's red fir forests.

In the northern Sierra, where the summit ridges are mostly under 9,000 feet, red firs often are the trees of the highest elevations, wooding the crest with extensive, almost pure stands. In the south, where the divide is much higher and more rocky, the firs fill in the protected places well below the summits, often on plateaus where soil has accumulated and winds are not too strong. Throughout the length of the range, the red firs form a distinctive high-mountain community, a true climax forest in which young firs succeed the old. In many ways this forest is the Sierran equivalent of the taiga or circumpolar boreal forests. Many of its birds, mammals, and plants are similar to those of Canadian spruce forests, reflecting an ancestral relationship. Others are uniquely Sierran, the product of eons of isolation and evolution.

Among the singular species is the red fir (*Abies magnifica*) itself, which grows only in the Sierra Nevada, the northern California Coast

Ranges, and the southern Cascades of Oregon. A virgin red fir forest has a mood all its own. The tall, straight trunks, rising 150 feet or more, massive as they reach four and five hundred years of age, are clothed in a deeply furrowed bark of the richest dark red. This mellow bark dominates the forest. Turning purplish red in the rain, chocolate red in flat light, it sets off vividly the trees' close-fitting needles and the wolf lichen (*Letharia vulpina*) that festoons trunks and limbs with luminous chartreuse, an accurate indicator of the height of the snow pack.

A number of the firs are characteristically topless, many the victims of lightning strikes. The upper halves of dead trees sometimes come crashing down unpredictably, giving them the reputation among foresters as "widow-makers." On the remaining stumps the bark clings for years. Throughout the forests where logs lie crisscross and splintered on the ground, their fast-rotting interiors powdery with decay, the rosy bark slabs persist in colorful intact chunks for decades.

In the densest stands of trees, the ground is thickly littered with fallen twigs and limbs, cone scales, needles, and humus. During the summer this collection sometimes becomes so compacted that it can be lifted from the soil in large mats. In these heavily shaded areas only a few plants will grow. Enough red fir seedlings survive to maintain the stand, and several species of gooseberry (*Ribes*) and snowberry (*Symphoricarpos*) exist.

Occasional wildflowers brighten the floor, snow plant (*Sarcodes sanguinea*) the most brilliant among them. Its stout fleshy stems, covered with reddish scales and crowded with bell shaped crimson flowers, push through the humus just after the snow has melted. Sometimes there are two stems to a clump, occasionally as many as twenty-two. Lacking green leaves, the snow plant cannot manufacture its own food as plants with chlorophyll do. It feeds indirectly on decayed organic matter in the soil through the medium of a microscopic fungus that completely covers its roots. The plant and the fungus share a symbiotic relationship known as mycorrhizal. As spring wanes snow plant flowers produce small red marblelike capsules. By September the parent has one or more well-formed young plants underground at its base, ready to emerge next spring at the first sign of melt.

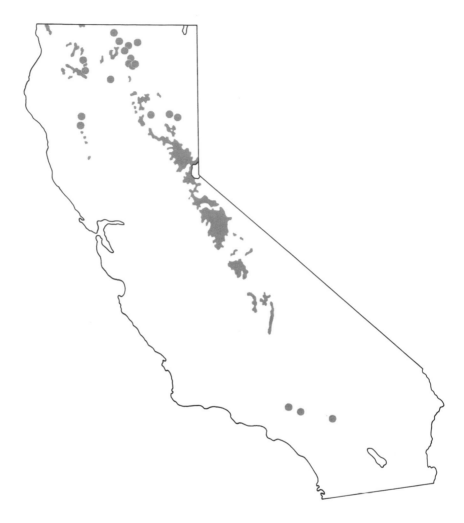

Red Firs and Lodgepole Pines
(map by Carla J. Simmons)

Other members of the heath family like the shady haunts as well:
the waxy white-flowered shinleaf (*Pyrola secunda*) with green-and-
white-veined basal leaves, the low twining pipsissewa (*Chimaphila
umbellata*), and the ghostly pinedrops (*Pterospora andromedea*). Lacking chlorophyll, pinedrops lives through fungi associated with the
roots of nearby trees. Its flesh-colored gummy stems, one to three feet
high, are partially covered by brownish scaly leaves and are topped

with clusters of minute ivory bells. Here and there rise brownish stems of another root saprophyte, the spotted coralroot (*Corallorhiza maculata*), carrying terminal clusters of quarter-inch flowers, each a miniature orchid, its lower lip white with purple spots. Even some green plants that seem self-sufficient, such as the shinleafs, are now known to be involved with or dependent on one or more types of fungi attached to their roots.

Of these shade-loving plants characteristic of the red fir and upper mixed conifer forests, the shinleaf, pipsissewa, coralroot, and pinedrops all range widely through boreal forests of the United States and Canada; shinleaf and pipsissewa occur also in Europe and Asia. Only the snow plant is of narrower western limits, confined to the Sierra and adjacent mountains of California and southern Oregon.

In the open glades, the sun-loving plants of the 6,000-to-9,000-foot belt become evident. Lodgepole pines (*Pinus murrayana*), Jeffrey pines, and occasional but constant western white pines (*P. monticola*) intermingle.

Mountain whitethorn (*Ceanothus cordulatus*), bush chinquapin (*Castanopsis sempervirens*), pinemat manzanita (*Arctostaphylos nevadensis*), and gooseberry add a shrub understory. On the gravelly open soils grow patchy gardens of white hawkweeds (*Hieracium albiforum*) on foot-high stalks, pussypaws (*Calyptridium umbellatum*) hugging the ground with rosy flowers and red spoonlike leaves, low blue lupines, golden asters (*Chrysopsis breweri*) in solitary heads, and the almost prostrate shield leaf (*Streptanthus tortuosus*), displaying tiny magenta flowers above leaves that completely clasp the short stems.

The climate of these open gardens is as different from that of the dense forest as are the two sides of a fir at forest edge. Hikers know this "bake or freeze" alternative. Sitting on the sunny open side of a mature red fir for twenty minutes heats you thoroughly. A 180-degree move around the trunk into complete shade provides nearly instant refrigeration. At first pleasantly cool, the air soon grows too cold for comfort, and within twenty minutes the sunny side of the tree is welcome once more.

In the frigidity of the shade, plants typical of more northern climes are at home; in the sunny places abound the plants more characteristic of the Sierra and other summer-dry Pacific slope mountains.

Among the conspicuous animals of the red fir forests are two scampering rat-sized rodents with black and white stripes on their backs and sides. The chipmunk (*Tamius*), the smaller and more delicate of the two, has a pointed face with stripes on the head; the chunkier golden-mantled ground squirrel (*Spermophilus lateralis*) lacks stripes on its copper-colored head and neck. Both are as much a part of western mountains as the timber itself. In the Sierra Nevada the golden-mantle lives principally in the higher forests, but chipmunks of one kind or another occupy nearly every habitat up and down both sides of the range. The eight chipmunk species look much alike except for the darkness of their color and the brightness of their stripes. Natural selection has obviously favored those patterns that blend with the environment. Chipmunks living in dense chaparral, where twig shadows are weak, have weak stripes; so do alpine chipmunks of the open talus slopes. The lodgepole chipmunks of the open red fir and lodgepole forests, where sunstruck twigs cast dark shadows, show well-demarcated light and dark stripes.

Depending for food on what the forest produces year after year, these spry little mammals are alert opportunists. Very fond of manzanita flowers, chipmunks in spring distend their stomachs with the sweet-smelling pink bells, leaving stumps littered with stripped flower stalks. Equally favored are manzanita seeds, which the chipmunks cram into cheek pouches until they seem ready to burst. Some seeds are carried into underground burrows; others, cached in small holes for later use, often sprout in clumps after a fire.

In years of bumper crops of mountain whitethorn, chipmunks rely on its seeds for nearly six weeks in late summer. They relish pine nuts, and some species climb high into the trees to get them. Cherished delicacies are the spiny-skinned wild gooseberries, which they manage to harvest without swallowing either spines or skin, and the tiny but sweet wild strawberries.

Burying whatever surplus seeds they can collect at harvest time in the fall, they eat some of these during the winter and seek the caches when emerging from hibernation the next spring. Failure of the autumnal seed supply means a serious spring food shortage. Since the animals are not leaf eaters, except as a last resort, new spring vegetation is of no use to them until it flowers. They fill in their spring diet with surface fungi, caterpillars dug out of leaf litter, and whatever other insects they can find. Rather fastidious eaters, after pouncing on the big brown carpenter ants of decaying logs, they decapitate their victims and discard the heads before swallowing the bodies. The little rodents seldom miss an insect influx that means easy protein. In the years when aphids infest young fir needles, chipmunks may concentrate on aphids for an entire month, swallowing them whole and utilizing them for over three-fifths of their diet.

On the evenings when the forest comes alive with wing-rattling termites streaming from slits in damp logs and taking to the air in mating flights, chipmunks appear everywhere as if on cue. Excitedly they run from hole to hole, grabbing the insects as they pop out. Approximately one of every twenty emerging termites disappears down a chipmunk gullet.

Although chipmunks and golden-mantled ground squirrels use similar holes and burrows under rocks and logs for shelter and nests, they coexist without serious competition because of different food needs and different ways of obtaining food. The squirrels are heavy leaf and fruit eaters and restrict their feeding close to the ground— with a few exceptions, like manzanita flowers, which they share with both chipmunks and black bears.

When golden-mantles emerge from hibernation in the spring, they crop voraciously on the green shoots of grasses and forbs, from tiny seedlings to tall ones, depending largely on the succulent leaves of green herbs until the plants begin to dry up in late summer. There is a kind of amazing precision in the way a golden-mantle squats on its haunches, holding a wild pennyroyal (*Monardella*) in its forepaws, and with quick bends of the coppery head nips off flower, leaves, and stem right to the ground like an automatic descending scythe.

When these squirrels turn to seeds, they eat primarily those they can get from the ground or that are in reach of boulders or logs. Hence they harvest the ground-level nutlets of mountain whitethorn and its matlike relative squaw carpet (*Ceanothus prostratus*), while the more agile chipmunks are climbing shrubs and trees to garner seeds higher up.

In the autumn of good years, conifer seeds become an important food, often amounting to one-third of the golden-mantle's diet. In bad years, when the forest floor is dusty and dry and most seeds have gone or have failed to set, only innumerable small pits in the ground give a clue to the one remaining source of rodent food. Every rodent around will have its stomach packed with truffles. These subterranean fungi thrive in the coniferous forests of the Sierra Nevada and southern Cascades in both quantity and variety. Their color may range from coal black, gray, brown, white, or orange to greenish or purplish; the consistency may vary from firm to soft or even gelatinous, and the aroma may be spicy, cheesy, garlicky, fishy, or fruity. But in one form or another, the truffles are present in the soil, well adapted to the long dry season and able to attain maximum numbers in the warm autumn when other foods often are gone. In protein content they compare favorably with conifer seeds: roughly 24 percent for truffles, compared to 21 percent for Jeffrey pine.

The ground squirrels apparently detect the fungi by smell and dig them out. Many small mammals besides golden-mantles and chipmunks feast on the delicacies—chickarees, California ground squirrels, gray squirrels, flying squirrels, woodrats, and deer mice, among others. During some years, when golden-mantles emerge from hibernation in advance of any new greenery, truffles left over from the previous fall provide their sole food for several weeks.

Ordinarily golden-mantles are not the insect eaters that chipmunks are, but an unusual insect outbreak can bring them running. The California tortoise-shell (*Nymphalis californica*) is a butterfly noted for sporadic population explosions in the higher forests of the Sierra. Some years its caterpillars completely defoliate mountain whitethorn and other ceanothus hosts. When this occurred in the northern Sierra in July 1951, Lloyd Tevis Jr. happened to be studying the chipmunks and golden-mantled ground squirrels of the infested area. What he saw was a concerted attack by the rodents on two stages of the butterfly's four-stage life cycle. After the spiny black-and-yellow caterpillars had gobbled up every leaf in sight on acres of whitethorn, they deserted the naked shrubs and migrated across the ground to nearby white firs. Here they pupated. En route on the ground, they were heavily attacked by golden-mantled squirrels, which fed on them to nearly two-thirds of their diet.

Chipmunks, evidently repelled by the bristles of the caterpillars, ate few in that stage. But after the caterpillars turned into ashy gray chrysalids hanging from the underside of fir boughs, chipmunks scampered nimbly over the branches to pick off and crunch the chrysalids for days. Some ate almost nothing else. Eventually the remaining butterflies hatched, swarmed over the forest, and drifted with the air currents up and over Lassen Peak to the north. Whitethorn regained its foliage within a month, and the rodents returned to more routine fare.

Chipmunks, despite their small size, will defend a radius of fifty yards around their nest, an area one-third larger than the golden-mantle's defended territory. Because both rodents forage over a much wider distance, they need to know well every burrow and escape route within reach, for their enemies are many. Among the most difficult to elude are the weasels. These relentless hunters, slender and short-legged, can slip down rodent burrows with ease and speed. Two kinds of weasels of roughly similar habits live in the Sierra. The short-tailed weasel or ermine (*Mustela erminea*), the smaller, shorter-tailed species of the high country, dens in rockslides and under tree roots. The much more common and slightly larger long-tailed weasel (*M. frenata*) inhabits all parts of the range, and much of North America as well.

Both weasels wear a summer coat of soft brown above and white below, and turn completely white in winter except for the tip of the tail, which stays black the year round. Since they require about a third of their weight in meat every day, they use their sharp, inquisitive eyes and sensitive noses in ceaseless prowls for small prey. Chipmunks recognize them instantly as enemies and immediately inform every animal within hearing.

One quiet July morning in the red fir forest at Glacier Point in Yosemite National Park, a terrific commotion broke loose among the heavy population of chipmunks and golden-mantled ground squirrels. The rodents began darting to right and left as though their very lives depended upon it. Some went into their burrows, others climbed stumps; every animal in sight took up a loud, continuous chatter that lasted for twenty minutes. Suddenly a weasel darted out from under a cabin, dashed to the left and to the right, then caught sight of three holes at the base of an old stump, smelled them, and disappeared into one. In a few seconds it reappeared with a young golden-mantle in its mouth. Repeating the performance, the weasel killed four squirrels within twenty minutes.[1]

Death comes quickly to a victim, by means of a bite through the base of the skull. That operation has to be repeated many times by a tireless mother weasel during the five weeks that she assumes sole responsibility for her litter. One female weasel that reared six young in a building in Sequoia National Park brought in a steady stream of small mammals during the thirty-seven days the youngsters were in the den: seventy-eight mice, twenty-seven pocket gophers, two moles, thirty-four chipmunks, three woodrats, and four ground squirrels.

Weasels, along with badgers and other carnivores, are among the controls that keep rodents from overrunning the woods and meadows. When weasels move into an area where fat, sluggish chipmunks are fed by campers, soon frantic chirpings and scufflings can be heard in the woodpiles and under logs as the lives of chipmunks pursued by weasels end in a few smothered squeaks. But in a week or so things quiet down. The weasels, having culled the surplus chipmunks, move into a nearby meadow to do the same job on voles (meadow mice). The chipmunk population rebuilds, eventually ready for another influx of weasels.

Their streamlined build and speed notwithstanding, weasels are not foolproof hunters; they work hard for a living. A weasel was observed chasing a shrieking golden-mantled squirrel down a road in Sequoia National Park; although it caught hold of the squirrel by the back of the neck four times, each time the squirrel threw it off. The squirrel finally rushed blindly into a pool of water, with the weasel right behind. The shock of cold water seemed to terminate the chase: both animals scrambled separately and single-mindedly to get ashore and went their own ways. Another golden-mantle eluded a pursuing weasel by dashing behind a bushy lodgepole pine and running four feet up into dense growth. The weasel, following chiefly by scent and about as fast as a man could run, missed the scent and continued straight ahead into the squirrel's empty burrow.[2]

Always a formidable enemy, weasels are especially fearless in defense of their young. A miner who owned a cabin in the red firs of the northern Sierra told me of hearing a plop in his rain barrel one day and of stepping outside to investigate. A young weasel was struggling in the water. On the edge of the barrel pranced the mother and another youngster. He moved closer to lift the weasel out, when to his amazement the mother started for him threateningly, and kept coming. Taken aback, he stopped. She turned away from him, dashed to the far side of the barrel's edge, leaned way down in, and managed to grasp the struggling weasel by the nape of the neck, then carried it a few feet with her teeth in its fur before she set it down on safe ground.

The weasel tribe is as well represented in the trees of the red fir belt as on the ground. Two of the finest arboreal artists of coniferous forests anywhere, the marten and the fisher, live in these woods. Of the two, the marten (*Martes americana*) is by far the more common. But a glimpse of its slim brown body running nimbly through the trees is rare enough to excite any naturalist anytime.

In summer martens prefer to hunt on the ground among the talus slopes of the high Sierra. A rich crop of animals lives in these rockslides—pikas, bushy-tailed woodrats, marmots, and deer mice—with chipmunks, voles, and golden-mantled ground squirrels nearby, as well as ample berries, all welcome to a marten's palate. At this season, martens will sometimes come into fishermen's camps at night and steal trout off a line, or in broad daylight rob a lunchbox left unprotected. They occasionally pounce on grasshoppers that are soaking up the warmth of the granite rocks in the chill of evening.

When the first snows of the long winter fall on the high country, martens retreat to the red fir forests. The winter storms that carry moisture from the ocean up the Sierra's western slope drop the heaviest total precipitation on the upper mixed conifer belt, with the greatest snowfall settling among the red firs. In the record year of 1906–1907, seventy-three and one-half feet fell at the 8,000-foot level near Tamarack in the central Sierra. Even in lesser years the snowpack ranks among the deepest in the United States.

In these snowbound forests the marten struggles to subsist for eight or nine months. Its golden-brown fur reaches prime pelage as temperatures drop. The patches of yellowish orange on throat and chest stand out against a darker foxlike head, dark brown bushy tail and feet. Its footpads grow a dense coating of hair that insulates them from snow and ice. Averaging two feet in total length, the animal is light, weighing only about three pounds, and it can bound over slightly crusty snow without leaving a track. In the trees it looks somewhat like and moves like a squirrel, but is faster and can leap wider gaps.

During the winter martens live principally on chickarees, flying squirrels, blue grouse, and woodpeckers. None of these is easy to find, and they take nimble footwork to catch. Hunting territories apparently aid in the search. Each marten seems to have several such territories that it alternates, with absences from each circuit lasting weeks at a time. On these rather well-defined "runs," an animal may travel as much as ten to fifteen miles in one night, following a very erratic pattern, going in circles, zigzagging, backtracking, but making general progress along a definite course. Sometimes other martens follow over the "trails" within a few hours; the well-developed anal gland probably serves as a trail marker. Some naturalists have been convinced that martens at times travel in small winter packs. The rugged, inaccessible winter terrain and the animal's primarily nocturnal habit make this difficult to check, since tracks so often lack definition.

In daylight, martens have been watched numbers of times chasing chickarees and capturing ground squirrels; on these occasions they are usually solitary. When hunting arboreal squirrels, they may travel through the trees for miles without descending to the snow. They are thought to rob woodpecker holes of birds or eggs at night by reaching in with a forefoot. This is the position in which martens often were caught in traps in the Sierra during the first half of the century. The season was closed in 1952 to permit their much diminished numbers to increase, but they are still a rare sight in the range.

Rarer yet is the fisher (*Martes pennanti*). Once present in numbers throughout northern forests and down the higher mountain chains from the Appalachians to the Pacific, fishers have dwindled to remnants in most parts of their former range. Their beautiful fur, known to the trade as North American sable, was heavily sought out by trappers until commercial trapping ended in California in 1961. Now fully protected in the Sierra, fishers maintain a sparse but stable population between Yosemite and Sequoia National Park.

When seen at a distance in the forest, the animal looks like a dark, oversized weasel. Slung low, like all the weasel tribe, with brownish black fur, black feet, and a grizzled head, the fisher averages about a foot longer and three times heavier than a marten, growing to a three-foot length and ten pounds. Its weight seems to add power and agility rather than bulk, for whereas a marten can overtake the fastest tree squirrels in full flight, the fisher can catch not only squirrels but martens as well.

The fisher's name is misleading: in the Sierra and most other areas the animal rarely goes after fish. The closest it comes to water is in following small creeks to seek out the aplodontia, or mountain beaver. Its usual haunts are the remote red fir and upper ponderosa pine forests, where it lives a solitary existence most of the year and travels at regular intervals over extensive territorial routes, principally at night.

When observed in the daytime, ordinarily it is pursuing chickarees or gray squirrels through the trees or stalking mice, rabbits, chipmunks, ground squirrels, or marmots on the ground. Its swiftness is extraordinary.

The trapper-naturalist W. H. Parkinson tells of a November day in the red firs and lodgepoles of the southern Sierra when he and his wife saw a fisher jump gracefully and slowly across an opening. Apparently in no hurry, it stopped to walk around a log, then disappeared into the forest. When they reached the place where it had vanished they saw their terrier, a great bear dog, looking intently up into a lodgepole. Forty feet above sat the fisher.

When it saw them, it started down, headfirst like a chickaree. Within fifteen feet of the ground, the fisher stopped and began scolding the dog "just as a big gray squirrel would do," hanging head downward, holding on with its hind legs and pounding on the trunk first with one forefoot and then with the other. All the while it gave out a kind of growl that terminated in a snarl or hiss, teeth white against the dark head.

To see what it would do next, Parkinson fired a bullet into the bark near it. The fisher leaped for the ground, landing fifteen feet from the tree and clear past the dog. The dog soon overtook it. For about three seconds there was "a blur of white dog and dark fisher." When the blur cleared, the fisher was fifty feet up a nearby fir; the game but dazed dog was bleeding with a dozen wounds from nose to tail. For the next quarter-mile, the Parkinsons "were treated to a rare spectacle." The fisher traveled through the treetops nearly as fast as they could run, leaping from a branch of one tree to a branch of another with "the ease and assurance of a bird." When it finally reached an extra-large red fir with a heavy crown, it climbed into the top and vanished. There they left it.[3]

Fishers seem to be the only predators to have mastered the art of killing porcupines; few animals are fast enough to accomplish this feat. Sharp slashes to the porcupine's face and head quickly finish it off and let the fisher rip open the soft underbelly with all its contents. Even the fisher often pays a price in embedded quills, but the quills do not seem to fester or harm as they do in coyotes, bobcats, and mountain lions.

The quills or hollow spines are sound reasons why the ambling, long-haired porcupine (*Erethizon dorsatum*) is left pretty much alone. One encounter discourages most aggression. When attacked, a porcupine drops its head between its legs, turns its rear to the enemy, and erects long sharp spines all over the back and tail. If approached too closely, it slaps violently with the tail, driving dozens of quills home. The quills, loosely attached and sharp-tipped, break off readily at the base when they enter flesh. Their back-slanting barbs continue to work in deeper and may eventually pierce a vital organ. Quills that have become loosened in a fight sometimes drop off the tail as it is flipped about, giving the mistaken impression that the animal throws its quills.

The spines are actually modified hairs. The lone baby, born in late spring, has a well-developed coat of hair and some spines at birth. The spines do not harden until later.

Generally considered a northern mammal because of its wide occurrence in northern and mountainous forests, the porcupine is really South American in origin. A few million years ago, when a land connection pushed up between North and South America after eons of

Porcupine in a red fir; hermit
warbler below

separation, the porcupine was one of the South American fauna that
attempted the crossing and passed through the Costa Rican filter.
Along with it came the capybara, armadillo, giant sloth, and many
others. Not all of them made it—or for long. The porcupine survived
and spread to become the only species of a South American–type rodent in the United States and Canada; its closest relatives are the
capybara, guinea pig, and chinchilla.

Vegetarians by nature, porcupines eat herbs and shrubs in summer,
the tender inner bark of young conifers at any season. In most areas
they play the role of natural forest-pruners, killing off by girdling
some of the young trees that would otherwise succumb in the com-

petitive thinning of a maturing forest. Their taste for terminal buds and shoots decapitates occasional treetops and causes disfigured trunks.

Their craving for salt and minerals drives them to gnaw deer antlers, ax handles, shovel handles, outhouse seats, saddles, and any other perspiration-touched gear around camps. Sometimes their choice of targets is bewildering. One summer in the Gold Lake country, I set out a salt block to attract porcupines for photography. Awakened about midnight by a loud gnawing, I grabbed the camera and stole quietly outside. The beam of the flashlight shone on a porcupine gnawing an empty brown cardboard carton, half eaten. Alongside, untouched, stood the white salt block.

After a summer night of feeding on the ground, porcupines pick their way slowly and deliberately to a fir or pine. Silhouetted against a dawn sky, they climb like bushy-haired mops to daytime roosts in the dense foliage above. Efficient climbers, they spend much of their time in trees, although some make dens in rocks. In the snowy Sierran winters, a porcupine sometimes lives in one tree for months at a time, sheltered from icy blasts by heavy foliage and its own hairy coat, resting in the crotch and eating everything within reach, preferably from a sitting position. Pine needles, buds, cambium layer, mistletoe all go into its grist mill; onto the snow below drop hundreds of one-inch pellets, each a compact oval of "pressed sawdust."

Not all animals of the red fir forests are as active during the long winters as porcupines, weasels, martens, and fishers. Even the mustelids (weasel family) curtail hunting during storms, holing up till the blizzards have spent their fury.

Other animals survive the winter by going underground into snug nests in burrows or dens or behind fallen tree roots. These hibernators and semihibernators handle their winter needs in several distinctive ways. Golden-mantled ground squirrels fatten up by heavy eating in the autumn and retreat to their underground nests with the first snows. There they curl up and fall into a deep sleep, or torpor. The heartbeat slows to a few beats per minute; breathing ebbs to a barely perceptible rate; body temperature drops to within a few degrees of the ambient temperature. Periodically, every sixteen days or so, they rouse and regain normal body temperature, move about briefly, urinate but do not eat, and then sink back into the torpid state.

Chipmunks deal with the winters quite differently. Instead of putting on a heavy layer of body fat, they store a quantity of seeds in their underground nest and nibble on these at intervals. The cold and snow that drives them to shelter seldom completely inactivates them, though they do become sluggish. Being "stubborn homeotherms," most Sierran chipmunks maintain a warm body temperature in the face of widely ranging environmental conditions. In many areas they come out when the ground is open in winter, inactive and lethargic in behavior and with slightly depressed temperatures, but they move around, basking in the sun if there is any, and then return to light sleep on top of their seed pile.

Another shallow sleeper is the black bear. After adding a 30 percent weight increase of fat in autumn, it retires to a den in a hollow tree or cave. Here, with no food stored in advance, the bear lives on its fat, staying lightly awake much of the winter in a kind of "carnivorean lethargy," and comes out occasionally. Photographers who have quietly lowered cameras into the opening of an inhabited den, hoping to photograph a sleeping bear, have been surprised more than once with slashed, bleeding hands.

It has been presumed that a combination of cold temperature and a lack of food causes animals to hibernate. Hibernation and prolonged sleep are efficient means of reducing metabolic rates so that a small amount of food energy goes far. If food is available, bears sometimes remain active at lower elevations in Sierran winters. In 1936, a year of unusually heavy snowfall and very low temperatures, six bears were observed in Yosemite Valley all winter. They spent considerable time around the incinerator, where scraps of food could be had.

Golden-mantled squirrels hibernate for different lengths of time at different elevations, the longer periods occurring higher up, an apparently clear adaptation to low temperatures and restricted food. However, their desert relative, the Mohave ground squirrel (*Spermophilus mohavensis*), which spends hot summers underground in a torpid state (estivation), has been discovered to maintain the same seasonal cycle when it is held at room temperature in a laboratory as when it lives in the field. This provides support for the idea of a biological clock somewhere in hibernators and estivators that runs their cycle on an inherent rhythm in a way we have yet to understand.

This inherent rhythm, unique to each species, is very evident among the animals of the mountain meadows. Thousands of meadows, varying from small seepages to spacious ranches, intersperse the midmountain and higher mountain forests. Each, in an unmatched setting of its own, is a serene open place where morning dew hangs heavy on the grass and sedge, midday sun dazzles, evening's coolness brings the deer. But each is much more than grass, wet soil, wildflowers, and deer at twilight. Each is an interlaced community of plants and animals whose lives affect each other intimately the year through, often in ways that barely show above the surface.

Most obvious of the meadow mammals is the mountain pocket gopher (*Thomomys monticola*), which signals its presence chiefly by the large mounds of fresh dirt it pushes out of its underground burrows and the earthen plug with which these are sealed. In its extensive tunnel system, the pocket gopher lives solitarily for most of the year, feeding on the bulbs, tubers, and roots of plants that it runs into as it digs. Sometimes it ventures a few feet from a temporarily open door to snatch a favorite plant before backing quickly into its den, but mostly it stays out of sight.

Superbly equipped for digging, with powerful shoulder muscles and long sharp claws on the forefeet, the pocket gopher also has small eyes and ears that do not get clogged with dirt, and sensitive vibrissae, or whiskers, that help find the way through dark tunnels. When burrowing becomes too difficult, the tough incisors bite through chunks of earth or roots that bar the path, a membrane behind the incisors keeping dirt out of the mouth.

The pocket gopher's most striking adaptation to the fossorial, or burrowing, life is a physiological one. Animals that live in narrow places need small hips so that they can turn around in the burrow. But if the hips are too small, the pelvic opening will not be wide enough to permit passage of the young at birth. The pocket gopher solves this neatly. Its pelvis is small, with right and left halves fused at the central pubic symphysis. In pregnant gophers, an ovarian hormone dissolves the pubic symphysis, changing the pelvic opening from an O shape to a U shape, through which the large-headed young pass safely. (The broad-footed mole [*Scapanus latimanus*], an insectivorous small-hipped fellow tenant of the meadow underground, handles the same problem quite differently. In moles the reproductive tracts lie in front of the pubic bones, allowing the young to be born without having to go through the slim pelvic opening.)

Pocket gophers establish definite territories in their meadows, in the shape of tunnels that radiate from a nest site. One acre of dry favorable ground frequently will support ten individuals and their home ranges. The animals' burrow systems must be large enough to provide for their food needs. Although their systems may lie close together, they evidently do not intersect; it is thought that they hear each other digging and thus avoid encroaching on each other's range.

When winter comes to the meadow, mountain pocket gophers lay out new burrow systems in the snow at ground level. Animals with the best-located summer ranges move into the snow just above the old tubes; others move in from adjacent areas of frozen soil. They construct well-insulated, ball-shaped nests of shredded grass in the snow and radiate snow tunnels from the nests. Safely hidden by the snow, they feed on green stems of grasses and sedges, caches of mountain whitethorn leaves, occasionally the bark of shrubs, as well as corms and tubers.

With the melting of the snow, the pocket gophers return to their underground burrows, which always need renovating and cleaning after a winter of vacancy. They push the earth that has settled and clogged their old burrows into the snow tunnels just above, packing them tightly. When the snow melts, these earth cores, some forty feet long, lie exposed like giant worms winding over the spring meadows.

Pocket gophers affect the life of mountain meadows in a good many ways. Their practice of plugging all entrances to the burrow maintains underground chambers with a temperature and humidity ideal for many other creatures. In weather extremes, toads, salamanders, snakes, mice, beetles, pseudoscorpions, and other arthropods frequently move in. Pocket gophers' continual burrowing exerts a significant plowing influence on the meadow. Lloyd Ingles found in one southern Sierran meadow that an individual animal brings up about one hundred pounds of earth per week; this amounts to tons per year that filter into the sod and enrich the soil. Subsoil brought to the surface weathers into topsoil much more rapidly than when below ground. The burrow systems have other favorable effects on the meadow. The heavy surface runoff each spring sinks into them, helping to reduce snowmelt floods down the mountains and to ensure a steady flow of springs later. Because the well-drained soil over the burrows dries out sooner each summer, grasses and forbs are able to grow, rather than sedges. Even the piles of pellets left in the "privies" near the snow nests undoubtedly add fertilizer.

On the Hoopa Reservation in northern California, pocket gophers served as agents of reforestation. Where overgrazing by cattle removed grassy turf from a range, allowing bulbs to invade, pocket gophers moved in after the bulbs and added their mounds and burrows. The bare earth that they tunneled up furnished the only successful seedbeds for a bumper crop of red firs the following year.[4]

The most numerous mammals of the meadow are unquestionably the montane and long-tailed voles, or meadow mice (*Microtus montanus* and *M. longicaudus*). About half the size of pocket gophers, they live in the damper places among the deep grasses and sedges, and are active day and night, winter and summer. Like pocket gophers, they construct underground tunnels and in winter continue life beneath the snow; but much of their summer activity goes on above ground in the runways they cut through vegetation close to the surface. In dense grass these paths can be seen only by getting down to mouse level. Strewn with green fecal pellets and rich nitrogenous urine, the runways are well fertilized. They wind through the varied herbaceous plants on whose stems and leaves the voles feed.

In years when these voles erupt in the cyclic population explosions typical of rodents, the small, brown mammals occupy every available space in the meadow, and sometimes nearly strip it of vegetation. At these times the endless runways are more evident than usual, and the voles often scurry about in full sight in daylight. If captured in the field and placed in individual cages for study during such an epidemic, the voles invariably die within a few days, even with natural food and water fully available. If caged with several other mice, a seemingly fat, healthy vole often dies within twenty-four hours. An autopsy usually shows a full stomach and no apparent parasites or injuries.

The reasons for these puzzling deaths are complex. Intensive field studies of lemmings, voles, and rabbits have been under way for decades in an effort to understand the entire cycle. Evidence indicates that animals living in extremely dense populations suffer from internal stresses brought on by the crowding. The stress seems tied to hormonal imbalance, and the adrenal-pituitary complex plays a critical role in eventual death.

Following a meadow vole population explosion, there is always a sharp die-off and a period when numbers are low before they gradually build up again. This gives vegetation a chance to recover as meadow sod, benefiting from the honeycombing burrows of the epidemic years that let in air and water, reestablishes itself.

Among the willow, alders, and creek dogwood (*Cornus stolonifera*) in the wetter parts of Sierran meadows lives a curious, much larger rodent that is fairly common locally but shy and seldom seen. The mountain beaver (*Aplodontia rufa*), about fifteen inches long and almost tailless, looks more like an oversized pocket gopher than a beaver. It has all the trademarks of a burrower: long, sharp front claws, small eyes and ears, long vibrissae, and thick, short brown fur.

Not related to true beavers, the mountain beaver is a relict rodent, the lone survivor of one of the most primitive living rodent families. Once widespread throughout the West, its range is now restricted to the Pacific Coast, where, as in the Sierra, it thrives near small streams or in wet meadows, always under dense plant cover. Here it digs underground tunnels as much as ten inches wide and three or four feet deep. Kept scrupulously clean, they are often damp, with water trickling through; in some places they drain the willows sufficiently to allow grasses to grow and other plants eventually to invade the meadow.

Like the montane vole, the mountain beaver cuts runways through the grass to reach its food supply. Often these surface tunnels run fifty yards or more to clusters of shooting star (*Dodecatheon*), wild vetch (*Vicia*), yellow monkey flower (*Mimulus guttatus*), and columbine (*Aquilegia truncata*). It clips off many kinds of plants near the burrows for food and climbs shrubs and small trees to prune and dine on both leaves and bark. Piles of these cuttings are often left to dry outside the burrow, and are taken into the tunnel when "cured."

Day and night appear to be all the same to the mountain beaver. It follows a rest and activity cycle of its own rhythm. After feeding for about thirty minutes, it retires to the nest for a three-to-four-hour nap. Upon emerging, it proceeds to its fecal pile. As it passes each of the half-inch-long, hard pellets, the animal takes the pellet into its mouth and tosses it onto the pile. Now and then it chews and eats a pellet, a habit common to some other rodents and some shrews, possibly a means of conserving minerals, vitamins, or other needed elements. The usual half-hour feeding period then commences, followed by the next sleep, the next defecation, and so on for six or seven alternating periods of rest and activity over a twenty-four hour day.

Winter snows probably interrupt this cycle only slightly. The animal caches some food in its burrows, climbs trees and shrubs for new supplies as needed, and burrows through the snow to strip young red firs and lodgepoles of needles and bark, thus somewhat discouraging meadow invasion.

In the same thickets and meadows where the aplodontia plods its cycle, tiny voracious insectivores whirl through their lives at a fast and furious pace. Six or more species of shrews live in various habitats of the Sierra, small slim creatures with long pointed noses, highly sensitive vibrissae, and minute eyes hidden in velvety fur that brushes either way. Darting along their paths under logs or grass cover, they quiver noses nervously and emit occasional high-pitched squeaks as they hunt earthworms, insects, and animal flesh mainly by scent or touch.

There is good reason for their nervous restlessness. As the smallest living mammals they have the highest metabolic rates—the living speed of mammals goes up as size goes down. To support this high rate of living and compensate for the heat that their small bodies lose rapidly, shrews must eat their weight equivalent each day. This means eating every two or three hours.

In summer, the shrews of the red fir forest meadows (*Sorex*) follow a built-in behavior pattern that accomplishes this feat with a minimum of effort. Three times during a twenty-four-hour period the shrew feeds especially heavily. The first peak comes in the coldest hours of early morning, when insects and spiders have crawled down sedges and willows into the meadow litter; sluggish, they are readily picked off. Later in the morning, these insects and arachnids warm up and crawl back up the sedges and grasses, but they are still slow moving and so continue to fall victim to the shrew. In the afternoon, however, the insects become lively and hard to catch, and it is then that the tiny mammal works least. During these hours, and at other slower-paced intervals, it breaks its almost ceaseless motion with short naps thirty to seventy seconds long. Stopping, it rests its nose on the ground, closes its eyes, and sleeps lightly, at times twitching its vibrissae and turning completely around while napping.

As the sun sets and a cool evening breeze begins to blow down the mountain, the wetwood termites emerge from rotten logs to fly to new locations. This signals the third feeding peak, as the shrew snaps up half a dozen termites on the spot and immobilizes fifty or sixty more for future use. Its saliva may contain a poison that partially paralyzes the victims.

Lloyd Ingles, whose Huntington Lake research uncovered this shrew cycle, found that shrews kept in captivity followed the same activity rhythm as those in the wild, in spite of the food constantly available. This would indicate that the shrew's pattern of behavior is inherent, "the result of ages of selection which have fitted the animal to its environment."[5]

The red fir meadow shrew does not hibernate. How it manages to find enough food to stoke its fast-burning body during the one winter in its life is still a mystery. Major staples undoubtedly are the eggs, larvae, and pupae of insects that winter at the same ground levels as the shrew. Cannibalism may be part of the answer, one high-strung little body refueling the other, although Ingles doubted that this happens in nature, having found many dead shrews without a mark on them.

Of eleven shrews that started the winter on 1.25 acres of overlapping home ranges at Huntington Lake, only two, a male and a female, were left by spring. Presumably these, the parents of the next generation, were the ones that most successfully defended their expanding territories as food ran lower and lower, until only they remained. "Theirs were the genes that determined next year's crop of young shrews," Ingles wrote. "Year after year, century after century, the shrews best adapted to win this annual territorial competition give rise to the next generation."[6]

Spring snowmelt exposes the meadows weeks before it clears the pack from the adjacent forests. By mid-May in most years, new green spears of sedges and grasses push through the water and soggy muck. The brownish shrub mat reveals faint red buds and the dash of an occasional gopher from one dry clump to the next. Corn lilies (*Veratrum californicum*), two to four inches high, burst their protecting leaf sheaths. Quaking aspens (*Populus tremuloides*) on the meadow's edge dangle catkins with crimson anthers; mountain chickadees glean food from cracks in the white barks. The sights and sounds of returning birds fill forests and clearings.

In the open meadow Brewer's blackbirds waddle once again among the six-inch-high blades of grass as robins cock for worms on the higher spots. In a saturated corner, a trim brown sparrow with finely streaked buff-colored breast pours out a vigorous three-part song. Delivered over and over—alternately from a clump of young lodgepoles, a stump, and a twenty-five-foot lodgepole, forming a rough triangle—it clearly denotes the territorial boundaries of the Lincoln's sparrow. A month later, the bird will be as shy and secretive as a mouse, slipping through the grass to its nest.

Spring brings the clear whistles of white-crowned sparrows back to the higher willows and the flash of black cap on yellow as Wilson's warblers flick through the moist thickets. As the snowmelt mosquitoes swarm and fade, and the meadows warm and dry, insects that escaped the ground hunts of moles and shrews are fed by meadow birds to their nestlings and are hawked by western wood-pewees and yellow-rumped warblers at the meadow's fringe.

Even these routine hunts hold occasional perils. Elisabeth Crenshaw and her daughters, while hiking near Long Meadow in Yosemite

National Park some years ago, were startled to see a young yellow-rumped warbler flying back and forth in the grass as if it were tied to a string. It had swallowed a stalk of grass, probably while swooping after an insect, and was firmly anchored. They caught the bird, freed its wings and body from the entangling grasses, and gently and steadily began to pull the stalk from its throat. When they finally got it out, the warbler sat blinking in hand for a moment, then flew into a lodgepole.

At twilight, bats take up the insect hunt, feeding until night temperatures quiet their prey in the upper and lower strata of forest and meadow. The leathery membrane that connects the bat's elongated hand bone to its legs and tail makes it our only mammal capable of wing strokes dexterous enough to capture the fastest-moving insects in flight. The bat locates them by echo responses of their bodies to the high-pitched sounds it emits.

Three kinds of bats, all rather widely distributed, fly commonly about clearings or among trees of the red fir belt in the Sierra. Two of them, the little brown bat (*Myotis lucifugus*) and big brown bat (*Eptesicus fuscus*), are gregarious, spending the day in large numbers in caves or hollow trees, hanging upside down by their hind claws in typical bat style. The long-eared bat (*Myotis evotis*) is solitary, as is the uniquely American but less common silver-haired bat (*Lasionycteris noctivagans*), which roosts in trees by day. The silver-hair's habit of flying low over lake shores or streams resembles the way in which bats generally drink, by skimming pools and scooping water into their open mouths while in flight. Now and then one gets caught by a trout.

Other predators lie in wait for the careless small mammal or bird of the meadow, day or night. Weasel families, a mother and half a dozen nearly grown young, sometimes fan out over a small area of the meadow, about a foot apart, and advance slowly, looking for voles. They find shrews less palatable because of the musky offensive odor given off by powerful scent glands in the skin, but rarely overlook a juicy pocket gopher.

Coyotes make the rounds of gopher diggings, standing for minutes at a time with head poised at a likely burrow entrance. A quick pounce, coming down with both front feet and mouth, sometimes produces a warm brown carcass. Pocket gophers are most vulnerable when they open the burrow to push out fresh earth; this movement may attract red-tailed hawks or goshawks. Badgers also occasionally dig them out. With all their enemies, it is not surprising that pocket gophers rarely live more than three years and that there is a complete turnover in a mountain meadow gopher population every four or five years. Juveniles, on leaving home, may stumble into a beautifully laid out tunnel system, freshly vacant, and take over.

Two large resident owls help create the vacancies as well. The great horned owl (*Bubo virginianus*), a forest dweller by day, often begins its nightly food roundup with a vigil in an open tree at the meadow's edge. Noiselessly it drops onto small moving forms, powerful talons snuffing out life. Voles, pocket gophers, woodrats, rabbits, grouse, and squirrels all fall victims—even malodorous shrews and skunks, which the owl, having a poor sense of smell, eats uninhibitedly. From foothill woodlands to the higher forests, this aggressive hunter culls nightly the surplus and the careless from bird and small-mammal populations.

The more rare great gray owl (*Strix nebulosa*) is a bird of diurnal habits. Found across the American and Eurasian arctic, it occurs sparingly in the Sierra, known best from the Yosemite region. Here in the red fir–lodgepole forests, the big owls sit on pines or firs along the meadow fringe early or late in the day, their bodies bent sharply forward as they watch for rodents. The great puffy round head with yellow eyes and lined facial disk seems immense; and the dusky, heavily feathered body and long tail, huge. Indeed, in overall size—twenty-seven inches on average—this is North America's largest owl. But the body beneath the fluffy feathers is slight: though five inches shorter, the great horned owl outstrips the great gray easily in weight. In disposition, also, these two owls differ. The great gray has a gentler mien, lacking the erectable feather tufts (or "horns") and the ferocious glare of the other; it sometimes allows human approach to within ten or twelve feet, when absorbed in catching and eating gophers.

A gopher, offered by the male great gray to the female and accepted by her, seals the pair's bond in courtship. Affectionate mates, they groom each other and cuddle throughout the nesting season. The nest, in broken tops of large dead trees, snags, or old goshawk stick nests, is located in old-growth red fir or mixed conifer forest with twenty acres or more of ungrazed, moist meadow nearby for hunting. Such habitat has become increasingly scarce in the Sierra, and the great gray's existence depends on it. California's endangered species list estimates their numbers at around fifty.

Other owls in the same old-growth-forest–meadow terrain combine to produce prime owling spots in some months of the year. The mellow whistles of saw-whet and pygmy owls, the flammulated's hoot, the barking of the California spotted owl, the great horned's hoot, and the deep booming *whoo* of the great gray are all possible when conditions are right. The Sierran subspecies of the spotted owl (*Strix occidentalis*), a close relative of the great gray, lives and hunts strictly among the trees—old growth or mixed old growth preferred—sleeping by day in a cool roost, on the wing for squirrels, wood rats, and deer mice at night.

Summer daytime birds bring the colors and sounds familiar to campers and hikers of the red fir–lodgepole forests: the red-headed yellow and black male western tanager, Steller's jays flying in at the first rustle of a sack lunch, dark-eyed juncos searching the ground for seeds or crumbs. The *pip-pip-pip* and ringing *hic-three-beers* of the olive-sided flycatcher are often the first sounds to greet the dawn from a red fir spire. I once counted eighty-five *pip-pip-pip* series in the eight minutes between 6:00 and 6:08 A.M. The nasal call of the western wood-pewee is just as early and nearly as frequent, often accompanied by the robin's cheery carol. Hermit thrushes send full, clear cadences into the cool air, each opening with a flutelike note that is held a moment. The ruby-crowned kinglet's song plays up and down the scale. The low thumping of the male blue grouse booms through the woods—seven deep notes in about four seconds, a pause of forty seconds, and another seven thumps, like someone pounding far away in an indeterminable direction.

Scattered among the forests are rocky promontories and boulder-strewn acres where Jeffrey pines (*Pinus jeffreyi*) rise as the dominant trees, often intermixed with small or extensive stands of high-mountain chaparral and Sierra junipers. Yosemite's famous windblown pine on Sentinel Dome was a Jeffrey. It died during the drought of 1976–1977, after surviving an earlier lightning strike.

Jeffreys resemble ponderosa pines sufficiently to have once been considered a variety of the more widespread species, and in Sierran regions where their ranges overlap they hybridize. But on dry rocky slopes from 6,000 to 9,000 feet, the beehive-shaped cones of the Jeffrey identify the tree beyond question. Six to ten inches long, larger and more rounded than the ponderosa's, Jeffrey cones have prickles that point downward and are not felt when the cone is held in the hand.

The Jeffreys of these open slopes are often massive trees with reddish brown bark, trunks clear of branches for a third of their height, then shaded by several large horizontal limbs and topped by smaller branches curving into flattened or rounded crowns. The crowns are a favorite singing perch of Townsend's solitaire, especially where they overlook great dropoffs. Here, in June, the slim gray thrush pours out a torrent of liquid notes, beginning with robinlike phrases that flow together in a continuous, breathless warble, inevitably ending with clear bell tones of penetrating depth. At peak ardor the bird sings for four out of five minutes. As late as mid-October, the solitaire's arresting song (minus its earlier fervor) floats out over the granite exfoliations of the rocky domes. With the winter snows the bird retreats to lower canyons and northern juniper woodland, but moves back up in early spring just as soon as it can find food, even if a twelve-foot snowpack is still on the ground.

Despite its treetop singing perch, the solitaire is a ground or bank nester. It, along with various other birds of similar nesting habits, finds cover and food in the brushy shelter of mountain chaparral patches amid scattered Jeffrey pines. Here abound berries of greenleaf and pinemat manzanitas, mountain whitethorn, serviceberry, bitter cherry, and tobacco brush (*Ceanothus velutinus*), the acorns of huckleberry oak (*Quercus vaccinifolia*), the chestnutlike burs of bush chinquapin, and the seeds of wildflowers and grasses.

Chinquapin's golden fuzzy leaves and the silvery-green leaves of whitethorn often hide green-tailed towhee and fox sparrow nests.

The loud bright songs of these finches liven the brush and open woods in June.

About this time the blue grouse, the Sierra's only forest grouse, leaves the trees to nest in the ground cover of broken forest-chaparral areas. The female's grayish brown mottled plumage conceals her perfectly on the nest. When she abandons it finally, proceeding at her deliberate walk, she does so with the chicks in tow, teaching them to feed on seeds and berries, to freeze or run for cover, to jump into the air after gnats, flies, grasshoppers, and other large insects.

As summer wanes, male grouse in small bands move higher up the mountains, followed by the hens and young. Winter snows drive them into the protected branches of dense conifers, where they feed on needle tips, well insulated from the cold by close-set body plumage and feathered legs. Summer finds them back on the brushy open-forested slopes.

On these same slopes mountain quail (*Oreortyx pictus*) build needle-lined nests on the ground under brush, filling them with ten to twelve buff-colored eggs in late May or June. If all goes well, the downy broods will in due course be scurrying from cover to cover after their straight-plumed parents, directed by various low clucking and whining notes that lead them to run and hide rather than fly. Sometimes, however, the eggs meet a different fate.

One June day in Yosemite Valley, Charles Wentz of the Yosemite Field School heard a mountain quail distress call. Investigating, he found a California mountain king snake (*Lampropeltis zonata*) at the quail's nest, in which lay three eggs. Picking up the beautiful red-black-and-white-banded snake, he carried it fifty yards down the road and well below road level and let it go. The snake traveled rapidly right back to the nest. Recapturing it, Wentz took it three times as far down the road and released it at the river's edge. Immediately the snake crawled up the bank and, in spite of his attempts to head it in another direction, persisted in returning to the nest. A third time Wentz tried, making a journey of a quarter of a mile down the road and one hundred feet up the mountainside before turning it loose. The snake headed right back down the mountainside and, following a route that was less direct than previous ones, eventually reached the nest. This time its perseverance gained it a dinner.

In addition to snakes and carnivores, which are always on the look-out for nests, some rodents also show an occasional taste for eggs and young. California ground squirrels, although primarily herbivores, have been observed sucking mountain quail eggs and carrying off the young chicks; at times they eat small animals that have been run over by automobiles or kill and carry off golden-mantled ground squirrels.

Cannibalism used to be a problem among certain game birds held in captivity, until it was discovered that their hunger for meat was caused in part by a salt deficiency. Meat eating in rodents may be a symptom of the salt hunger common to deer, cattle, porcupines, and probably other herbivorous species of the salt-poor high Sierra. High-mountain birds, such as Cassin's finch, sometimes eat mud at mineral springs and, along with red crossbills and pine grosbeaks, pick up minerals from campfire ashes. Minerals lacking in the soft water of mountain lakes and streams may be acquired by the wildlife in what-ever form they can be found. Clark's nutcrackers and ravens com-monly peck away at squashed carcasses of chipmunks and chickarees on high mountain roads, obtaining both food and minerals.

The red fir–lodgepole pine forests of the Sierra Nevada share a good many birds with the lodgepole pine–subalpine fir–Engelmann spruce forests of the Rocky Mountains: Steller's jays, western tanagers, olive-sided flycatchers, western wood-pewees, mountain chickadees, her-mit thrushes, Townsend's solitaires, and yellow-rumped warblers, to name a few. The wetter summers in the Rockies affect the decay rate of forest humus more than they influence the bird life. By mid-August of most years, Sierran forests are so dry that the surest place to find birds is near springs or creeks or lakes, where they come to drink and bathe.

One August in the Gold Lake district of the northern Sierra, a part-ner and I maintained a dawn-to-dusk vigil at a creek fed by a spring in an open red fir forest, with a small meadow nearby. It was barely light when we arrived at the pool and took stations behind young red firs. The chill of night lay heavy and wet.

At 5:13 A.M., the first calls of wood-pewees and olive-sided flycatchers rang through the woods, a half-minute apart. The gray-and-white shape of a porcupine ambled across a clearing and clambered, scraping and scratching, up a western white pine to the first side limb twenty feet up, where it sat back on its haunches.

At 5:17, a dark-eyed junco visited the pool; at 5:25, a brown creeper crept out on the lower log, hopped down, and drank; at 5:30, a young yellow-rumped warbler took the first bath of the day. In the next fifteen minutes it was followed by bathing hermit warblers, Nashville warblers, mountain chickadees, and an orange-crowned warbler in for a quick sip. This was the start of a parade that continued with varying intensity all day. At one moment the water lay empty; the next it was asplash with birds, and then its encircling firs were crowded with preening, feather-shaking, disheveled creatures.

At one time, in the water or above, were two hermit warblers, two mountain chickadees, a Wilson's warbler, two red-breasted nuthatches, two Nashville warblers, and a yellow-rumped warbler. Most drank first, then bathed. Some, like the tanager, only bathed. Chickadees, yellow-rumped warblers, and juncos mixed it either way; they appeared often, the steadiest users by far. Some of the scarcer visitors—Lincoln's, white-crowned, and chipping sparrows, and the white-headed woodpecker—left after a single drink, as did the painted lady butterfly (*Vanessa cardui*) and pine siskin.

Occasionally the air was alive with song: the lively, strident warble of a male Cassin's finch, the *chick-adee-dee* notes and gurgles of the mountain chickadees, the mew of a green-tailed towhee, and the distant *pip-pip-pip* of the olive-sided flycatcher. Again all was quiet save for the buzz of bumblebees, the movement of flies, a golden-mantle nipping seeds from a pennyroyal (*Monardella odoratissima*), and the click of a junco.

As evening approached, at 6:45 the three steadies—mountain chickadees, juncos, and yellow-rumped warblers—finished a very active bathing and drinking bout, leaving the pool clear. From a near fir out hopped an evening grosbeak, looking large and lordly compared to the smaller birds; it drank four times with pauses, then left in direct, propelling flight.

By 7:15, the damp cold waves of night were no longer intermittent; the pennyroyals quivered in the currents. Pewees and the olive-sided still called; a yellow-rumped warbler hawked an insect two feet from my ear.

By 7:30, visibility was becoming poor at the pool. There was quiet over all except for the distant roar in the treetops and the trickling of water. Suddenly a junco chucked, sounding very loud, and dipped its bill in the water.

By 7:40, all was still. At the creek pennyroyals, an underwing moth moved in and out of the flowers that the bumblebees had taken care of by day; the bees were now five black sleeping forms on the leaves.

Lodgepole pines, with their relatively water-tolerant roots, play a successional role in red fir forests by pioneering into meadows. The lodgepole's sun-loving and shade-tolerant seedlings may be succeeded by shade-loving firs or hemlocks, but they often succeed themselves. Throughout much of western North America's mountain region, lodgepoles form extensive pure forests of their own.

In the Rockies the stands often consist of pole-sized trees growing close together, the result of fire, which opens tightly sealed cones and causes young trees to sprout in profusion. But in the higher reaches of the Sierra, lodgepoles grow tall and husky, with trunks four feet across on mature specimens. From scattered tongues that extend down into cold or wet pockets of the ponderosa pine belt, the trees reach nearly to timberline. They ring lakes, border streams, spread over moist slopes, surround and invade meadows from small ones to the largest.

In the light shade of the scaly thin-barked older trees, their silver branches densely clothed with short green needles, two to a bunch, rise young lodgepoles of all sizes and shapes, some bent by snow. Patches of corn lilies and shooting stars lie tucked away in wet glades; among grasses by fallen logs sway purple asters, white bistorts, blue lupines, larkspur, and yellow senecios in season. In June there are usually Williamson's sapsuckers and mountain chickadees nesting in nearby stump holes and pine grosbeaks whistling from the treetops.

For as long as humans have known them, the lodgepole forests of the Sierra Nevada, especially in the drainages of the upper Tuolumne and Merced Rivers, have been subject to periodic outbreaks of a tiny insect that turns them temporarily into ghost forests. During epidemics and for years afterward, thousands of defoliated trees stand bleak and gray, their hollowed-out needles lying in piles on the ground.

The cause of this shedding is a quarter-inch mottled gray moth, the lodgepole needle miner (*Coleotechnites milleri*), which follows a two-year life cycle intimately linked to the lodgepole. Appearing in late July of alternate years, the moths lay barely visible yellow eggs on the twigs and in old excavated needles, bud scales, and needle sheaths of mostly older lodgepoles. The eggs hatch in late summer into quarter-inch-long pinkish caterpillars that bore into the tips of the needles, feeding there until winter. As the caterpillars grow larger during the two springs and summers of their twenty-one-month span, they move from one needle to another, mining out the tender inner contents, turning the needles from green to yellow to brown. Each caterpillar destroys from three to five needles in its lifetime. Although small as individuals, during an epidemic their total numbers become enormous. By the time the caterpillars pupate and emerge as adult moths in the second summer there may be as many as five hundred moths flitting about a single lodgepole branch.

Adults mate and lay eggs, and the cycle continues. Five successive two-year generations of needle miners can cause as much as 90 percent needle loss in infested forests. Heavily defoliated lodgepoles die within a few years; trees weakened by the needle miner often succumb secondarily to mountain pine beetles (*Dendroctonus*).

Needle miner outbreaks have occurred periodically in the Tuolumne Basin of upper Yosemite National Park throughout the centuries. Each time, the miners left forests of bleached snags in their wake. And each time, thousands of young lodgepoles surged up in the new openings to replace the dead trees.

As the needle miner cycle waned, yielding to natural controls, the forests slowly regrew as pure lodgepole stands. Within fifty years or more they would be fit targets for new needle miner invasions. In hastening the death of mature lodgepoles, needle miners triggered their replacement by younger ones, ensuring both the continuity of lodgepole forests and a food supply for future generations of needle miners.

Along with the needle miners, all the other wildlife of the lodgepole forest food chain—mountain chickadees, woodpeckers, chipmunks, bees, beetles, Cassin's finches, pine siskins, shrews, and the rest—depend on a steady supply of dead and dying lodgepoles.

Some tiny parasitic wasps attack only needle miners and are so intimately associated with them that their own life cycles synchronize perfectly with the two-year cycle of their host. Insectivorous birds, like mountain chickadees, which consume caterpillars by the hundreds, play an important role in keeping pest numbers below the threshold of explosion.

What once appeared to be a catastrophic epidemic has turned out to be a self-healing natural cycle in the red fir–lodgepole pine forests of the Sierra Nevada.

Sugar pines dangle the world's
longest pine cones, often up to
twenty inches, throughout the
midmountain forests of the Sierra
Nevada, but face a nemesis in
white pine blister rust.

The western foothills abound in spring with masses of wildflowers. Meadow foam fills the wet spots with a white haze (*top foreground*), while tidytips (*middle*) cover the drier areas.

California poppies spread their brilliant orange.

In May the white blossoms of
California buckeyes (*foreground*)
lead the way up slopes to gray
pines on the ridgetops.

The foothills are the home of the
scrub jay, an omnivorous feeder
and noisy alarmist.

In the next higher mountain belt
lives the large bushy-tailed gray
squirrel, which relies heavily on
acorns of California black oaks.

The pink bells of greenleaf manzanita bloom in mid-mountain forests in March (*top*), followed by dogwood's showy display in May (*bottom*).

The chickaree cuts down and caches large clusters of white fir cones for its winter food supply.

Ponderosa pines' orangish trunks
characterize the midmountain
forests of the Sierra.

Opposite: Snow plants push
through mid-Sierran soils in early
summer like giant asparagus heads
and mature into striking crimson
clusters.

A fresh winter snowfall on Half
Dome, with the Merced River
below, enhances Yosemite's
magnetic beauty (*above*) and rims
the branches of the black oaks
(*opposite*).

The heavy snows that pile up each year in the red fir forests above Yosemite Valley (*above*) erupt in the spring melt into mighty waterfalls (*opposite*).

The rocky granite outposts
favored by Jeffrey Pines, as at Taft
Point in Yosemite (*top*), also
furnish good dens for yellow-
bellied marmots (*bottom*).

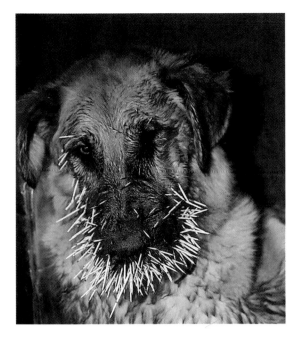

Porcupines are regular residents of the high mountain forests, but rarely do we see evidence of how they defend themselves. Dogs either learn to stay away from porcupines on their first encounter, or they never do. This dog had just been quilled by a porcupine's tail for the seventh time.

Bears have become increasingly bold in Sierran residential areas in recent years, emptying garbage cans and sometimes entering garages or cabins.

High mountain meadows, as at
Highland Lakes at 8,000 feet
elevation, fill with corn lilies,
lungwort, senecios, and myriad
wildflowers in summer.

Opposite top: Corn lilies display
cream-colored blossoms on tall
stalks near the lakeshore in late
July.

Opposite: Yosemite toads are
among the amphibians ominously
declining in numbers in the high
mountain lakes of the world. The
female shown here is darker and
larger than the male.

The golden and coral leaves of aspens bring a spectacular glow to the high country in October.

Opposite: Giant sequoias, the most voluminous trees known, occur in isolated groves in the Sierra. Nearly all the old-timers show scars of past fires.

Prescribed burns now play a recognized role in forest management in most parts of the range. They simulate natural fires, help prevent fuel buildup, open up the forest, and add nitrogen to the soil.

Opposite top: Sage grouse cocks put on a bizarre courtship show at traditional areas in east Sierran sagebrush in early spring.

Opposite: Black-tailed jackrabbits were formerly corralled by Native Americans in great drives and utilized for robes and food.

The lower eastern slopes of the
Sierra carry woodlands of squat
pinyon pines and junipers in a
land adapted to little rain.

Opposite top: Mule deer occur all
through the range, migrating to
high meadows for summer,
retreating on well-defined paths to
the foothills in late autumn.

Opposite: The skies above Mono
Lake greet many an eastern
Sierran dawn with spectacular
clouds.

Higher elevations on both sides of
the range are dominated by richly
colored red firs in a belt of heavy
precipitation.

Opposite top: Pinedrops are among
the shade-loving wildflowers of
the red fir forests that lack green
leaves and feed on soil nutrients
through a fungal network.

Opposite: Lodgepole pines often
line the shores of high Sierran
lakes, being very adaptable to
varying water levels. They require
sunny, open areas for germination.

Companion trees in the subalpine realm are western white pines and mountain hemlocks. The bark of mature western white pines (*left*) breaks up into a distinctive cell-like pattern. The young mountain hemlock shows, at this early stage, the drooping terminal shoot that marks most older trees of its kind.

Opposite top: The irrepressible Douglas squirrel, or chickaree, romps up and down Sierran forest trees of the midmountain and higher levels, aggressively and vocally defending its territory.

Opposite: Steller's jay assertively flaunts its brilliant royal feathers from the foothills on up, keeping an alert eye on all activities.

Two conspicuous rodents live in the red fir–lodgepole pine forests. The larger golden-mantled ground squirrel, with a solid copper-colored head (*top*), feeds at ground level. The smaller chipmunk, with stripes on its pointed head (*bottom*), often finds insects and seeds in the trees. Eating different foods, the two compete very little.

Above: Both rodents, along with rabbits, gophers, and mice, often fall victim to the bobcat's stalk and pounce, anywhere from the foothills to timberline.

The cougar preys primarily on larger animals, such as mule deer, going after smaller game only in an emergency.

Burrowing Belding's ground squirrels (*top*) live in high mountain meadows (*middle*), as do the badgers who dig them out (*bottom*). A badger can dig itself out of sight in less than two minutes.

Sierra junipers favor high
mountain rocky outposts where
the chief water supply is
snowmelt. Their rich cinnamon
bark is shredded by deer mice,
chipmunks, and squirrels for soft
nest linings.

Whitebark pines dominate most Sierra Nevada timberline areas in either erect or mat form, thriving here at 10,000 feet on Tioga Pass.

Opposite top: Among the colorful wildflowers of the subalpine heights are the explorers gentians, blooming most years in August.

Opposite: By contrast, riparian areas of midmountain forests put on a fragrant, luxuriant show of western azaleas in early June.

The Sierra Nevada provides bird diversity through the seasons. Roving flocks of band-tailed pigeons (*top*) may fly in at any time of year to feed on acorns and berries. These two arrived in a blizzard.

Bottom: Major winter snowstorms turn Sierran forest landscapes into nodding "nuns"—the range of light transformed briefly into a magical range of white.

Six

ALONG THE SUMMIT OF THE Sierra Nevada extends an area nearly two hundred miles long and twenty miles wide known to thousands of hikers and backpackers as the high Sierra. Lying above the level of continuous forest, this spectacular belt stretches from Pyramid Peak near Lake Tahoe to Cottonwood Pass south of Mount Whitney, and includes all of the central and southern high country from approximately 8,000 feet to the tops of the loftiest peaks. From Yosemite south it is a roadless realm, accessible only by trails, and then only in summer and autumn. Plainly written on this wild, rugged landscape is the history of recent intense glaciation. The angular peaks sculptured by rock-plucking glaciers, the massive granite slabs planed and polished to mirror brilliance, the erratic boulders weighing thousands of pounds stranded where only moving ice could have left them, all speak of an age when rivers of ice overpowered the land.

During the Pleistocene three glacial periods separated by long warm intervals occurred in the Sierra. Unlike the one huge ice cap that covered much of northeastern North America, the Sierran glaciers were discontinuous. Some parts of the range had none, and in northern areas only small ice patches nestled in basins or cirques of the taller peaks. But from Donner Pass south to the upper Kern River, ice fields varying in size from a few to many square miles sent trunk glaciers flowing down valleys to the east and west. Formed in the high mountains when more snow fell annually than could melt or evaporate, and compacted year after year into ice, the glaciers eventually became heavy enough to move slowly downslope, usually following preexisting stream valleys. As they moved, they plucked rocks from weak joints in the sides and floor of their path, scratching and scouring surfaces with them.

Over time, this action rounded V-shaped river valleys into U-shaped glacial valleys. Rivers and creeks pouring into the valleys from the side sometimes had their entrance channels carried away by the glaciers, which left them hanging high above the deepened gorge. When the ice later melted, the rivers descended in cascades or plunged over the brink, as in the leaping waterfalls of Yosemite Valley.

The three glaciers that carved out Yosemite Valley flowed at one stage for thirty-six miles, reaching slightly below El Portal in the Merced River canyon. The first stage, three thousand feet thick opposite Glacier Point, submerged all but the tops of Half Dome, El Capitan, and a few other peaks. It deposited at the base of Sentinel Dome huge boulders of a different type of granite from that on which they now rest. Their point of origin was miles away, across a chasm that only an ice river three thousand feet deep and nearly a mile wide could have bridged. The last glacier left a terminal moraine across the valley near El Capitan. As the ice melted, this moraine dammed the valley to form Lake Yosemite. The lake gradually filled to become the meadow and open forest that the first humans in the area encountered.

In modified form the glacier story was repeated in the San Joaquin, Kings, Kaweah, Kern, and other rivers of western and eastern slopes. Everywhere glaciers carved and smoothed surfaces, swept away soil, enlarged stream channels, and dug lake basins, leaving their bold imprint on the land. Then, as the climate warmed a few degrees and brought the Ice Age to a close around ten thousand years ago, the glaciers melted away, filling thousands of tarns with their waters, the rivers with turbulent roar.

Today's high Sierra retains only miniature versions of the powerful ice forces that shaped it. The sixty "glacierets" present on Mount Lyell, the Palisades, and other high peaks are products of a recent cooler period that occurred about four thousand years ago. Although all of them are less than one and one-half miles long, these small glaciers that cling to shady high-mountain cirques exhibit all the characteristics of greater ones: crevasses, bergschrunds, glacial tables, and moraines. Their bases pour out a steady stream of "glacial milk," meltwater whitened by finely ground rock flour. In late summer, when the snow is soft and the crevasses gape two hundred yards long by four feet wide, with no bottom in sight, and serrated icicles hang like long spears thirty feet into the bluish-white depths, these glaciers seem frigidly arctic in their setting among 13,000- and 14,000-foot peaks.

Although most of the high-country rock base is granite, much of it a white granite that reflects intense light, the whiteness is broken by green splashes of mountain meadows and trees, by the blue of lakes, and by black volcanic crags and red-brown or purple metamorphic peaks. Red mountains such as Dana and Gibbs carry metamorphic versions of summits originally formed under the sea, through which the ancient Sierra arose, and contain marine fossils to prove it.

From 10,000 feet to the crests of higher peaks cling the hardy low flowers of the range's highest plant community, alpine fell-fields. Below them, interspersed wherever trees can get a footing, stand the subalpine forests from 9,000 feet to timberline. Subalpine trees are not many in kind: conditions of the heights are too rigorous for more than a handful of species.

In lower subalpine areas, mountain hemlocks (*Tsuga mertensiana*), achieving heights of up to one hundred feet, associate with red firs, lodgepole pines, and western white pines in tall, beautiful forests. These narrowly conical trees have soft bluish green needles that look starlike in sprays; the terminal shoots of young trees perennially droop a little. Sometimes living where snow lingers well into the summer in north- or east-facing canyons, hemlocks form almost pure open groves, cool retreats vibrant with mature reddish purple barks and saplings snow-bent to the ground but straightening resiliently when freed.

Brushing shoulders with them, or standing alone on rocky overlooks, western white pines lift characteristically swirling upper branches and needles that at times shimmer like silver. So distinctive is the sound in the wind of this and the other Sierran pines that John Muir claimed he could tell where he was by pine music alone if he were set down blindfolded anywhere in the mountains. Climbing this tree to listen closely to the needles, he found that they gave out a well-tempered, winglike hum, about 250 vibrations per minute, each needle in the cluster of five remarkably free from clicking against the others except in storms. The finest pine music, said Muir.

Closely attuned to the granite domes are the cinnamon brown–trunked, shreddy-barked Sierra junipers (*Juniperus occidentalis*). Climbing over windswept ridges, pushing roots into every soil-collecting crevice, they are often almost the sole species spaced over miles of solid rock. Blasted by gales, weighted by snow, scored by lightning, junipers twist and turn in all the picturesque shapes of trees subject to the elements. Where they bend with the wind, their bleached windward trunks provide a buffer for the low green growth in the lee. In the shelter of boulders trunks rise to boulder height, then spread a tough horizontal mat of scaly green leaves sometimes twenty feet across, sloping like a roof to deflect the wind up and over. Other junipers stay erect, with rounded or flattened crowns.

The tendency of some trees to assume low matted forms on approaching timberline while others remain upright has been noted for a long time. The rigors of subalpine environments do not force all trees into the same habit of growth. Lodgepole pines, for example, generally remain at tree heights normal for them practically to the tree's upper limits. Studies just east of the Sierra Nevada crest found the most important factors determining tree growth to be inherited. Mountain-tops provide tremendous laboratories for investigating evolution. The changes in genes, or mutations, that are evolution's working tool are caused in part by oxygen deficiency, extremes of heat or cold, and radiation. All of these prevail with great force high in the mountains.

Working at Slate Creek Valley, the timberline station of the Carnegie Institution of Washington, plant biologist Jens Clausen classified over 36,000 individual trees according to their growth form and the altitude at which they reached tree line. Clausen found three major conifers—mountain hemlock, lodgepole pine, and whitebark pine (*Pinus albicaulis*)—struggling up the moraines, talus, screes, and gravel beds of this glacial hanging valley from 10,000 to 12,000 feet. The climate in which they live is among the most severe in the temperate zone. It has ten-month long winters; spring, summer, and fall telescope into two months from mid-July to mid-September; frost can occur any night of the year.

At the bottom of the valley, the three species of trees all attain full forest size. Lodgepole grows predominantly with a single trunk, whitebark primarily with more trunks, hemlock with either one or more. As the conifers climb they reach a belt two to three hundred feet below their own specific tree lines at which they assume one or more of three different growth forms: tall trees, low mats called elfinwood, or intermediate forms composed of several short erect trunks on a mat base. This is the border zone between subalpine and alpine, a kind of no-man's-land where conditions of the austere heights above begin to be felt. Into this testing arena the three trees drop seeds containing their genetic potential. Their chances for survival higher up depend on producing genetic combinations or mutations for plant forms that can exist under alpine conditions. Alpine conditions eliminate tall and intermediate trees and select for flat-growing mats.

Whitebark pine, with all the requisite genes, attains the highest tree line within the valley, 10,800 feet on south-facing slopes, and has evolved an elfinwood race that climbs at knee-high level up 12,000 feet. On east slopes mountain hemlock shows a parallel evolution, its gnarly matted alpine forms ranging a thousand feet beyond its tree line of 10,250 feet. Only lodgepole persists as a tall tree to its timberline at 10,500 feet on south slopes. But it, too, is in the process of evolving an alpine mat form, as pockets of elfinwood clearly indicate.

In the southern part of the high Sierra, thriving in the most inhospitable places on rocky benches, grows the only other major subalpine tree, the foxtail pine (*Pinus balfouriana*). From Mount Whitney, where they share timberline with lodgepoles, to Onion Valley, foxtails form groves that usually stand apart from other trees. They meet the demanding climate with thickset reddish brown trunks that taper to a bleached tip, the foliage often borne asymmetrically, the branches clothed densely at the end somewhat like a fox's tail.

In the rocky substratum where foxtail roots anchor around large boulders, and in similar rockslides throughout timberline areas, live two of the high Sierra's most common mammals, the yellow-bellied marmot and the pika.

A fat, grizzled yellow-bellied marmot (*Marmota flaviventris*) stretched out on a boulder, basking in the sun, is a familiar sight to hikers. Any attempt to approach it closely, however, inevitably triggers a sharp whistle of alarm, followed by the marmot's quick disappearance into an impenetrable pile of rocks. If the presence of blackish, half-inch-long droppings reveals that this is a regular lookout, a quiet wait at a distance will usually be repaid by its black face with white forehead patch peering cautiously out of a dark opening. When it has determined that all is well, the basking resumes, alternating during the summer months with foraging trips to nearby meadows.

Feeding on tender green vegetation, the big rodent puts on a thick layer of fat to carry it through a long winter of hibernation. Unlike its fabled eastern North American relative the woodchuck or groundhog, it does not usually emerge until April or May, lean and hungry for fresh green shoots.

The smaller pika (*Ochotona princeps*), though less often seen, is commonly heard in its rockslide niche throughout the high country. Nasal bleats ring out at any time of day, warning other pikas to keep out of the territory; the pika marks its territorial boundaries with secretions from eye and cheek glands. The calls are especially frequent just before dusk, when these little gray "rock rabbits" perch on their favorite lookout posts, usually backward-slanting rocks with overhead protection, and sound off. As many as six animals per acre may claim home ranges along the margins of talus slopes. Sitting hunched up with the back higher than the head and feet tucked under the body, they look like tailless bundles of fur. With each bleat the whole seven-inch body jerks forward and the round ears twitch upward. Although squat in appearance, reminiscent of a small guinea pig, the pika is very agile. The hairy soles with bare toe pads give superb traction on the rocks over which it bounds; in an emergency, the pika can spring ten feet.

It is as haymakers that pikas are best known. Near the jumbled rocks where they live are always small meadows or soil patches that hold clumps of wildflowers, grasses, sedges, or shrubs. During the brief summer season the pika feeds on these and harvests enough of them to last through the long winter. It works energetically at the task, cutting off stems and branches near the ground, loading them into bundles, and carrying them in its mouth to a sun-drenched shelter near its den. Each animal builds its own hay pile, adding new cuttings daily, and allows the hay to cure slowly; a female and her young sometimes make a group cache. In special bursts of enthusiasm, an animal may bring in fifteen loads of hay in an hour, adjusting the plants on the pile with its teeth. The front feet, used for washing and grooming the fur, never gather or manipulate the food. Dried feces of neighboring marmots sometimes add variety to the food pile.

When winter snows cover the rockslides, pikas retreat to the seclusion of their dens, remaining active, moving short distances under the rocks to eat from their hay piles, which continue to be as natural in color and as fragrant as well-cured hay. Occasionally in winter the animals may be heard calling from under the snow.

The pikas' link to snow and cold is an ancient one, for they are among the creatures known as glacial relicts. Widely distributed during the Ice Age, they now occur only where the climate is still similar to the Ice Age type, and hence are scattered disjunctively in the far North and on mountains in North America and Eurasia. The largest alpine areas in the world today occur on the Tibetan plateau and in the adjacent Himalayas; here live forms of pikas, pipits, rosy finches, horned larks, marmots, and sheep related to those found in mountains of the Western Hemisphere. Much evidence indicates that alpine species originated on the Tibetan plateau and later spread into the higher mountains of Europe and North America. The first pikas in North America probably crossed over the Bering land bridge in

Miocene times and expanded south through the Cascades, Sierra Nevada, and Rocky Mountains as far as northern New Mexico, all areas where they occur at the present time.

Also known as conies or rock rabbits, pikas show their relationship to rabbits in their rabbitlike hop and rabbitlike nose and teeth. Rabbits have four upper cutting teeth, instead of two as in rodents, and a lower jaw so narrow that the teeth can meet on only one side of the face at a time. Pikas and rabbits both chew with a sideways motion, alternately chewing on the two sides.

Two rabbits are occasionally seen in the high country. The snowshoe rabbit (*Lepus americanus*), ranging south from the northern boreal forests, is partial to forest and streamside thickets of the northern Sierra. The white-tailed jackrabbit (*L. townsendi*) occurs over open alpine flats and sparsely wooded terrain up to 12,000 feet, as well as in sagebrush areas east of the mountains. As rabbits go, it is enormous, one and one-half times the size of the common black-tailed jackrabbit (*L. californicus*) of the foothills, with tail and feet always white and with a warm protective coat that turns white in winter. Technically, the snowshoe, whitetail jackrabbit, and blacktail jackrabbit are all hares. Hares have precocial young, born fully furred and with eyes open; rabbits have altricial young, born naked with eyes closed.

The whitetail's favorite daytime resting hollows ("forms") are among boulders or under matted whitebark pines at timberline; here their droppings accumulate. Primarily nocturnal, they are only occasionally seen by summer hikers. Winter records on any high-altitude species are scarce, but Orland Bartholomew, who spent most of the winter of 1929 above 9,500 feet in the southern Sierra, observed white-tailed jackrabbits haunting the windswept crests to the very summit of Mount Langley.

It was a year of normal snowfall. At a time when the snowpack averaged four feet or less, he found southern exposures of canyons bare and Mount Tyndall and Mount Whitney with naked summits and little snow on their slopes. Many streams were flowing; most lakes were frozen. In addition to the white-tailed jackrabbits that were out foraging on the high slopes, mountain chickadees were "cheery companions to the last stick of timber"; Clark's nutcrackers and chickarees foraged below 10,000 feet; pikas and weasels were about; and martens raided foodbags at night, "in one case pilfering a whole pound of precious butter."

White-tailed jackrabbits, being animals of the open spaces, have less to fear from martens than from the red fox. Despite their speed, they sometimes fall victims. Lowell Sumner and Joseph Dixon reported seeing fresh tracks in the snow at the head of the Kern River that told a clear story of ambush. One of a pair of foxes had lain in wait behind a pile of boulders while the other fox rushed the whitetail and drove it toward the partner. The tracks of foxes and rabbit crisscrossed round and round the boulders to a bloodstain where rabbit tracks ended. After the kill, the foxes sat in the snow for a while, then went over the ridge carrying the rabbit.

There is no dearth of food for herbivores like the pika, yellow-bellied marmot, and white-tailed jackrabbit in the high Sierra. Interspersed among the bare granite summits are timberline meadows and alpine fell-fields that carry a lush succession of shorthair sedges (*Carex*) and wildflowers in the brief summer. On moist slopes, among dry gravels, or tucked away in damp crevices grow colorful gardens, less showy in dry years, luxuriant following abundant winter snows. Some hold individual flowers that are large and striking; others shelter tiny "belly plants" that require a chipmunk-eye-level view for full appreciation. Most plants are perennials, blooming year after year from the same sturdy roots; the growing season is too short to allow time for more than a few quick-cycling annuals to produce the seeds necessary to perpetuate themselves.

All are adapted in one way or another to the elemental forces of alpine climate. The habitat in which they live is really a high mountain desert. The solar radiation is intense, dehydration severe; the only water source is from melting snow and occasional summer rains. In many areas soil is completely lacking; where soil exists, it is thin, predominantly disintegrated granite, and sheds water quickly; much of the soil is unstable, subject to avalanches, rockslides, and the constant effects of freezing and thawing. Then there is the nearly omnipresent wind, which regularly attains velocities of up to fifty miles per hour, sucking up precious moisture, battering and sandblasting. The daily temperature extremes also play a role, averaging 22°–62°F on the summit of Mount Whitney in September, dropping to –2°F in Gaylor Lakes timberline basin in winter.

Sierran alpine plants meet these forces with the same adaptations as alpine plants everywhere. Some grow as low mats or cushion plants, countering the wind by hugging the ground, countering the cold of night by trapping daytime heat within the close-knit foliage. Interiors of cushion plants have been measured to be as much as twenty degrees warmer than the outside air. All resist evaporation in one way or another with leathery leaves, waxy leaves, leaves reduced in size, or leaves that are densely glandular, sticky or covered by a fuzz of hairs.

Some hardy specimens, like the rare snow willow (*Salix nivalis*), poke their one-to-four-inch-high stems primarily through the old metamorphic or unaltered volcanic soils that occupy scattered strips in the Sierra. Others frequent granitic soils. A good many plants show no soil preference.

When the Sierra was overrun by glaciers in Pleistocene times, scattered alpine areas escaped the ice. Mount Darwin, the Dana Plateau, Koip Peak, and Mount Whitney, among others, kept their heads above it and still show an ancient preglacial surface. These areas are believed to have served as refuges, or refugia, for plants during the glacial stages. Later they served as bases from which recolonization took place. Today most of the more than two hundred species in the Sierran alpine flora live where they do irrespective of glaciated or unglaciated surfaces.

Among them are plants with affinities to far-flung places—the yellow hawksbeard (*Crepis nana*) of Asiatic origin, the snow willow of the American Arctic, several phlox, gentian, and waterleaf species of the Rocky Mountains, even John Muir's favorite creeping white heather (*Cassiope mertensiana*), which is found also in the Canadian Rockies north to Alaska. "White heather grows where angels have trod," says an old Scottish fable; when several acres of north slope on the highest of the Echo Peaks are covered with the plant's white bells in mid-July, the fable is easy to believe.

The alpine Sierra holds a number of species that are entirely or nearly its own. Among the endemics is lovely sky pilot (*Polemonium eximium*), raising clusters of light blue phloxlike flowers on dry rocky ridges near the highest passes from 12,000 feet to the very summits. Appearing when the snow melts, it flowers quickly and is at its peak usually for only a day.

Among chaotic masses of granite blocks, especially in the southern Sierra, grow gardens of Sierra primrose (*Primula suffrutescens*), their magenta flowers rising from rosettes of spoon-shaped leaves.

Under overhanging rocks bob the yellow-centered bluish flowers of alpine stickseed (*Hackelia sharsmithii*), reminiscent of forget-me-nots. Here and there can be seen the yellowish heads of many species of senecio, reminding some people of goldenrods; the nodding purple blossoms of the alpine shooting star (*Dodecatheon alpinum*); the cream-colored flowers of alpine columbine (*Aquilegia pubescens*); the rosy bells of mountain heather (*Phyllodoce breweri*); the small yellow drabas on dry gravel (*Draba sierrae* and *D. lemmonii*); the pinkish blossoms of the dwarf bitterroot (*Lewisia pygmaea*); and several kinds of spring beauty (*Claytonia*), which in the West all are mountaintop dwellers.

As robust as any high Sierran herb is the yellow composite *Hulsea algida,* growing on nearly every high peak and pass from Yosemite to Mount Whitney, where it extends up to 14,000 feet. Standing ten inches tall, the plant often has fourteen heads in flower simultaneously. Glandular-sticky all over, except for the rays, it gives off a pleasant scent of balsam when touched and is the favorite alpine food of bighorn sheep, which eat all parts of it, including the roots.

The only birds that nest abundantly in the alpine zone of the Sierra Nevada are the gray-crowned rosy finches. Chocolate brown with a pinkish wash on wings and rump and a light gray head patch, these sprightly finches spend most of the year above timberline. The size of house sparrows, they move about in large flocks that swoop down with twittering noises to alpine turf, harvest the sedge and grass seeds, then with a few throaty chirps burst into undulating flight that takes them off among the peaks. Strong fliers, they handle the winds with great skill, riding them on rather long pointed wings until the precise instant for a sudden turn and landing.

Along the edges of alpine lakes they hunt for mayfly larvae or for caddis flies freshly emerging from chrysalids. Winter or summer, they salvage seeds of plants and glean snowfields and glaciers for the thousands of insects that each year appear as a kind of manna from heaven. Whether these beetles, flies, butterflies, and others fly up or are caught in updrafts and blown up, they eventually reach the heights. The frigid air soon numbs their flight muscles and drops the paralyzed creatures as dark sprinklings on the snow.

During the ten years that Charles (Bert) Harwell, then a park naturalist at Yosemite, was one of a team measuring glacier melt, he found that the surface of the Mount Lyell glacier lowered about four feet a year, exposing enormous quantities of frozen, embedded seeds, spiders, pollen, and insects, there for the finding by searching birds. He discovered that rosy finches by no means had the alpine heights to themselves. There were dippers feeding with them at glacier fronts, golden eagles soaring above, and kestrels catching grasshoppers on the tops of peaks. He saw small flocks of pinyon jays flying over glaciers, and American pipits wagging their tails on the ice. He found eared grebes in alpine lakes and sharp-shinned hawks often about. While he was at 12,400 feet on the Kuna glacier one day, a noisy, intense twittering caught his attention. "Here came a mad band of some fifty rosy finches chasing a sharp-shinned hawk off their mountain. The hawk made no attempt to do anything but escape."[1]

The archenemy of the rosy finch, however, is not a hawk but the most conspicuous bird in the high country, Clark's nutcracker. During the breeding season, rosy finches build nests in caves or crevices on the faces of cliffs or under rocks of the talus slopes below, preferring cool, shaded places. The cliff nests are virtually inaccessible to anything but birds. The big gray, black, and white nutcracker forages regularly along the craggy cliffs, examining every hole and ledge, eating eggs when it finds them or carrying out and devouring fledglings.

Young rosy finches leave the nest when they can barely navigate; they hide, beautifully camouflaged, among adjacent boulders until able to fly well. During this interval they are vulnerable to both the nutcrackers and weasels, which search the jumbled rockpiles persistently. There are other temporary hazards. The early California ornithologist William Dawson discovered one precocious young finch that had fluttered into a bergschrund, the crevasse at the head of a glacier, and

Clark's nutcracker extracting nuts
from a whitebark pine above a
resting snowshoe hare

was chirping cheerfully thirty feet down in the icy chasm as his mother swept in and out to feed him.

Clark's nutcrackers winter regularly at lower altitudes, often nesting in the pinyon-juniper forests of the eastern slope in March, when the land is still covered with snow, and feeding largely on pinyon nuts, fruits, and berries. In June parents and young move up to the high country, where their raucous calls roll out from the tops of lodgepoles and whitebark pines as one of the familiar sounds of timberline. The nuts of the whitebark form a staple part of the bird's diet. The long sharp bill works like a pickax in splitting cones open to extract seeds; at times it is used as a crowbar, prying out seeds while one foot steadies the cone on the branch. Whitebark nuts are large and sweet, a dark chestnut brown, and unlike most pine seeds are wingless. What the wind cannot do in distributing the seeds, the nutcracker does. In harvesting, the bird occasionally flings seeds about the parent tree, but it pulls most of them into a pouch on the floor of its mouth, often as many as 150 seeds at a haul, and flies with them across ridges and chasms ten or more miles from their source. Here, on specially selected cache sites, it buries the seeds and covers them with litter.

Upon spring's return to the high country, the nutcrackers show remarkable memories in relocating 60 to 90 percent of their caches. Many of the unrecovered seeds grow into new groves of whitebark pines, bringing to full circle a singular ecological relationship.

Nutcrackers are not as tame in the Sierra as they are at Crater Lake, Oregon, where they come down to feed at tourists' feet. William E. Colby wrote that in the years when sheepmen pastured their flocks at Tuolumne Meadows the big birds fed on scraps and became as tame around camp as pets. When the sheepmen left the park for good, the nutcrackers reverted to their former wild, unapproachable state. Omnivorous like their relatives the crows and jays, nutcrackers hunt carrion and any small prey: grasshoppers, beetles, grubs, even moths and butterflies.

Climbing a western mountain has often been compared to traveling north from the Great Plains; each thousand-foot increase in elevation brings the approximate ecological equivalent of terrain lying 300 miles northward; far enough up or far enough north, you reach tree line and beyond. The rugged environments at sea level in the Arctic and on mountaintops farther south are similar enough to require the same sorts of biotic adaptations for survival, and they share a glacial history. As the Pleistocene glaciers retreated, butterfly species that were cold-adapted followed them northward and to the mountaintops, producing the discontinuous distribution of today.

Butterflies of the high Sierra include both wide-ranging cosmopolitan species such as the painted lady, mourning cloak (*Nymphalis antiopa*), and California tortoise-shell and rare types whose nearest relatives can be found only on other isolated mountaintops or in the arctic tundra. Some species, such as the Ivallda arctics (*Oeneis ivallda*), erratic fliers of Sierran summits, have come to resemble exactly the texture and color of the particular rocks on which they alight. Near the crest of the range, where jumbles of metamorphic mountains tinted in subdued browns and reds contrast with peaks of pale gray granite, Ivallda arctics fly among the boulders, often leaning with the wind on landing, their mottled wings blending into patches of lichen. Gray forms occur on granite, brown forms on metamorphic rock, their caterpillars feeding on grasses.

The subalpine meadows are hosts to a variety of butterfly species. An intense bit of color on the wing is the lustrous copper (*Lycaena cupreus*), a fiery orange-red flier with dark edgings. Most characteristic are the gray blues (*Agriades glandon*) that sometimes swarm about shooting stars and settle among the grasses and sedges as soon as the sun drops behind the western peaks.

Although the host plants on which eggs are laid and caterpillars feed are unknown for a good many Sierran species, one known host is that of Behr's sulfur (*Colias behrii*), the only greenish butterfly in the Sierra. For a number of years around the turn of the century Jean Baptiste Lembert, a pioneer homesteader in Tuolumne Meadows, held a virtual monopoly on this butterfly. Only he and the Indians knew where to find it in this subalpine country, at 8,600 feet, then highly inaccessible except by a long and arduous trek. The butterfly, being rare, was much in demand by natural scientists, and Lembert supplied it in quantity to universities and museums.[2]

When the Tioga Road opened the area in 1915, naturalists soon discovered the secret of this smoky-edged sulfur's haunts. Its larvae feed exclusively on the Sierra bilberry (*Vaccinium nivictum*), tying the butterfly's distribution to this dwarf heath that turns the meadows red in autumn. Although Tuolumne and adjacent meadows form the primary base, smaller colonies of Behr's sulfur have been found to the south at Mineral King and at Rock Creek.

Characteristic of the dry high meadows are pert little mammals familiar to every camper and backpacker. Belding's ground squirrels (*Spermophilus beldingi*) signal the approach of any intruder with short piercing whistles of alarm. Standing stark upright, resting on hind feet and tail, at a distance they look very much like pickets driven into the ground to tether a horse. At closer range, the "picket pins" show bright inquisitive eyes, wiggling noses, and dangling forelegs as they gauge the threat and decide whether to dash for their burrows.

These foot-long grayish yellow rodents with a reddish brown band down the back fade into the surrounding grasses of late summer. The most terrestrial of Sierran ground squirrels, they feed primarily on grasses, depending little on the large seeds, nuts, and roots sought out by the California ground squirrel of lower elevations. Along the margins of meadows, their range occasionally overlaps that of the forest-loving golden-mantled ground squirrel, but the golden-mantle rarely strays far into the open short-grass country where the Belding's is at home.

Named for Lyman Belding, the Stockton naturalist who first collected it in 1885, this high-elevation squirrel spends nearly eight months of the year underground, often hibernating from September to April, though this varies somewhat with the weather. Its young are born in July, as many as six in a litter, and on emerging from the nest are watched over carefully by the mother; at her single sharp warning note, they disappear into the burrow, sometimes all trying to crowd through the two-inch hole at once. When they later disperse, they dig their own burrow systems, occasionally appropriating the tunnels of mountain pocket gophers. One tunnel that was excavated totaled fifty-four feet in length. Soil moisture limits the tunnels' depth; most burrows checked have been less than a foot beneath the surface.

No depth, however, is much protection from the squirrels' occasional enemy the badger, once it has found one of the little rodents at home. Excavating a series of surface holes along the tunnel, the badger appears to see, hear, or smell its prey as it moves quickly from one opening to the other until it finally captures the luckless victim.

Formerly common in plains and mountain meadows of the West and east to the Great Lakes, badgers (*Taxidea taxus*) have been exterminated from much of their range by settlement, cultivation, and poisons. A 1915 University of California mammal survey of a cross section of the Sierra named the badger the most numerous carnivore in Tuolumne Meadows. Badgers are now neither common nor numerous in the Sierra, occurring in meadows here and there, through timberline.

When it comes to digging skill and speed, it is doubtful whether any American mammal can match a badger. Although many naturalists have seen the animal in action, one of the prize Sierran accounts is certainly Walter Fry's.

> On September 2, 1912, while at Mitchell Meadow, Sequoia National Park—elevation 8500 feet—we came suddenly upon a large badger some 100 yards from his den. We shut off his return to his burrow and chased him for a few moments on horseback. No sooner did we stop our chase than the badger dug into the ground, and did the fastest job of digging I have ever seen. Although the ground was hard and somewhat crusted with sod, the badger dug himself completely from our sight and plugged the hole behind him with dirt in less than one and one-half minutes. In excavating, his whole being was brought into action. He used all four feet, as well as mouth, with great skill and determination.

The badger's equipment for digging could hardly be more superb. Built low, with short legs and a broadly flattened body somewhat on the lines of a turtle, the animal is close to the ground to begin with. Its black feet, armed with powerful claws, are backed by stout muscles. The tough hide of long grizzled hair hangs loosely behind a face marked by a conspicuous white stripe running from the nose over the head to the shoulder, with contrasting black cheek patches. All of its two-and-one-half-foot length and more than twenty pounds are thrown into its search for food. Catching gophers, ground squirrels, mice, and chipmunks in one meadow until they become scarce, it then moves on to new territory, digs a burrow for shelter, and takes up the food search anew. It is courageous and powerful like its larger cousin the wolverine, knows no fear when cornered, and will use claws and teeth to devastating effect in its defense.

The wolverine (*Gulo gulo*), never plentiful in California, is now an extremely rare high Sierran mammal living from Lake Tahoe south to the Kern gap. Here in the southernmost outposts, occasional sightings of animals or tracks represent the few human contacts of the past three decades with this solitary powerhouse of the far North. A low-slung, heavy-bodied animal about three feet long and weighing up to forty pounds, the wolverine is generally dark brown, with a yellowish band extending along each side from shoulder to tail base and a gray patch across the forehead. It carries its head and tail low beneath a slightly humped back.

What little is known of its Sierran habits comes largely from observations in the early 1900s by trappers and naturalists, especially Walter Fry, who encountered the animal at scattered intervals during thirty years of field work in the higher regions in and near Sequoia National Park. Fry rated the wolverine "king beast of the Sierras," a creature that knows no retreat from any animal except man and "not only expects the larger animals to let him alone but requires them to give up their own prey to satisfy his gluttonous appetite." Fry saw three large coyotes that were feeding on a horse carcass vacate immediately upon the approach of a medium-sized wolverine; and he watched a large and a medium-sized cougar that were feeding on a deer they had killed give way to a medium-sized wolverine after much growling and threatened resistance on the part of the larger mountain lion.

At Buck Canyon, seven miles east of the Giant Forest, he happened onto a rare experience. His party had just made camp when they heard the growling of bears. Making their way to a nearby cliff edge, they looked down on a small grassy opening some 150 feet away where two large bears, one black and the other brown, were standing on the decomposed carcass of a cow disputing the right of possession. After much fussing and growling, both bears settled down to eat side by side.

About fifteen minutes later a large wolverine emerged from the brush one hundred yards to the rear and above the bears. It ambled along with occasional glances to either side, lay down for a few minutes, then got up and turned over a fairly large log under which it located a few snails and ate them. From the base of a large fir it picked and swallowed a good sized fungus, then caught and gulped down frogs from nearby small pools. Suddenly the wolverine sprang onto a boulder, nose pointing in the direction of the carrion; looking over at the two bears, it eyed them and the intervening space. Sliding to the ground, it sat hunched over for a few seconds, then began the advance, cautiously but quickly moving to the shelter of a large rock within thirty feet of the bears. Here it stood up, rigid, and peered around one side of the boulder. "His black, beadlike eyes glittered," recounted Fry,

> while the hair on his neck and back was erect and rough like that on a dog when going into a fight, and his short, bushy tail was hoisted to an almost perpendicular angle. Then, after having bristled himself up to what appeared double his natural size, in this queer and picturesque attitude the wolverine shot down the mountainside, landed directly on top of the carcass between the two bears, and, growling ferociously, snapped his powerful jaws and teeth in their very faces. Never in all my mountain experience have I seen wild animals more suddenly and thoroughly frightened than were those two bears. . . . Every combative impulse gave way to hysterical fright.

The brown bear in three enormous leaps reached a fir and climbed to the top. The black bear turned a complete backward somersault, landing on its feet with head downhill, and departed in a cloud of dust. The wolverine began to devour the carcass, crushing and swallowing even the large bones "as if they were mere chalk."

Filling up voraciously when food is plentiful undoubtedly carries wolverines through the periods when prey is scarce or dormant. In the timberline and red fir areas, which they hunt ceaselessly, winter and summer, wolverines take whatever they can find or catch—marmots and bushy-tailed woodrats in the rockslides, Belding's ground squirrels, pocket gophers, and voles in the high meadows, even porcupines on occasion. Rapid diggers when seeking a rodent in a burrow, they do not dig burrows for themselves but sleep, according to Fry, at random under shelflike rocks or at the base of a tree. The wolverine, shunning people and living in the most remote high areas, requires only a large enough untouched wilderness for a hunting range— something that is becoming increasingly scarce.

In some parts of the wolverine's terrain, glacial action and subsequent weathering have left low rocky ridges, sinks, and shallow bogs interspersed with meandering streams and small lakes. In the high mountain spring of May or early June, these wet meadows have resounded over the centuries with the mellow trills of Yosemite toads (*Bufo canorus*) and the *krek-it* of tiny Pacific tree frogs (*Hyla regilla*). Emerging from hibernation as soon as snowmelt pools form in the meadows, these amphibians waste no time commencing breeding. The choruses set up by male toads soon attract wandering females, which are much in demand since they are on the short end of a ten-to-one ratio. So eager are the males that they sometimes clasp and ride the backs of other males momentarily. Despite the distinct color difference in the sexes, the larger females showing many dark blotches on a pale background, the males a nearly uniform greenish tan, sex apparently is recognized more on a trial-and-error basis than visually. Females submit to clasping, whereas the protest notes and escape struggles of clasped males soon win their release. The eggs are laid in jellylike strings in the shallow water of silty pools surrounded by sedges and rushes. Tree frogs often breed in the same pools, preferring the deeper parts, while neighboring mountain yellow-legged frogs (*Rana muscosa*) select deep areas of lakes or slow streams. After the breeding season, adults of all three amphibians can be found side by side at the edges of lakes or ponds.

Temperature is known to exert a potent influence on the rate at which amphibious animals develop; at high altitudes it becomes critical. For eggs laid in water of 45° to 73°F to hatch into tadpoles and for the tadpoles to become frogs and toads in the course of a short subalpine growing season requires special acceleration. The mountain yellow-legged frog takes two seasons to accomplish its metamorphosis: it overwinters as a tadpole and matures the second summer. Living in the deeper lakes and streams that do not freeze makes this possible for the yellow-leg. What happens, though, to tadpoles of Yosemite toads living in shallow meadow ponds that sometimes dry up before the summer is over?

Ernest Karlstrom, who studied the toads intensively at elevations between 9,000 and 10,000 feet near Kaiser and Tioga Passes, discovered a number of ways in which the growth cycle was speeded up. The toad's habit of laying eggs in water usually not more than three inches deep gives the eggs a warmer microenvironment than their cooler surroundings; both the shallow water and adjacent ground surface pick up heat from the intense high-altitude sun, and the silty bottom of the pool is a good absorber of sky radiation. The tadpoles, in turn, tend to congregate during daylight hours in the warmer margins of the pond, where their black color absorbs solar heat. In years when high Sierran temperatures remain warm at midday into September and early October, many Yosemite toad tadpoles apparently reach adulthood before winter.

The adult toads show an equal number of adaptations for survival in the cold subalpine meadows. Unlike most toads, they are diurnal. Night's cold temperatures force them to seek shelter in rodent burrows, and on cool mornings they may not emerge until midday, spending much time at the entrance of a burrow basking in the sun.

The Yosemite toad poses an intriguing study in speciation, the way in which new species are formed. Occupying about 150 miles of the high Sierra, from Ebbetts Pass to south of Kaiser Pass, mostly above 9,000 feet, it is surrounded by the western toad (*Bufo boreas*), the common dusky garden toad of wide western North American distribution. Obviously closely related, the two toads show distinct differences, such as the whitish dorsal stripe on the western toad and the large parotoid glands of the Yosemite toad.

At only one known area, the Blue Lakes of Alpine County, do their ranges overlap. Outside the Yosemite toad's range, the western toad occupies similar mountain areas, indicating an adaptability to varied terrain. In speculating on how this situation came about, Karlstrom compared François Matthes's glacial map of Yosemite with locations of the two toads. The Yosemite toads' localities closely approximated areas that were never invaded by glaciers. From this evidence, Karlstrom drew a hypothetical historical picture.

During the late Tertiary period a generalized western toad type was probably widespread over the low mountains that composed the Sierra. The extensive uplift of the range and subsequent glacial carving of Sierran river systems fragmented the meadow habitats. Unglaciated islands suitable for toads remained between tongues of ice at intermediate elevations from 6,000 to 8,000 feet. On these, in geographic isolation, the Yosemite toads evolved their own specialized characteristics, later moving crestward as the glaciers receded.

There are indications of somewhat parallel developments in two other Sierran amphibians. The mountain yellow-legged frog occupies higher elevations, above the foothill yellow-legged frog (*Rana boylei*) of lower western slopes (though the latter has been pretty well supplanted by the introduced bullfrog in recent years). And in the central high Sierra lives the Mount Lyell salamander (*Hydromantes platycephalus*), a granite-matching rarity of rock fissures and seepages, with a more generalized relative, the limestone salamander (*H. brunus*), occupying the western foothills.

Within the past few decades, amphibians in the high Sierra, as well as in the Colorado Rockies and pristine high mountains throughout the world, have shown ominous drops in their numbers. A high Sierran survey of thirty-eight lakes where mountain yellow-legged frogs once leaped into the waters revealed the frogs remaining in only one lake. A similar story unfolded in fourteen lakes at the 11,000-foot level in the Colorado Rockies where tiger salamanders (*Ambystoma tigrinum*), formerly numerous, lost two-thirds of their population in nine years, a decline linked directly to acid rain and snow.

The acid precipitation resulting from the burning of fossil fuels that was shown to be killing thousands of lakes in Sweden, Canada, and the eastern United States in the 1970s spread to the western United States in the 1980s and continues to endanger more than 10,000 western mountain lakes, including those in Yosemite and Sequoia/Kings Canyon National Parks. In California, nitrogen oxides from automobile exhausts, converted in the air into nitric acids, form the chief contaminants. Carried by the westerlies to the high mountains, they descend with the snow. With the spring melt, they pour into the lakes, raising the lakes' acidity at the very time when aquatic insects are hatching and amphibians' jellylike eggs are especially vulnerable. As I describe it in *California Forests and Woodlands*, "The results are deadly. Even a minor change in a lake's acid content can decimate the plankton that forms the food base for all aquatic life. Frogs, toads, and salamanders, with their highly permeable skins, readily absorb toxic substances in their watery environment. Like canaries in a mine, they unwittingly act as barometers of their habitat's well-being."

Holes in the Earth-protecting ozone layer also allow the intense ultraviolet light of high altitudes to penetrate lakes and kill life. In some lakes, introduced trout also take a heavy amphibian toll. Whatever the combination of causes, the dramatic plunge in the numbers of amphibians has produced serious concern among ecologists. As herpetologist David Wake put it, "Amphibians have been around for over 100 million years. They're survivors. They survived whatever knocked out the dinosaurs. So if they're beginning to check out, we'd better take it seriously. The same water that no longer supports amphibian populations in the Sierra Nevada is the water we drink in Berkeley and San Francisco. It seems to me there's a message here somewhere. We'd better figure out what it is."[3]

One message seems abundantly clear: We must reduce and recycle our pollutants and eliminate the chemicals in refrigerators, air conditioners, and other appliances that cause holes in the ozone layer, along with reducing the carbon dioxide that affects global warming.

Amphibians are not the only forms of life that are at stake. Trees and other plants of the high mountain meadows suffer stress and stunting from acidic buildup in their soils, and the meadows themselves are in many places only slowly recovering, with Park and Forest Service protection, from the sheep herds of the 1800s and more recent heavy overgrazing by cattle. Overgrazing and pounding hoofs break up the sod. Spring meltwaters then cut through and form gullies.

Gullies drain the moisture that is essential to maintain the meadow. Once the water table is lowered, lodgepole pines invade. Too many cattle at any elevation stamp out riparian vegetation totally, leaving only bare-edged, muddy creeks.

A recent study in the Highland Lakes area of Ebbetts Pass found that the rare Yosemite toad and the mountain yellow-legged frog are both adversely affected by grazing. The same is true of mule deer on the Kern Plateau and of golden trout on the Whitney Allotment bordering Sequoia National Park. Cattle grazing threatens biodiversity in much of the Sierra. Economically, the grazing fee formula on federal lands has always been a winner for cattlemen and a loser for the Bureau of Land Management, the Forest Service, and taxpayers.

In addition to meadows, the high country is sprinkled with more than 1,500 lakes that nestle in rocky basins scooped out by glaciers, in steep-sided cirques, and behind glacial moraines. Other lakes of the past have already filled with gravel, sand, and soil from entering streams, to become in turn marshes, meadows, and eventually forests. At some, garter snakes (*Thamnophis*) probe the grassy edges and frigid depths looking for frogs; spotted sandpipers teeter on the surrounding beaches calling a sharp *peet-weet* into the solitude; algae, water beetles and other aquatic insects, along with a few crustaceans and mollusks, form a sparse but interconnected chain of life.

None of the high lakes held fish after glaciation; waterfalls excluded them, confining the native fish to the lower streams, with the probable exception of golden trout. The native fish fauna in the Yosemite and Sequoia regions totaled six species: three minnows, hardhead (*Mylopharodon conocephalus*), Sacramento squawfish (*Ptychocheilus grandis*), and California roach (*Hesperoleucus symmetricus*); a riffle sculpin (*Cottus gulosus*); the Sacramento sucker (*Catostomus occidentalis*); and rainbow trout (*Oncorhynchus mykiss*).

Over the entire range trout were the primary cold-water fish, with three kinds of native trout originally distributed in separate drainage systems. East of the crest in the Lahontan Basin, served chiefly by the Carson, Truckee, and Walker Rivers, abounded the cutthroat trout (*Oncorhynchus clarki*), marked by two red stripes on its lower jaw. In cool streams west of the crest swam the gamy rainbow with a reddish violet side stripe and many black spots on the upper part of its body.

To the south in a few high streams of the Kern River drainage, fishermen of the 1870s caught a golden trout, olive green above peppered with large black dots, a crimson line down the center of its belly, reddish lower fins and gill flaps, sides a flashing crimson-gold and gray. Directed by President Theodore Roosevelt to investigate the golden trout (*Oncorhynchus aguabonita*) and make certain that it was not exterminated, Barton Evermann explored the Kern Plateau waters in 1904. The fish, he theorized, had once been a Kern River rainbow trout but had become isolated by volcanic barriers above the main Kern River. Living in Golden Trout Creek, which contains masses of lemon yellow and orange tufa, the trout had over time evolved the colors of its native streambed.

Hybridizing readily with rainbows, the goldens produce infinite color variations in the many high Sierran streams and lakes in which they have been planted, earlier by enthusiastic fishermen and Sierra Club members, later by Fish and Game field crews. Colonel Sherman Stevens made one of the first transplants in 1876, carrying thirteen golden trout in a coffeepot four miles from a Kern River tributary to Cottonwood Creek near his sawmill. The fish thrived in their new home and later served to stock the Cottonwood Lakes.[4]

From the turn of the century through the 1940s, California Fish and Game extended the range of goldens one hundred miles north of the Kern drainage, hauling the trout over mountain passes by twenty mule pack trains. Specially oxygenated tank trucks now carry fingerlings and "catchable" trout from hatcheries to roadside streams; airplanes drop the fish into back-country lakes.

Where there is running water for spawning, goldens and rainbows are often self-sustaining. Brown trout (*Salmo trutta*), introduced from Europe in 1895, and the eastern brook trout (*Salvelinus fontinalis*) occur in some waters along with the natives and in some alone. The brook trout are at their best in high lakes, where they spawn in seepage areas around the shore or in springs emerging from the lake bottoms.

The streams that carry snowmelt down the western slope formerly caused heavy flooding below in the Central Valley in winter or spring.

Check dams in the mountains now reduce this hazard; additional dams impound water for irrigation, hydroelectric power, and distant-city water supplies, creating artificial lakes at middle and lower elevations. Although these reservoirs with their fluctuating shorelines lack the natural beauty of mountain lakes, they often are pleasant places for family recreation and are well stocked with squirming trophies for the angler. Depending on their elevation and plantings, the reservoirs hold brown and rainbow trout, kokanee salmon, blackbass (*Micropterus*), catfish (*Ictalurus*), crappies (*Pomoxis*), bluegills (*Lepomis macrochirus*), and other Fish and Game imports. Some of these fish also live in adjacent streams.

Reservoirs usually occupy canyons or valleys, making use of the river's natural walls. Where the canyons and rivers are of special beauty, their selection as reservoir sites by cities or municipal utility districts has led at times to stormy controversy over what is the highest use of land and water. In 1914, a reservoir for the city of San Francisco was created in the sunlit meadows and oak and pine forests of Hetch Hetchy Valley in the "Grand Canyon of the Tuolumne," twenty miles north of Yosemite Valley. Today's human demands for the precious one-by-seven-mile space of Yosemite Valley point up that earlier choice to inundate Hetch Hetchy as an action against the long-term national interest, just as John Muir and the Sierra Club said it was in 1914. Now underneath a hundred billion gallons of water, Hetch Hetchy over the years could have brought outdoor pleasure to millions of people. Similar choices hang in the balance at regular intervals for the other remaining wild rivers of the Sierran slopes, each issue fought out by environmentalists versus developers both in the political arena and in the courts.

Water competition in California has always been a conflict between the public interest and private gain. The latter view, blind to our role as a part of nature, is equally blind to our feel for the roar of a wild river's cataracts, the churning of its white water, its clear pools and fellow forms of life.

In such riparian haunts in the Sierra, you cannot go long without meeting a plump slate-gray bird that bobs and dips in the shallows or on some half-submerged rock in midstream. Dippers are year-round residents of most permanent streams in the mountainous West. Water is their element, and they are never far from it. Over it they fly a low whirring course; within range of its spray they build their dome-shaped mossy nests; in and around and through cascades and waterfalls they whirl and flit, jumping from rocks to catch mayflies in the air, diving headfirst into foaming eddies. Flying to the middle of a rushing river, the bird alights daintily on the surface, then with a quick fluttering turn of the wings disappears beneath the torrent. Walking on the bottom, it probes for caddis fly larvac, flatworms, and hell-grammites, and on bouncing to the surface flies abruptly up and away.

A songbird with unwebbed feet, the dipper claims as its chief aquatic adaptations waterproof feathering, maintained by an oil gland ten times larger than that of most land birds, and nostril covers that can be closed underwater. Musical at any time of year, it sometimes sings out above the river's roar on winter days when snow banks a frigid land. Chained by neither temperature nor altitude, it runs the gamut of Sierran waters, equally at home along montane streams or at the margins of alpine lakes, bobbing with rosy finches.

Seven

IN THE RAIN SHADOW

The winds that carry Pacific Ocean moisture to the Sierra Nevada drop most of it on the upper ponderosa pine–red fir forests of the western slope. What is left whitens the summits, leaving only a token for the east side. The lower eastern slope is consequently arid, its foothills and valleys merging inseparably into the Great Basin desert that stretches nearly a thousand miles across eastern California, Nevada, Utah, Colorado, and Wyoming to the Rocky Mountains.

This high desert, varying from 4,000 feet to 6,000 feet at its Sierran border, hot in summer, cold in winter, is a wide-open land from which you can look up much of the year to nearby snow-covered peaks and, eastward, to tawny rounded mountains. Dominating the rolling expanse of space and clear dry air is the low sagebrush scrub plant community. Composed of several species of silvery-green sagebrush (*Artemisia*), grasses, allied shrubs, and wildflowers in season, it clothes the Sierra's eastern flank for most of its four-hundred-mile length. In the deep, pervious soils, big sagebrush (*A. tridentata*), the largest form, reaches heights of seven feet or more. All the way to 9,500 feet or higher, this tough, aromatic shrub carries the imprint of the desert up the eastern slope, crossing over in places onto the west side of the range.

As the raven flies it, this valley-to-mountaintop distance is not very far. For the eastern escarpment is so steep in its southern section around Mount Whitney that there is a two-mile, almost vertical drop from alpine meadows to desert flats. It is this proximity of desert valleys and snow-capped peaks, with all the variety of plant and animal life packed between them in the short distance, that gives the eastern Sierra its uniqueness.

The eastern slope, with a gradient in places ten times as steep as the western gradient, compresses into approximately six miles plant communities whose counterparts may spread out over sixty miles on the west. This makes the east-side zonation much more compact and less distinct. Plant communities sometimes jam together, or are missing, or pop out above or below their usual sequence. Variations in local topography, moisture, exposure, temperature, slope, and history determine the actual configuration.

The rivers that cascade down east-side canyons, following paths once filled by glaciers, have cut through glacial moraines at nearly every bottom. Side roads now wind alongside many an old glacial path, each approach distinct from the others as it leads across the mountain's sagebrush shoulder into the foothills and forests above. From road's end trails zigzag upward to lakes lying in minaret-rimmed basins, to green meadows, snow-filled cirques, and jagged peaks of the high country; and many of the trails link with the John Muir Trail, which follows the crest of the range.

The eastern heights harbor essentially the same plant and animal communities as those we have seen in the high Sierran west. Below the alpine fell-fields grow subalpine forests of whitebark and lodgepole pine, western white pine and mountain hemlock, with foxtail and occasional limber pine (*Pinus flexilis*) to the south. Below these, red firs rise in cool deep-shaded stands, intermingling with lodgepoles and, at their lower borders, with white firs and Jeffrey pines. Aspens appear in groves anywhere from sagebrush country, where they grow along streams, to the fir-lodgepole forests.

The same sounds echo throughout the red fir forests of east and west: the distant spiral of the hermit thrush, the ruby-crowned kinglet's miniature symphony, the scold of the chickaree. Among the red firs of the Mammoth Lakes region, only the pumice on the ground would signal that this is the eastern slope rather than the western. Pumice, a kind of grayish, featherweight, spongy volcanic cinder, covers much of the approximately twenty-five-mile area from Mammoth to Mono Lake. Hurled out of vents as a frothy lava some five to twelve thousand years ago, it overlies hundreds of feet of solid lava that built the 2,400-foot-high Mono Craters, Mammoth Mountain, and dozens of ridges, hills, and obsidian domes. Devil's Postpile National Monument represents an outstanding example of basaltic lavas that fractured into immense polygonal columns as they cooled.

Just below the fir belt, this same region contains the largest Jeffrey pine forest in the world, some two hundred square miles of superb trees. Jeffreys generally fill the role on the eastern slope that ponderosa pines fill on the western, occupying middle elevations slightly above the foothills. North of Lake Tahoe, both species occur together in some east-side spots; but south of Tahoe, Jeffreys are the only stately pines growing, from scattered patches in sagebrush up through the foothill woodlands into pure stands of open forest at the middle levels.

The orangish brown, large-plated trunks of mature trees, sometimes smelling in the crevices of vanilla or pineapple, often rise clear of branches for many feet. In places they tower over hillsides of mixed chaparral—the varnish-leafed tobacco brush covered with sweet-smelling white flowers in early summer, currant, bush chinquapin, bitterbrush (*Purshia tridentata*), the twisting forms of greenleaf manzanita. The story goes that a one-hundred-dollar reward was once offered to anyone who could find a piece of manzanita twelve inches long that was straight. The reward was never claimed.

The unusually large Jeffrey pine forest east of the Mammoth Lakes owes its existence to a break in the Sierran wall. The crest, which elsewhere prevents most moisture from reaching the east side, drops lower at the Mammoth gap. Pacific Ocean storm clouds can here move directly over the saddles of Minaret Summit and Mammoth Pass, dropping their rain and snow east of the crest. This gives the Mammoth Mountain red firs and ski slopes their deep snow cover and provides the water for the adjacent Jeffrey pine forest to thrive on what otherwise probably would be dry, sagebrush-covered hills.

Highway 395, which runs the length of the east side, winds for miles through this parklike Jeffrey pine forest on either side of Deadman Pass (8,041 feet).

At Sherwin Summit and other inclines, the road bisects pinyon pine woodland, and near Lee Vining passes alongside Mono Lake. "Lonely tenant of the loneliest spot on earth," Mark Twain called Mono Lake in the 1860s. He had nearly drowned trying to row a wooden boat across it, getting caught in a storm. Avian visitors view it differently. On days when piles of cumulus clouds reflect from its blue surface and thousands of Wilson's and northern phalaropes spin round and round in the shallow waters stirring up food, the lake is far from untenanted. Rimmed by tufa pinnacles along segments of the white shore, with the snow-capped Sierra Nevada to the west, sagebrush desert to the east, and the grayish black Mono Craters to the south, Mono Lake carries a stark beauty all its own.

That beauty, along with the one million waterfowl and songbirds that traditionally stopped in the Mono Basin during migration over the centuries, began to disappear in 1941 when the Los Angeles Department of Water and Power dammed four of the five Sierran streams that fed the lake and sent the water south to city faucets. Because the lake has no outlet, its salt content doubled through evaporation. An alkaline border formed around its thirty-mile rim, and loose dust blew chokingly on windy days. Over the next four decades Mono Lake's level fell catastrophically, exposing the California gull nesting colonies on Negit Island to attacks from coyotes crossing a newly formed land bridge. Trout disappeared as creeks dried up. Marshes, lagoons, and riparian vegetation vanished. The fresh water that formerly lay on the surface of the heavier salt water was no longer there for shovelers, pintails, and other waterfowl, and their numbers plummeted.

In the mid-1970s, a group of college students and concerned conservationists led by David and Sally Gaines decided to fight for the lake. Forming the Mono Lake Committee, they publicized the lake's desperate plight and its magnetic appeal through calendars, photographs, articles, and bird-a-thons. Against seemingly impossible odds, they won a sixteen-year legal battle with the Los Angeles Department of Water and Power. In 1995 the State Water Resources

Control Board ruled that Mono Lake must be allowed to rise seventeen feet, to 6,392 feet above sea level—enough to restore a healthy ecosystem in the lake and its basin. This was assuredly one of the major environmental victories of the decade in the West.

Too salty for most life, Mono Lake is perfect for a certain few. It teems with brine shrimp, tiny crustaceans that swim and breed in the shallows and have sometimes been harvested by the California Department of Fish and Game as trout food. The shoreline darkens at times with small flies that swarm by the millions. These are the famous "koo-chah-bee" flies (*Ephydra hians*), whose pupae were relished by the Indians for food. The larval cases of the flies were attached to rocks on the bottom in shallow water. In late summer, when the winds washed great quantities of pupae onto the shore, the Indians collected them in masses, dried them, and removed their cases. The inner meat, resembling yellow grains of rice, was stored and eaten as a delicacy, reputed to have a flavor like nutmeat and shrimp. William Brewer, on his survey of California geology in 1863, described the pupae as "oily, very nutritious and not unpleasant to the taste" and wrote that they would make a fine soup if one did not know the source.

Koo-chah-bee were important trading items as well. The band of Paiute Indians who lived near Mono Lake and traded salt, obsidian, koo-chah-bee, and other articles across the Sierra apparently became known to their western neighbors the Yokuts as the "Monos" or "fly people" because of this food staple.

The Indians of Yosemite Valley were very fond of koo-chah-bee. Tabuce, the beloved Indian who demonstrated tribal customs to Yosemite Museum visitors during the 1940s, occasionally used to make acorn-flour pancakes for her guests. Just before serving she would lightly sprinkle a concoction over the top pancake, smiling and saying, "Something special." Later they learned it was koo-chah-bee.

The foothills of the eastern Sierra are dominated by the only one-needled pine in the world. Like spots on a leopard's back, single-leaf pinyon pines (*Pinus monophylla*) spread in a water-determined mosaic over the arid rocky elevations from 6,000 to 8,000 feet. Covering themselves when young with the stiff, curved, sharp-pointed needles, pinyons form compact balls and triangles of soft-toned blue-green. At maturity they stand less than twenty-five feet tall, more flat-topped and irregular in shape, but still usually offering scant shade. Sometimes, as near Rock Creek, they grow in almost pure, rather lush stands; occasionally they intermingle with Sierra junipers or Jeffrey pines, more frequently with the desert-loving Utah juniper (*Juniperus osteosperma*), desert mahogany (*Cercocarpus ledifolius*), or bitterbrush. North of Lake Tahoe, they taper off into a juniper-sagebrush woodland that persists into Oregon.

The pinyon's affinities lie primarily with the dry desert mountains of the Great Basin and the Southwest. Pinyon-juniper woodlands occur in the White-Inyo Mountains just east of the Sierra and in mountains of Nevada, Utah, Colorado, and Arizona. In the last three states the pinyon is mostly a two-needled species (*Pinus edulis*) rather than the one-needled tree of the Sierra. Fossil evidence indicates that many parts of the Mohave Desert south of the Sierra, now occupied by scanty shrubs, supported pinyon-juniper woodlands as recently as nine thousand years ago.

This evidence was contributed unwittingly by the woodrat, which ranges widely throughout the deserts and mountains of the region and has done so for a long time. The woodrat by nature collects a great diversity of plant materials within a limited foraging area for its house or den, which in arid regions is usually inside a cave or rock shelter. Here it assembles woody branches, spiny twigs, leaves, fibrous bark, old animal bones, fruits, seeds—an astonishing variety of things from available plants. Usually placed in relatively dry and secluded crevices, these plant materials have often mummified and remained well preserved for thousands of years. Studied, they provide a fairly detailed inventory of an earlier local flora. Woodrat middens from the Mohave Desert range in radiocarbon age from 4,000 to 19,500 years. Nearly all of them contain records of former juniper or pinyon-juniper woodland in the abundant fossil twigs and seeds of Utah juniper, leaves, cone scales, and seeds of single-leaf pinyon pine.

Pinyon pine woodland today grows in mountain areas having ten to twenty inches of precipitation, with desert scrub of less than half

Pinyon Pine–Juniper Woodland
(map by Carla J. Simmons)

that amount of rainfall at lower elevations all around it. The fossil evidence suggests that wooded corridors once existed continuously between the higher desert divides. Along these corridors, woodland trees could have migrated in wetter times to the isolated or disjunct stands where many of them occur today.

Pinyon jays, probably the most characteristic birds of the pinyon-juniper groves, wander freely from one woodland area to the next much of the year. The size of robins but looking and acting more like

Pinyon pines share a close
relationship with pinyon jays

dull blue crows, these gregarious jays forage in loose flocks of four to
forty or more at all seasons. They even nest in colonies, building twiggy
nests with deep felted cups in pinyons and junipers. While feeding,
there is much "conversational" mewing, chattering, or nasal cawing
among them. They feed their young grasshoppers and other insects,
but nuts of the pinyon are their preferred food when available. And this
preference links them to the pinyon pine in a very special way.

In years when pinyon seeds are plentiful, the jays eat them abundantly and carry as many more in an expandable esophagus to communal cache sites in their nesting groves. Here they screen the seeds carefully before planting them, selecting only dark brown shells that contain
firm meat and have a solid ring when clicked in the bill. The benefits to
both tree and bird are obvious: the jay garners superb food, nesting sites,
and shelter; the pine gains an efficient seed dispersal service.

The plump, sweet pinyon nuts were the staple food of the Indian
tribes of the eastern Sierra until the 1860s. Trespassing on another

band's pine-nut territory seems to have been the chief cause of quarreling among otherwise relatively peaceful people. Two tribes of Indians shared the Sierra's eastern shoulder. The Washo occupied the area just east of Lake Tahoe, from the lower tip of Honey Lake south to the Walker River Valley. North and south of the Washo, as well as east into the Great Basin, lived the Paiute. The two tribes spoke different languages, the Paiute being related by language and culture to the Shoshone and Bannock peoples of the Great Basin, the Washo apparently to California tribes of the Hokan stock.

In appearance neither was the tall, high-cheekboned, aquiline-nosed warrior of the Great Plains. They generally had straight black hair and a robust roundness. Both led an uncertain existence in a harsh land, and both learned to know its every source of food and water through the variable seasons. In years when the pine-nut crop was good, hopes ran high in the camps for a winter when all might eat. Ground pine-nut meal formed their basic survival food; it was made into a mush to which would be added any seeds, meat, insects, berries, or other flavorful tidbits available.

Gathering in the pinyon groves in autumn, the Indians worked in small groups, knocking the cones from the trees and gathering them in baskets. Timing was important. The cones had to be harvested before they opened and shed their nuts naturally, and before the pinyon jays, Clark's nutcrackers, ground squirrels, and other nut pickers secured too heavy a share. To open the cones the Indians sometimes spread them in the sun to dry, then beat or shook them vigorously in a basket; or they heaped brush on a pile of cones and set the brush afire. The light scorching removed the pitch and popped the cones open, exposing the large meaty brown nuts.

Pinyon nuts, rich and oily and delicious raw, will not keep long in a fresh condition. They had to be precooked to last through the cold weather ahead. The tribes usually spent a month intensively collecting and preparing tons of nuts to be stored against the coming winter. Then they began the trek downhill to winter camps, carrying the baskets of nuts on their backs. In good years some groups spent the fall and winter in the pinyon belt, but much of the region was subject to heavy snow and held few springs. Most families moved to the lower foothills or high ground in the valleys along the eastern edge of the Sierra, near water. Here they set up winter camps and collected firewood—great piles of it, higher than their winter houses—to combat the coming snows and cold.

Autumn was also the time for Washo rabbit and deer hunts. The black-tailed jackrabbits of the sage flats, still fat from their summer feeding, were an inviting target. Hunters sometimes shot them individually with bow and arrow, but the most productive means of securing a large number of animals was a rabbit drive. Almost every Indian family owned a rabbit net, several yards long and three feet wide, made of sage fibers. When a number of families combined their nets and supported them on sticks, a semicircular barrier many hundred yards long could be erected. While some of the group waited behind the nets, others walked across the flats toward them, scaring up and driving before them hundreds of rabbits. Once in the nets, the big jacks, weighing several pounds apiece, were killed with ease.

Hunts like this were held wherever the rabbit population was high and until the rabbits temporarily vanished. During the drives the Indians feasted on all the freshly broiled rabbits they could eat. They skinned, cleaned, and dried hundreds more into dehydrated mummies, and during the winter these dried rabbits, according to James Downs, "would be pounded into powder and added to soups or to pine nut and grass seed mushes." The woven-together skins provided the most important clothing and bedding that the Washo had, the rabbit-skin blanket. Soft and warm, it wore out quickly and required frequent replacement.

Both tribes hunted the mule deer that inhabited their winter range. Sometimes they stalked the deer in small groups, other times individually. A Washo stalker often wore a disguise, a stuffed deer head with the skin draped over his shoulders. Keeping downwind, he approached the herd, expertly imitating the actions of a buck mingling with its fellows. When within a few feet of his quarry, he threw off the disguise and shot his arrow, aiming for the area just behind the shoulder. Here it would penetrate the lungs and usually break off, as the animal reared and plunged away with the arrowhead and foreshaft in its body. Lacking the explosive power of a bullet, even a well-placed arrow could seldom kill a deer outright. Pursued, the wounded buck might run for miles. The Washo hunter whose arrow had struck home avoided a long search by simply sitting down to wait. If he found bloodstains, he mixed the blood with saliva, made a fire, heated a stone, and put the mixture on the stone. When the liquid boiled away, he extinguished the fire and went after his quarry. He often found it a short distance away, dead or dying. Dried deer meat provided one more insurance against the long winter.

Pronghorn (*Antilocapra americana*) were more sporadic visitors but numerous when they came. In their former range over the semiarid plains of the West, they occurred in numbers comparable to the bison.[1] During the Indians' tenure in California, antelope roamed in great herds through the central and southern valleys and eastern sagebrush steppes, eating grasses and leafy plants in summer, bitterbrush and their favorite sagebrush in winter.

Keen-eyed and extremely fleet, pronghorn can detect danger at a great distance. Raising the long white hairs on the rump patch when alarmed, alerting others in the band, they dash away with these white spots bouncing. Variously clocked at thirty-eight to sixty miles an hour, they run gracefully and seemingly enjoy it. They are North America's fastest native mammal. At rest, their coat patterns of reddish tan marked with white and black break up the body outline so that at a distance they blend indiscernibly into the range.

Despite these defenses, the antelope has two weaknesses that allowed the Indians to hunt it successfully. It is exceedingly inquisitive, and its herd members remain together even in the face of danger. Hunters today often can lure pronghorn within gun range by waving a white cloth on a stick; curiosity overrides caution, and the animals eventually move in to investigate this unusual sight.

The Indians, armed only with bows and arrows, had to bring the animals in even closer. They did it by a corralling method similar to a rabbit drive, but with refinements. When a herd of antelope was discovered in the vicinity, word quickly went out to form a communal hunt. A circular corral was built of brush or rope made of sagebrush bark, frequently with wings extending out from the opening and people on hand to fill in any spaces at the time of the hunt. Young men of the tribe then sneaked into position on the far side of the herd, away from the corral, and began to drive the antelope slowly toward the trap. Keeping out of sight, the drivers crept close. One at a time they suddenly stood up, then just as suddenly disappeared. These strange actions made the herd nervous and pushed it gradually toward the corral. As it came closer, more Indians appeared in every direction except that of the trap, until finally the antelope were stampeded into the corral and the opening was closed.

Although pronghorns often leap when in flight and can broadjump twenty feet, a good three-foot fence will hold them. Once the animals were caught, the Indians usually celebrated with ritual dancing and singing that lasted all night. The confinement and the noises surrounding them panicked the antelope into running round and round the corral; by dawn, when the slaughter began, they lay played out. A herd might supply food for a large group of Washo or Paiute for a week. "One such hunt," says Downs, "usually exhausted the antelope population in an area and would not be repeated there for several years."

For their tools of bone, wood, or stone, the Indians used whatever was at hand. They made bows out of juniper or occasionally desert mahogany, arrows of willow. Obsidian arrowheads were wrapped on with sinew, which was sealed with a sticky exudation from sagebrush. Looped willow stems furnished traps for small animals; plant fibers made nets for fishing. They wove willow baskets for every purpose: collecting food, cooking, storing food, winnowing, seed beating, and, after the insides were waterproofed with a coating of pitch, as water containers. With big game such as deer, antelope, and mountain sheep to furnish occasional breaks in their diet, the Indians lived chiefly on pine nuts, small game, insects, and seeds.

Washo hunting and gathering habits were almost identical with those of the Paiute most of the year. The Washo country was perhaps the most verdant of the eastern valleys. East Sierran streams generally disappear rather quickly into lakes and sinks of the low desert. The Carson and Walker, the larger rivers in Washo territory, flowed during the entire year. There were green belts along the rivers and around the sinks. Waterfowl fed in the sinks; sage grouse, ground squirrels, gophers, and field mice abounded. Compared with the bone-dry country to the east, Washo land was a haven. But in summer the valleys grew hot and dry very early, and Washo life moved upmountain to the blue lake they called Tahoe, meaning "big water" or "high water." Lying at 6,239 feet in a basin between the main crest of the Sierra and the Carson spur range to the east, Tahoe was a revered Washo place.

The huge rock along the eastern shore was the site of a sacred cave; the creeks flowing into the lake, certain stands of trees, and rock outcroppings were tied to the sacred myth of the creation of the Washo world. The lake itself gleamed like an enormous gem set among illimitable tall conifers, sugar pines dangling long cones full of small sweet seeds, Jeffrey pines, white and red firs, incense cedars. The waters seemed alive as they changed color during the day from emerald to cobalt blue to deep purple. Never freezing over completely even in the coldest winters, they held a supply of fish vital to the Washo diet.

As soon as the snow melted from foothill trails in the spring, the young people of the tribe began the trek up the steep east-side passes. Arriving on the still-snow-covered shores of Lake Tahoe, they lived in caves, gathering spring plants for vegetables and fishing for mountain whitefish (*Prosopium williamsoni*), which they brought back to the rest of the tribe in starvation years. As summer approached, the lowland families left winter camp and one by one moved up to the lake. By early June the entire east-side Washo population was encamped on Tahoe's shores.

They arrived in time for the spawning runs of the large lake fish. The Lahontan cutthroat trout (*Oncorhynchus clarki henshawi*) and Tahoe sucker (*Catostomus tahoensis*), in particular, swam out of the deep lake waters into the side streams by the thousands, sometimes so thick that their bodies filled the streams from bank to bank. Men, women, and children armed with baskets waded into the streams, scooped up the swarming fish, and tossed them onto the shore. There, others split and boned them, producing two fillets. Female fish were stripped of their roe, which was eaten raw or spread out to dry, and everyone feasted on broiled fish, the first fresh protein since autumn for most of them. At the height of the run fishing went on through the night, torch lights reflecting off the shiny backs of the fish. During the two weeks or so of the spawning runs, the Washo ate and dried enormous numbers of fish. Had they known how to smoke them, as the Indians of the northern coasts did, they could have lived nearly the year round on the resources of Lake Tahoe's streams. As it was, the dried fish spoiled if taken into their foothill and desert valleys, and so were edible only as long as the tribe remained in the cool mountains.

This they did for most of the summer. When the spawning runs diminished, families left their lakeside camps and headed into the higher mountain meadows. The meadows offered a wide variety of bulb and root plants, greens and berries, which the women, armed with a digging stick and a burden basket, sought and gathered. Granite boulders pock-marked with mortars still show where they sat pulverizing dried fish roe and grinding seeds and berries.

In the higher meadows grew an early summer native sunflower whose seeds could be ground into flour. From damp spots came the new shoots, roots, and seeds of the common cattail. Before the cattail grew fluffy its seeds could be wrapped in leaves and cooked; they made a brown paste that was eaten like candy and with equal zest. Another confection was the sugary exudation for which the sugar pine is named. Hard white crystals of "sugar" form on the upper side of wounds in the tree's wood. They contain resin and have cathartic properties, but are as sweet as cane sugar. Adults and children alike picked these "sap balls" from the bark and chewed them.

Wild strawberries and gooseberries were eaten fresh as they appeared at successively higher elevations in July and August, the strawberries sometimes mashed into a thick drink. Wild onions and wild rhubarb grew in profusion. Small game was available—pocket gophers in the meadows, chipmunks and golden-mantled ground squirrels in the open pine and fir forests. The men and boys fished wherever the lakes and streams held prospects. In the upper reaches of the Carson and Truckee Rivers, minnows by the hundreds were caught in shallow pools with winnowing baskets and baked in an earthen oven. Water and food were plentiful, shelter and firewood readily obtainable, temperatures comfortable. Excursions to the subalpine meadows and rockslides above yielded an occasional deer or plump marmot to vary the menu.

As summer waned, many Washo dropped back down the eastern slope to the foothills and valleys, where grasses were ripening and the seed harvest was at hand. Seeds of wild mustard, pigweed (*Chenopodium*), rabbitbrush (*Chrysothamnus nauseosus*), saltbush (*Atriplex*), and certain grasses were especially prized because they kept so well; every ounce of surplus summer food that would store was a bonus against the nonproductive winter.

A few Washo families often climbed the crest above Lake Tahoe and descended to the western foothills to collect ripening acorns. Occasionally, if early snows made a return hazardous, they wintered on the western side alone or moved into Miwok villages. But most of them were back in the eastern foothills for the vital autumn pinyon-nut harvest.

The discovery of gold in the Sierra's western foothills in 1849 brought the first serious trespass of cross-country emigrants on Washo and Paiute lands. A decade later, with the finding of gold near Mono Lake and silver in the Comstock Lode at Virginia City east of Lake Tahoe, the eastern slope began to fill up with mining camps, boomtowns, and "strike-it-richers." Cattlemen and sheepmen moved their stock onto the Indians' best wild-seed lands and brush slopes. The newcomers preempted game and fish and cut pinyon and Jeffrey pines for fuel.

The Washo accepted their fate stoically, managing to exist marginally between invader and land. Some of the Paiutes fought back in the year-and-a-half Indian War of 1860–1862. Eventually, to survive, they were forced to go to work for the white man. Some took jobs at the ranches springing up in the better-watered valleys; others became drivers of the flotillas of logs that now rumbled down the Carson River each spring.

The logging boom was shifting into high gear in the Sierra. The demand for wood seemed insatiable. The first transcontinental railroad line crossed the range in the 1860s, using Sierran timber and fuel from California to the Rockies. Each mile required 2,500 ties; immense quantities of lumber were needed for viaducts, bridges, trestles, and tunnels. Thirty-seven miles of snowsheds alone took 65 million board feet.

The mines of the Comstock and the cities that sprang up around them devoured even more wood than the railroad. Geologist William Brewer, visiting the Gould and Curry Mine at Virginia City in 1864, was amazed at the lumber hidden in the depths. The timbering to prevent cave-ins surpassed anything he had imagined: stout pieces a foot square ran across the mine in every direction, with additional braces where the pressure was greatest. Estimates went to 600 million board feet buried underground in the shafts and tunnels of the silver mines—enough to build a city of six-room houses for 150,000 people. And when the towns that mushroomed on the barren hills went up in smoke, as Virginia City did on October 26, 1875, it was timber from Tahoe and Truckee that rebuilt them.

For a third of a century lumbermen went after the tall timber. The streams were bordered with their camps and choked with floating logs. At one place along the Truckee River, there were twenty-five sawmills in operation. Most east-side river canyons were too narrow and winding for logs to be floated down without catching on snags. The East Carson was an exception, and each spring, on the receding water after the spring flood, an unbroken flow of high-country logs moved downstream, kept free from obstructions by Paiutes and French Canadians maneuvering nimbly on the edges of the flotilla. Millions of board feet and hundreds of thousands of cords of wood snaked down the Carson in this manner.

Getting the big sugar and Jeffrey pines, the finest lumber, up and out of the Tahoe Basin and down the eastern slope to the mills was often brutally exciting work. Skid roads made of logs were sometimes used, with teams of six or eight oxen rolling a train of logs onto the skidway, then hauling it down. Wanting a speedier way, Truckee loggers invented the chute, a well-greased gutter between skid logs. In this track the logs plummeted down self-propelled. From the mountains above each lumber center, torpedoes of pine and fir came smoking down the chutes at a hundred miles an hour, smacking into the ponds at the bottom of the slides with a bombardment like cannon fire, hurling spray a hundred feet.

The next step was to use water for the rapid transit. Taking a tip from miners who dug or built aqueducts to divert water for hydraulic mining, lumbermen built flumes. These V-shaped wooden troughs, up to three feet across, were strong and reasonably watertight. Angled at a slight incline and mounted on trestles, they could carry logs across gulches and chasms or along mountainsides for short or long distances to a mill.

By 1875 narrow-gauge railroads joined the flumes in carrying away the trees of the Tahoe region. Twelve large lumber companies worked steadily, cutting down the colossal specimens of pine and fir, clearing one piece of ground, then moving mill and camp to the next stretch of timber, until they had nearly encircled the lake. A narrow-gauge railroad climbed the steep grade from smoke-shrouded Glenbrook on the eastern shore, where three sawmills ground away night and day, to Spooner Summit; from the summit, twelve miles of flume carried the lumber and wood down to Carson City for use along the Sierra's east side.

The Tahoe destruction was part of a general logging havoc throughout much of the Sierra. By the time public outcries reached national proportions at the turn of the century and brought about the creation of national forests and parks, Tahoe had come close to ruin. As George and Bliss Hinkle described it, "The great expanses of naked, brush-covered mountain, the hundreds of thousands of acres of second growth, the slashings, punk and trash in young forests, the eroded gullies, the diminishing streams, the desiccated mountain lakelets. These are the souvenirs of the Comstock. What the demolition did to the Tahoe-Truckee watershed cannot be contemplated without a shudder and probably will never be assessed."

One of the consequences of this environmental degradation was the virtual extinction of the Lahontan cutthroat trout in Lake Tahoe and in the lake's only outlet, the Truckee River. Native to the Truckee, Walker, and Carson River drainages of the eastern Sierra, this yellowish olive fish with black spots on the upper body and red stripes under the jaw was also known as the Tahoe trout because of its great abundance in the lake. In its heyday, specimens weighing up to thirty-five pounds plumbed the clear waters.

One or more of the many adverse changes in its environment killed it off. Logging, forest fires, overgrazing, and water diversions all devastated its watersheds, causing stream erosion and ruining spawning beds. On the east fork of the stripped and burned Carson River,

Marsden Manson in 1896 recorded a scene in which summer showers had sluiced off the ashes and soil to such an extent that tons of trout were killed; he could, he said, have loaded a four-horse wagon with the dead fish.

Pollution of the Truckee River by paper mill wastes and sawdust made it at times inhospitable to life. In addition, insurmountable dams were built in the Truckee River, at the Lake Tahoe outlet, and on Tahoe tributaries that prevented the migratory spawning runs of the fish. Commercial fishermen pulled hundreds of tons of trout from the big lake, many of which were shipped to San Francisco; millions of trout eggs collected on Tahoe's tributaries were sent to other areas. To try to improve the fishery, various exotic fish—including Atlantic, king, and silver salmon, rainbow, brown, golden, brook, and lake trout, and Great Lakes whitefish—were introduced haphazardly into the lake from the 1880s on, with little or no knowledge of the lake's ecosystem or what the foreign species would do to the natives. Fishing declined rapidly after 1900, long before commercial fishing of the native trout was stopped in 1916.

Nothing that was done improved the lot of the cutthroat; between 1922 and 1928, they died off in enormous numbers, leaving windward beaches "white with dead fish."[2] The cause of the die-off was unknown, although disease brought by the introduced fish was considered a possibility. In addition to the disease toll, lake trout took a predacious toll. By the early 1930s the Lahontan cutthroat trout, which once packed side streams from bank to bank in spawning runs, was extinct in Tahoe waters.

Of the introduced fish only the lake trout, or Mackinaw (*Salvelinus namaycush*), brought from Michigan in 1895, established themselves in numbers. "Frequently seen" in 1911, they were reported as "fairly plentiful" by 1923 and flourishing in 1938.[3] Today lake trout dominate the Tahoe deepwater fishery. Dark gray with pale spots, they patrol unchallenged the depths to five hundred feet, where the cutthroat once swam. Not needing side streams for spawning, the lake trout drop their eggs onto the loose rock on the lake bottom.

The shallow waters harbor rainbow trout on a stocked, non-self-sustaining basis. Small numbers of brown trout, native mountain whitefish, brook trout, and kokanee salmon (*Oncorhynchus nerka*) round out most of the game list. Native non-game fish such as Tui chub (*Gila bicolor*), Piute sculpin (*Cottus beldingi*), and the bottom-feeding Tahoe sucker largely provide forage for the lake trout.

Tahoe has always been renowned for the unusual clarity of its waters. In 1883 John Le Conte noted in the *Overland Monthly* that he could see a white dinner plate at a depth of well over one hundred feet.[4] The role of this clarity in the lake's food chain has been explored in recent decades.

Fish and game specialists Ted Frantz and Almo Cordone discovered a number of mosses, algae, and liverworts living as far as 300 feet below the surface and forming unique deepwater plant beds of a type unknown elsewhere except at Crater Lake, Oregon. Most of the beds are at depths of 200 to 350 feet, occasionally as shallow as 20 feet, rarely as deep as 500 feet. They furnish food and shelter for the small-animal life of these depths, harboring stonefly nymphs and snails, abundant crayfish (*Pacifastacus leniusculus*), small trout, and non-game fish hiding out from the big lake trout that lurk about the greenery. The zones where the plant beds grow are the very zones where lake trout reach their maximum concentrations. Hence, the ecology of the lake's major game fish may be intimately linked to the deepwater plant beds whose lifeline descends through the clear water from the sun.

If that water were to become cloudy from silt, sewage, or the growth of surface algae, light would no longer penetrate to the necessary depths to keep the vital plants alive. Decaying mats of these plants on the beaches over past years indicate that such has definitely been happening. The growths of algae on the rocks and in pools along the shore and on the hulls of boats left in the water tell the same story. Tahoe's water is gradually turning from clear blue to turbid green.

Limnologist Charles Goldman has been studying Tahoe for over thirty years and recognizes the continuing problem as a steadily increasing fertility leading to more algae, less clarity, and destruction of much of the lake's esthetic appeal. In the natural geologic aging process, lakes tend to become more fertile as they gradually fill with fragments of dead aquatic plants and animals and debris eroded from their watersheds. This increase in fertility, known as eutrophication, ordinarily proceeds slowly, but has been dangerously accelerated by human actions in numbers of lakes worldwide.

If Tahoe's small watershed had been left to nature, the lake could have remained crystal clear for thousands of years. But at Tahoe, continual disturbances of the watershed have had a major influence on the lake. Lumbering, fire, overgrazing, and road building started the trouble by laying bare the mineral soil. Nutrients leached out of the soil by rains flowed in creeks and tributaries into the lake, beginning the fertilizing and silting process.

The tremendous urbanization of Tahoe in past decades has brought with it heavy air pollution from cars, garbage dumps, septic tanks, leaky sewage that escaped the mass pumped out of the basin, and effluent. Each spring runoff has added to the ever-increasing fertility of the lake and its resultant algae. Land disturbance has brought the erosion of roadcuts, subdivisions, ski slopes, and land leveling—the removal of soil-protecting vegetation. This both increases the leaching of nutrients directly into runoff waters and moves tons of loose soil into the lake, causing turbidity, mud flows, and deltas at the mouths of some streams. All of this has proven to be too rich a diet for a primeval lake. Tahoe's clarity has been dropping about one foot a year. If further pollution is not arrested, the long-term future of the big blue lake in the sky may be grim.

Attempts to spare Tahoe this fate have proceeded on embattled grounds for decades between the bi-state Tahoe Regional Planning Agency (California and Nevada share the lake), the League to Save Lake Tahoe, and concerned community groups. Some progress has been made. Much more is needed. The search for solutions is ongoing.

Despite its transition from a native's Eden to a flamboyant recreation area during the past century, Tahoe is still a precious spot to the Washo Indians. Living in Nevada and California east of the lake, Washo families frequently visit the lake in summer, to look at its blue waters, to recall at the great rock and at special creeks and beaches their history and myths.

Many things, in addition to the lake and its second-growth forests, have changed on the east side since Native Americans in numbers lived there in tune with the land. Beavers were originally not native to the Sierra Nevada. Three geographical varieties of one species of beaver (*Castor canadensis*) occurred in California, the Sonoran beaver along the Colorado River, the golden beaver in the Central Valley, and the Shasta beaver in northern California. Trapped almost to extinction by 1900, they were given full protection from 1911 to 1946 and came back from the brink. Between 1945 and 1955, the California Department of Fish and Game transplanted Shasta and Idaho beavers into most streams of the Sierra, east and west. Since then beaver colonies have existed along nearly all Sierran streams, expanding their range wherever circumstances allow.

Beavers need a continuous supply of water in which to live, and they quickly create this condition on shallow creeks by building a series of dams. Constructed of aspen, poplar, willow, and fir cut by the rodent's large orange incisors, and filled in with mud, sticks, wire, and rocks, the dams can be quite solid structures. The pools behind them, where the beavers live, form a habitat very different from the former fast-flowing creek. As they silt in, they become suitable for cattails, sedges, rushes, water buttercups (*Ranunculus aquatilus*), pondweed (*Potamogeton*), duckweed (*Lemna minor*), and other aquatic plants and, in turn, provide a haven for waterfowl, muskrats (*Ondatra zibethica*), and large trout.

Where beavers flood meadows and dam irrigation ditches that conflict with ranching, block culverts under highways, damage ornamental trees, domestic water supplies, and campgrounds, flood trails, and multiply beyond the carrying capacity of their area, their numbers are controlled by trapping. Nothing less usually discourages a beaver from dam building. The story is told of a rancher who tried several times to remove a beaver dam from a creek on his property. The animals repaired it faster than he could tear it down. Finally he hit on what seemed a foolproof idea: he drove a one-and-a-half-inch pipe through the dam to drain the water off. The next day the pool was at normal water level. The beavers had fitted a limb into the pipe and cemented it in place with sticky clay.

Since 1932 an introduced partridge, the chukar, has made itself a part of the east Sierran foothill fauna. A member of the red-legged partridge family native to the Mediterranean and southern Asia, the chukar is of an Indian strain. Looking much like a big pale gray quail with a white throat edged with black, black and white barring on the sides, red beak and legs, it lives in large flocks or coveys most of the year. In summer the birds usually stay within a mile of water, coming in to drink in early morning. Chukars use the same waterholes as quail, doves, and rabbits compatibly, and seemingly do not compete with the natives for food, frequenting more open knolls and flats than the others. Their diet is broad and includes the seeds, leaves, and stems of a great variety of grasses, as well as seeds of Russian thistle (*Salsola kali*), rabbitbrush, sagebrush, buckwheat, lupine, and mountain rose (*Rosa*). Their call, repeating the bird's name, *chuck, chuck, chuck, chuckarr, chuckarr,* carries a long distance in the clear, dry air. Rapid fliers and strong runners, they seem well able to take care of themselves on the rocky east Sierran slopes, in spite of loss of some eggs to ravens.

The native grouse of the region, the sage grouse, is a bird of completely different character. Confined to sagebrush country, where in fall and winter it feeds exclusively on sagebrush leaves, this largest of the North American grouse puts on one of the most unusual spring courtship displays of all game birds. In mid-March, depending on the weather, male grouse from several miles around gather on their ancestral strutting grounds. These assembly grounds, known as the arena or lek and used year after year, are usually flat areas in a meadow with good visibility on all sides. Here the cocks take up stations twenty-five to forty feet apart, occupying a swathe several hundred yards wide for as long a distance as there are birds to fill it; on large arenas, four hundred cocks may spread over half a mile, with as many hens about.

Each morning at predawn for weeks the arena is the scene of weird sounds and a kind of shadowboxing. The Crowley Lake arena often fills with more than one hundred dancing, booming sage grouse by 4:00 A.M. On moonlit nights you can see the big cocks arching their spiked, spread tails, drooping their wings stiffly, raising the white feathers on each side of the breast into a huge cape framing the dark head, and turning to right and left as they partially inflate the yellowish air sacs on the neck. Strutting about with the sac region bouncing, they inflate and deflate the sacs in rapid succession, producing an effect something like two large sunny-side-up fried eggs appearing and disappearing, with curious plopping sounds as the air is expelled. During the strut the wings scrape downward over the breast with a swishing noise. A steady chorus of booms, clucks, swishes, and cackles fills the night air and continues until sometime after dawn as the cocks strut on their territories. Occasionally the birds fight at territorial boundaries, but it is a ritualized fighting, largely bluff, with feints and prolonged glaring at the rival.

This daily fighting and displaying over a number of weeks gradually builds within the flock a social hierarchy in which a dominant cock, the best strutter and fighter, occupies the top rung. In large flocks there are several dominants. This master cock takes over the primary mating area, the territorial prize, a spot about six to ten feet in diameter that is used year after year. Here he mates with over three-fourths of the hens. Half his size, they walk to his station through groups of lower-ranked males and squat with wings spread in invitation, sometimes, if traffic is heavy, quietly waiting their turn. Master cocks have been observed to breed twenty-one times in a single morning, forty times in a day. Flocks often display in late afternoon also.

Near the master cock stands his chief rival, the subcock, who takes over some matings when the master is occupied. Farther away the guard cocks, a step lower in the hierarchy, keep lesser-ranking males out of the select circle and sneak in an occasional mating on the rare occasions when the system breaks down. Since only the most vigorous, most aggressive, and larger males attain the rank of master cock, natural selection tends to perpetuate these traits in the offspring. The breeding season lasts four to six weeks. At its end, the hierarchy crumbles. The hens move to nesting areas, the cocks to summer feeding grounds.

The fantastic displays of the sage grouse were once widespread each spring throughout the sage region of the western United States and along the eastern shoulder of the Sierra Nevada. At one time the big grouse were not infrequent on the east side of Lake Tahoe; Sagehen Creek, north of Truckee, recalls in name their former presence there.[5] The species, however, suffered the usual heavy decrease in numbers as livestock grazing, settlement, and agriculture engulfed its land. The tens of thousands of cattle driven into east Sierran valleys in the 1860s and the nomadic sheep bands that followed the "Great Circle" route up the east side between 1865 and 1907 caused complete destruction of much virgin range. Eating the palatable grasses and forbs and ignoring the sage, the stock grazed meadows to ground level. As they overgrazed and destroyed the grasses and herbs, sagebrush and unpalatable plants invaded. Years of little rain aided the sage, which can tolerate drought better than grass. What had been a sagebrush-grass country gradually came to support nearly pure stands of sagebrush.

It was 1930 before Inyo National Forest, established in 1907, was able to achieve some control of range use and livestock numbers on the east side. In about 1934, sage grouse, which had earlier dropped close to the extermination stage in eastern California, began to come back. Today their best populations are in the northeastern part of the state, in the Crowley Lake area and scattered eastward to the White Mountains. The grouse are not found at all uniformly throughout sagebrush range. The localities that have grouse possess the four basic habitat types the birds require: nesting areas, brood areas, strutting grounds, and winter range. The nesting areas usually are in sparse sagebrush from two to three feet high and within one mile of wet meadows or streams. Brood areas, used by hens and young as summer range, are along meadow edges near permanent water, with tall sagebrush adjacent for escape cover. Strutting grounds most commonly occur along meadow edges in short sagebrush, where visibility is good. Winter ranges require south slopes or rocky ridges where wind blows the snow clear from sagebrush two to three feet high.

Among the other variations of the sagebrush country are the areas, usually somewhat elevated, where bitterbrush abounds. Growing in a great variety of rigidly branched shapes and heights, with grayish bark and leaves whitish beneath, bitterbrush is at a distance not easily distinguishable from sagebrush except when in bloom. In June, when the last pink glow of desert peach (*Prunus andersonii*) is fading, bitterbrush blossoms envelop the shrub in a creamy-yellow haze. The fragrant flowers, somewhat like miniature single roses, place it in a distinctively western North American genus of the rose family, with two very similar species that intergrade in some east Sierran areas (*Purshia tridentata* and *P. glandulosa*).

The wedge-shaped leaves and young twigs are a favorite winter food of the mule deer herds that migrate down from the high passes with the first snowfall. They furnish the only natural food in the area that sustains the deer for prolonged periods. In earlier years they were a staple of the pronghorn as well; the shrub is still sometimes called antelope bush. Antelope in California are now restricted to the northeastern corner except for small but growing herds reintroduced by Fish and Game into Mono County in 1949 and, since 1982, onto other former historic ranges.

The seed of bitterbrush is popular with many birds and rodents. Deer mice, chipmunks, ground squirrels, pocket mice, kangaroo rats (*Dipodomys*), and woodrats all relish it. The rodents sometimes spread the shrub by caching its seeds in shallow burrows well away from the parent plant, but they also steal the Forest Service blind in attempted new field plantings of bitterbrush by seed.

On southeastern Sierran slopes adjacent to Owens Valley, bitterbrush has proved in recent years to be a preferred food of tule elk (*Cervus elaphus nannodes*). This light-colored and smallest race of American elk once occurred in numbers that "darkened" the open grassy valley of central California, its native habitat. Herds of up to two thousand animals, containing bulls of over seven hundred pounds carrying magnificent antlers, were described in 1846. From gold rush days onward, settlers and market hunters decimated the elk, until by the early 1870s only a remnant of the race remained, hiding out in the tules of Kern County in the southern valley.

By good luck, those southern lands were the large ranch holdings of Miller and Lux. "The elk were here before we were," Miller told his ranch hands. "Protect them."[6]

As the elk increased in numbers over the years, they were transplanted to more than twenty different places around the state, including Yosemite and Sequoia National Parks, in attempts to keep the species alive and, vainly, to find a permanent suitable home. In 1932, a Tule Elk Refuge was established by the state and Kern County near

Tupman, not far from the elk's last wild stand on the Miller ranch; this later became a state park and today includes a semitame, artificially fed, fenced-in herd of animals. A free-roaming herd also survived at Cache Creek in Colusa County.

In 1933–1934, through the efforts of Walter Dow of Lone Pine and California Fish and Game, fifty-five tule elk were successfully transplanted to the Owens Valley. Lying between the Sierra Nevada and the White-Inyo Mountains, with plenty of open range, little ranching, and few people (primarily because the water of the area was owned by Los Angeles and carried away in its aqueduct), Owens Valley seemed ideal for animals that like dry open spaces. Dow obtained permission from Los Angeles for the elk to run free on its land.

The elk thrived. In September the bugling of the bulls could be heard in the willows along the Owens River bottoms. Natural browsers and grazers of green vegetation, the elk had no trouble finding a wide variety of food. But as their numbers grew over the years, so did the protests from a handful of cattlemen that the elk were competing for their winter cattle feed, breaking down fences, trampling and wallowing in irrigated alfalfa fields. To appease the ranchers, Fish and Game authorized several hunts to keep the elk total between one hundred and two hundred animals.

Alarmed at what an epidemic might do to such a limited species stock, a citizens group, the Committee for the Preservation of the Tule Elk, formed in 1960 to press for a larger, safer number. Largely because of their work, in 1971 the California Legislature passed a bill prohibiting tule elk hunting until the statewide population reached 2,000 and requiring Fish and Game to establish new elk herds in suitable habitats. Around 2,700 animals currently exist in more than twenty herds throughout the state, including some in the bitterbrush zone of the eastern Sierra's lower foothills.

At higher, more remote elevations of the same region bighorn sheep also join the bitterbrush brigade part of the year. The California race of bighorn (*Ovis canadensis californiana*) once occurred regularly along the Sierran crest. Reduced by hunting and the overgrazing and diseases of domestic sheep, the Sierran population has had its ups and downs over the years. Today it is split among several herds in the craggy southeastern section. After summering in the alpine heights, the bighorns in late autumn descend the eastern scarp, traveling three to seven miles in distance, dropping five thousand feet in elevation. This is the breeding season, when rams fight for possession of a band of ewes. The clash of horns can be heard a long way off as the big rams rear and charge from a distance of thirty feet, butting their massive horns again and again until one of them has had enough. Attempts to relocate bighorns to Lee Vining Canyon, Wheeler Ridge, and Mount Langley have met with heavy declines. Avalanches, fragmented ranges, disease, lack of corridors, no genetic exchange, and mountain lion predation may all be contributing factors.

Since the primary species of plants used by bighorns, deer, and tule elk are in general the same as those used by cattle, priorities have to be established on national forest land. Cattlemen and sheepmen of past decades so maimed the range that much of it can never again support the game and livestock once possible. A close look at ecosystem balance is needed for the entire eastern Sierra Nevada.

Eight

THE MASSIVE EARTH MOVEMENTS that thrust the Sierra Nevada to its present height one to two million years ago even then carried traces of earlier life. On the high metamorphic peaks lie fossils of marine mollusks embedded when the range was below the sea. The geological impacts produced the steep eastern escarpment, the singular granite domes, and the glaciated river canyons. The combination of these in a great single block range is uniquely Sierran.

Equally characteristic is the sequence of plant communities that we have traced up and over the range. Sierran plants of today are the survivors of past migrations from the north and from the south and of major land and climate changes. These plants have been isolated long enough to develop individuality. Sierran boreal forests differ from Rocky Mountain and northern boreal forests in that they have no spruce trees. Sierran forests contain the only groves of giant sequoia on the planet, as well as sugar pines, incense cedars, and red firs of a distribution virtually limited to California.

The interplay of plant and animal life—and the effect on this of man-made environmental change—is pointed up vividly by the mule deer's role in Sierran ecosystems. Mule deer are just as linked to black oak seedlings and other green plants that they eat as they are to mountain lions, which in turn consume them. Deer are linked to logging and to new highways, which produce edge openings and fresh browse. Deer are also tied to livestock and rodents that compete for food, to periods of good seedling reproduction, to heavy winter snows, and to campers who feed them scraps and kill the snakes that would have reduced the ground squirrels that compete with deer for food. They are linked to trampling of any origin, whether by people, cattle, sheep, or themselves; trampling affects water infiltration into soil and inhibits the root growth of young green shoots. They are linked to disease that comes from crowding and malnutrition. They are linked to fire, which stimulates new green growth on a rich mineral-ash soil—and to many more processes that we haven't yet discovered.

Under wilderness conditions, a more or less closed food chain probably existed in the Sierra. Minerals were absorbed from the soil by plants, passed on into ground squirrels, pocket gophers, deer, and other plant eaters, transferred to grizzly bears, cougars, coyotes, badgers, and other carnivores when they ate the herbivores, and were returned to the soil through the death of the carnivores. The Native Americans fitted into the food chain at several points. What they took as food was usually consumed nearby; when they died, their bones enriched the soil. Their numbers were few, their imprint on the land was a management that sustained it, primarily in the form of annual burning that kept meadows open and slowed succession in some areas.

The miners, loggers, and stockmen who followed them left a different mark. In addition to their devastation, all these reversed the natural pattern of returning to the soil vital minerals borrowed for a lifetime. Logs that were shipped away left no decaying elements to nurture saplings. Sheep and cattle by the millions each autumn carried off to the lowlands minerals acquired in mountain meadow grasses. Erosion added to demineralization. Mountain soils gain new minerals only from the weathering and breakdown of rocks, an exceedingly slow process. The mineral drain from Sierran national forests has gone on for more than 150 years—and continues.

Other individuals left as their legacy Yosemite, Sequoia, and Kings Canyon National Parks, the national forests, the giant sequoia groves, the state parks, the John Muir Trail. Some handed down Hetch Hetchy reservoir, where a beautiful mountain valley had been.

Today's ecologists and concerned citizens continue to fight the battle on many fronts. The ten-year Sierra Nevada Ecosystem Project funded by Congress and conducted by a select scientific team concluded in 1996 that the Sierra Nevada has been badly degraded. Among the areas of concern pinpointed were loss of old-growth forests, almost to extinction on the east side; loss of western-foothill woodland and riparian habitats; damage from logging, overgrazing, dams, roads, placer mining, ozone, and acid rain; and a decline in populations of fish, amphibians, and songbirds. Project participants emphasized the urgent need for regionwide planning to preserve the range's most valuable resource, water; the need to restore fire to its natural role in old-growth ecosystems; and the value of large blocks of forest reserves connected by habitat corridors.

If the will is there and actions follow, options still exist to prevent further irreversible loss of the range's unique biodiversity, and to regulate our numbers so that there will always be room in the Sierra Nevada to renew our ties to the earth.

APPENDIX: FINDING YOUR WAY

The roads over the northern and central Sierra offer a cross section of the range's plant communities, which differ considerably with each highway. On some roads the foothills stretch out for twice as many car miles as on others, where you gain altitude sooner and enter ponderosa pine forests more quickly.

The highest road across the range, and a route that, if followed from one side to the other, goes through all plant communities except alpine fell-fields, is the Tioga Pass road (Route 120) in Yosemite National Park. Yosemite can be entered from the west by any of three main highways: Route 41 (out of Fresno), 140 (at Merced), or 120 (at Manteca). These all cut for miles through woodland and chaparral of the western foothills. Route 140 follows the Merced River canyon in its approach to Yosemite, and on reaching the park entrance at Arch Rock Ranger Station passes through mixed evergreen forests of Douglas fir, nutmeg, canyon live oak, and California laurel. All three roads lead to Yosemite Valley's meadows and ponderosa pine forests at 4,000 feet.

The road from Yosemite Valley to Glacier Point, which overlooks the valley from 3,200 feet higher up, gives close views of sugar pines, white and red fir forests, lodgepole pines, and the mixed Jeffrey pine–chaparral areas that blue grouse, mountain quail, and Townsend's solitaires like. A branch of the Glacier Point road goes to the Mariposa Grove of giant sequoias at the southern end of the park. Another road from Yosemite Valley is the Tioga Pass road mentioned above. The Tioga road winds through red fir forests, around granite domes, past glacial polish on the rocky borders of Tenaya Lake (best seen in early morning and late afternoon light) to wide-open Tuolumne Meadows at 8,600 feet and over Tioga Pass among subalpine white-

0 10 20 30 40 50 miles

Redding

N

44

Lassen Volcanic
National Park

36

*Fredonyer Pass
(5,748)*

99

32

36 Susanville

CALIFORNIA
NEVADA

5

70

Quincy

395

99 Oroville

70

*Yuba Pass
(6,701)*

49

Marysville

*Donner Pass
(7,240)*

*Beckwourth Pass
(5,212)*

70

49

80

Reno

99

80

Sacramento

*Echo Summit Pass
(7,382)*

Placerville

Lake Tahoe

50

50 Carson City

99

49

50

*Carson Pass
(8,573)*

Ione

88

395

Stockton

Calaveras Big
Trees State Park

*Ebbetts Pass
(8,730)*

Manteca

4

Sonora

108

*Sonora Pass
(9,626)*

Modesto

99

120

Yosemite
National Park

Northern Sierra Nevada
(map by Bill Nelson)

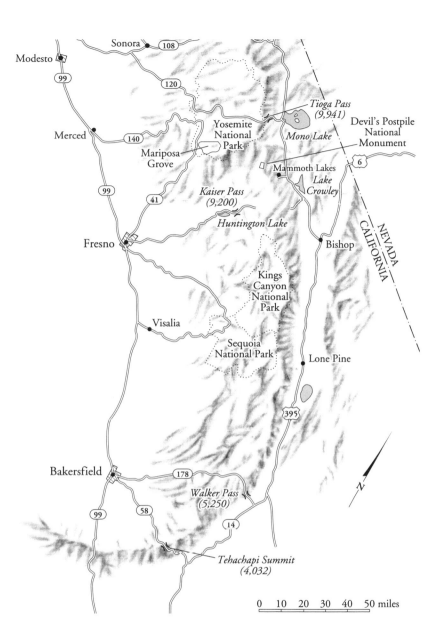

Southern Sierra Nevada
(map by Bill Nelson)

bark pines at 9,941 feet. In the Tioga Ranger Station area, a climb of a thousand feet on foot will bring you above timberline into alpine fell-fields. Ask the rangers for a suggested route. From Tioga Pass, the road makes a quick eastern descent through pinyon pines and sagebrush to Mono Lake.

The Sonora, Ebbetts, and Carson Pass roads also offer largely unspoiled Sierran cross sections reaching into subalpine forests. Donner Pass is a freeway, and Echo Pass almost is one. The northern passes all are lower, as is the most southerly pass, Walker. For visiting giant sequoias, the largest groves are in Sequoia National Park, in the Mariposa Grove of southern Yosemite National Park, and in Calaveras Big Trees State Park on Route 4.

NOTES

INTRODUCTION

1. Quoted by Francis P. Farquhar in *History of the Sierra Nevada* (Berkeley: University of California Press, in collaboration with the Sierra Club, 1965), pp. 15–16. Distant snow-capped mountains to the east had been observed from the Central Valley in 1772 by Captain Pedro Fages and Fray Juan Crespi and mentioned in their diaries. Crespi had even made a quaint drawing of rivers emerging from the mountains. Pedro Font, in 1776, was the first to map the range and to give it a name—a descriptive one that took.
2. François E. Matthes, *The Incomparable Valley,* ed. Fritiof Fryxell (Berkeley: University of California Press, 1956), p. 43.
3. John Muir, *The Mountains of California* (Garden City, N.Y.: Doubleday, 1961), pp. 2–3.

1. THE WESTERN FOOTHILLS

1. This and subsequent quotations are by S. B. Parish, quoted in W. W. Robbins, "Alien Plants Growing Without Cultivation in California," [*University of California Agricultural Experiment Station at Berkeley*] *Bulletin,* no. 637 (July 1940).
2. John Woodhouse Audubon, *Audubon's Western Journal, 1849–1850* (Cleveland: Arthur H. Clark, 1906), p. 219.
3. This salamander is named for Johann Friedrich Eschscholtz, a surgeon and naturalist on two Russian expeditions to explore the western coast of North America, including California, in 1816 and 1824. The dance has been observed and

described by Robert C. Stebbins in *Amphibians of Western North America* (Berkeley: University of California Press, 1951).

4. This information about chamise was reported by Z. Naveh in "Mediterranean Ecosystems and Vegetation Types in California and Israel," *Ecology* 48 (spring 1967). James K. McPherson and Cornelius H. Muller found that the toxins accumulated on the surfaces of chamise leaves as a result of normal metabolism during the summer months and washed into the top inch of soil with the first rains ("Alleopathic Effects of *Adenostoma fasciculatum,* 'Chamise,' in the California Chaparral," *Ecological Monographs* 39 [spring 1969]).

5. Howard L. Cogswell, "The California Chaparral," in *The Bird Watcher's America,* ed. Olin S. Pettingill Jr. (New York: McGraw-Hill, 1965), p. 110.

6. The two Fry episodes are from Lowell Sumner and Joseph S. Dixon, *Birds and Mammals of the Sierra Nevada* (Berkeley: University of California Press, 1953), pp. 413–414.

7. Tracy I. Storer and Lloyd P. Tevis Jr., *California Grizzly* (Berkeley: University of California Press, 1955), p. 17.

2. MIDMOUNTAIN FORESTS

1. John Muir, "Proceedings of the Meeting of the Sierra Club (Nov. 23, 1895)," *Sierra Club Bulletin* 1 (Jan. 1896): 283.

2. Michael is cited by Arthur Cleveland Bent in *Life Histories of North American Birds of Prey,* pt. 2, Bulletin 170 of the U.S. National Museum (Washington, D.C., 1938), pp. 415–419.

3. Reported in "Deer-Coyote Incident," *Yosemite Nature Notes* 25 (April 1946).

3. GIANT SEQUOIAS

1. Quoted by Francis P. Farquhar in *History of the Sierra Nevada* (Berkeley: University of California Press in collaboration with the Sierra Club, 1965), p. 87.

2. Quoted by Walter Fry and John R. White in *Big Trees* (Stanford: Stanford University Press, 1938), p. 27.

3. Both species of redwoods have been widely planted over the world since the 1850s. They have thrived especially in Europe, Britain, and Australia, where some individuals are nearing an age of 150 years. Most are specimen trees. (From a University of the Pacific Faculty Research Lecture given by Ernest E. Stanford at Stockton in 1958.)

4. Richard J. Hartesveldt, letter to author, October 7, 1969.

4. FIRE ECOLOGY

1. The legend is told by Jean-Pierre Hallet in *Congo Kitabu* (New York: Random House, 1965), pp. 120–121.

2. From Theodora Kroeber, *Ishi in Two Worlds* (Berkeley: University of California Press, 1962), pp. 185–187.

3. From Omer C. Stewart, "Barriers to Understanding the Influence of Fire by Aborigines on Vegetation," *Proceedings, Second Annual Tall Timbers Fire Ecology Conference* (Tallahassee: Tall Timbers Research Station, 1963), p. 123.

4. Morton is quoted by Emil F. Ernst in "Forest Encroachment on the Meadows of Yosemite Valley," *Sierra Club Bulletin* 46 (Oct. 1961): 26–27.

5. Galen Clark's letter of August 30, 1894, to the Commissioners of Yosemite Valley is quoted by Ernst in "Forest Encroachment," p. 27.

6. The Miwok practices are described by Irene D. Paden and Margaret E. Schlichtmann in *The Big Oak Flat Road: An Account of Freighting from Stockton to Yosemite Valley* (Oakland: Emil P. Schlichtmann, 1955), pp. 121, 158.

7. James W. McFarland, "A Guide to the Giant Sequoias of Yosemite National Park," *Yosemite Nature Notes* 28 (June 1949): 75.

8. Floyd L. Otter, *The Men of Mammoth Forest* (Ann Arbor: Edwards Bros., 1963), p. 36.

9. W. Storrs Lee, *The Sierra* (New York: Putnam, 1962), pp. 204–206.

10. Quoted by Linnie Marsh Wolfe in *John of the Mountains* (Boston: Houghton Mifflin, 1938), pp. 173–174.

11. Mark Twain, *Roughing It* (New York: Harper, 1871), p. 140.

12. John Muir, *The Mountains of California* (New York: Doubleday, 1961), pp. 113–114.

13. Galen Clark, "A Yosemite Plea of 1907," *Yosemite Nature Notes* 6 (Feb. 1927): 13–14.

14. Harold Weaver, "Observations of Short Time and Long Time Effects of Prescribed Burning in Ponderosa Pine" (manuscript read at Teaford Forest Field Day, May 1966), p. 12.

15. Quoted by Edwin Way Teale in *The Wilderness World of John Muir* (Boston: Houghton Mifflin, 1954), pp. 221–222.

5. RED FIRS AND LODGEPOLES

1. The field observation of an unnamed ranger-naturalist in *Yosemite Nature Notes,* Feb. 1950.

2. Sequoia National Park observations are from Lowell Sumner and Joseph S. Dixon, *Birds and Mammals of the Sierra Nevada* (Berkeley: University of California Press, 1953), pp. 318–319.

3. Parkinson's story is quoted by Joseph Grinnell, Joseph S. Dixon, and Jean M. Linsdale in *Fur-bearing Mammals of California* (Berkeley: University of California Press, 1937), 1: 223–225.

4. From Lloyd P. Tevis Jr., "Pocket Gophers and Seedlings of Red Fir," *Ecology* 37 (April 1956).

5. Lloyd G. Ingles, *Mammals of the Pacific States* (Stanford: Stanford University Press, 1965), p. 96.
6. Lloyd G. Ingles, "Territoriality of Shrews and Men," a lecture given at Fresno State College, Fresno, California, 1964.

6. TREE LINE AND BEYOND

1. Charles Albert Harwell, "Some Birds of the Sierra Nevada," in *The Sierra Nevada: The Range of Light,* ed. Roderick Peattie (New York: Vanguard Press, 1947), p. 308.
2. For more on Lembert, see William E. Colby, "Jean Baptiste Lembert—Personal Memories," *Yosemite Nature Notes* 28 (Sept. 1949).
3. Wake is quoted by Elliot Diringer in "Scientists Link Animal Deaths to Acid Snow," *San Francisco Chronicle,* Feb. 19, 1990.
4. The activities of Evermann and Stevens are covered by J. H. Wales in *Trout of California* (Sacramento: California Department of Fish and Game, 1957).

7. IN THE RAIN SHADOW

1. Alexander C. Martin, Herbert S. Zim, and Arnold Nelson, *American Wildlife and Plants: A Guide to Wildlife Food Habits* (New York: Dover, 1961), p. 274.
2. *Angler's Guide to Lake Tahoe* (Reno: Nevada Fish and Game Commission, 1968).
3. Almo J. Cordone and Ted C. Frantz, "The Lake Tahoe Sport Fishery," *California Fish and Game* 52 (October 1966): 242.
4. John Le Conte's account is recorded by Charles R. Goldman in "The Bad News from Lake Tahoe," *Cry California* 3 (winter 1967).
5. George Wharton James, *Lake Tahoe* (Chicago: Charles T. Powner, 1956).
6. Quoted in Verna R. Johnston, "The Return of the Tule Elk," *Pacific Discovery* 31 (Dec. 1978).

PRINCIPAL REFERENCES

INTRODUCTION and
I. THE WESTERN FOOTHILLS

Axelrod, Daniel I. 1957. Late Tertiary floras and the Sierra Nevadan uplift. *Bulletin of the Geological Society of America* 68: Jan.

———. 1958. Evolution of the Madro-Tertiary geoflora. *Botanical Review* 24: July.

Bakker, Elna. 1984. *An Island Called California.* Berkeley: University of California Press.

Barbour, Michael, Bruce Pavlik, Frank Drysdale, and Susan Lindstrom. 1993. *California's Changing Landscapes.* Sacramento: California Native Plant Society.

Biswell, Harold H. 1961. Ecology of California grasslands. *Journal of Range Management* 9: Jan.

Busch, Robert H. 1996. *The Cougar Almanac.* New York: Lyons and Burford.

Gankin, Roman, and Jack Major. 1964. *Arctostaphylos myrtifolia,* its biology and relationship to the problem of endemism. *Ecology* 45: autumn.

Ingles, Lloyd G. 1965. *Mammals of the Pacific States.* Stanford: Stanford University Press.

Johnston, Verna R. 1994. *California Forests and Woodlands: A Natural History.* Berkeley: University of California Press.

Lawrence, George E. 1966. Ecology of vertebrate animals in relation to chaparral fire in the Sierra Nevada foothills. *Ecology* 47: spring.

Niehaus, Theodore F., and Charles L. Ripper. 1976. *A Field Guide to Pacific States Wildflowers.* Boston: Houghton Mifflin.

Ornduff, Robert. 1974. *Introduction to California Plant Life.* Berkeley: University of California Press.

Pavlik, Bruce M., Pamela Muick, Sharon Johnson, and Marjorie Popper. 1991. *Oaks of California.* Sacramento: Cachuma Press.

Peacock, Doug. 1996. Once there were bears: the rise and fall of the California grizzly. *Pacific Discovery* 49: summer.

Raven, Peter H., and Daniel Axelrod. 1978. *Origins and Relationships of the California Flora.* Berkeley: University of California Press.

Schoenherr, Allan A. 1992. *A Natural History of California.* Berkeley: University of California Press.

Stebbins, G. Ledyard. 1967. The Ione island of plant life. *California Native Plant Society Newsletter* 3: July.

Stebbins, G. Ledyard, and Jack Major. 1965. Endemism and speciation in the California flora. *Ecological Monographs* 35: winter.

Stebbins, Robert C. 1954. *Amphibians and Reptiles of Western North America.* New York: McGraw-Hill.

Whitney, Stephen. 1979. *A Sierra Club Naturalist's Guide to the Sierra Nevada.* San Francisco: Sierra Club.

Wolfe, Linnie Marsh. 1938. *John of the Mountains.* Boston: Houghton Mifflin.

2. MIDMOUNTAIN FORESTS

Barbour, Michael, Bruce Pavlik, Frank Drysdale, and Susan Lindstrom. 1993. *California's Changing Landscapes.* Sacramento: California Native Plant Society.

Basey, Harold E. 1976. *Discovering Sierra Reptiles and Amphibians.* Three Rivers, Calif.: Yosemite and Sequoia Natural History Associations.

Belisle, Anne M. 1951. Death of a scorpion. *Yosemite Nature Notes* 30: Sept.

Blackburn, Thomas C., and Kat Anderson, eds. 1993. *Before the Wilderness: Environmental Management by Native Californians.* Menlo Park: Ballena Press.

Garth, John S., and J. W. Tilden. 1963. *Yosemite Butterflies.* Arcadia, Calif.: Lepidoptera Foundation.

Gibbens, Robert P., and Harold F. Heady. 1964. *The Influence of Modern Man on the Vegetation of Yosemite Valley.* Manual No. 36. Berkeley: University of California Agricultural Experiment Station.

Grinnell, Joseph, and Tracy I. Storer. 1924. *Animal Life in the Yosemite.* Berkeley: University of California Press.

Hansen, Kevin. 1992. *Cougar: The American Lion.* Flagstaff: Northland Publishing.

Ingles, Lloyd G. 1965. *Mammals of the Pacific States.* Stanford: Stanford University Press.

Jameson, E. W., Jr., and Hans J. Peeters. 1988. *California Mammals.* Berkeley: University of California Press.

Kinloch, Bohun B., Melissa Marosy, and May E. Huddleston, eds. 1996. *Sugar Pine: Status, Values, and Roles in Ecosystems.* Proceedings of a symposium presented by the California Sugar Pine Management Committee (March 30–April 1, 1992, University of California, Davis). Oakland, Calif.: University of California, Division of Agriculture and Natural Resources.

Koenig, Walter D., and Ronald L. Mumme. 1997. The great egg-demolition derby. *Natural History* 106: June.

McLean, D. D. 1954. Mountain lions in California. *California Fish and Game* 40: April.

MacRoberts, Michael. 1974. Acorns, woodpeckers, grubs and scientists. *Pacific Discovery* 27: Oct.

Munz, Philip A. 1969. *California Mountain Wildflowers.* Berkeley: University of California Press.

Ritter, William E. 1938. *The California Woodpecker and I.* Berkeley: University of California Press.

Sierra Nevada Ecosystem Project Report (SNEP). 1996. Davis: Centers for Water and Wildland Resources, University of California, Davis.

Stewart, Bob. 1997. *Common Butterflies of California.* Point Reyes Station: West Coast Lady Press.

Young, Stanley P., and Edward A. Goldman. 1964. *The Puma.* New York: Dover.

Zwinger, Ann H. 1996. *Yosemite: Valley of Thunder.* San Francisco: Collins.

3. GIANT SEQUOIAS

Berland, Oscar. 1962. Giant Forest's reservation: the legend and the mystery. *Sierra Club Bulletin* 47: Dec.

Giant Sequoia Symposium. 1994. *Proceedings of the Symposium on Giant Sequoias: Their Place in the Ecosystem and Society* (June 23–25, 1992, Visalia, Calif.). Albany, Calif.: Pacific Southwest Research Station.

Grinnell, Joseph, and Tracy I. Storer. 1924. *Animal Life in the Yosemite.* Berkeley: University of California Press.

Hartesveldt, Richard J., H. T. Harvey, H. S. Shellhammer, and R. E. Stecker. 1975. *Giant Sequoias of the Sierra Nevada.* Washington, D.C.: Government Printing Office.

Harvey, H. Thomas, H. S. Shellhammer, and R. E. Stecker. 1980. *Giant Sequoia Ecology.* Washington, D.C.: Government Printing Office.

Ingles, Lloyd G. 1965. *Mammals of the Pacific States.* Stanford: Stanford University Press.

McFarland, James W. 1949. A guide to the giant sequoias of Yosemite National Park. *Yosemite Nature Notes* 28: June.

Otter, Floyd L. 1963. *The Men of Mammoth Forest.* Ann Arbor: Edwards Bros.

Peattie, Donald Culross. 1953. *A Natural History of Western Trees.* Boston: Houghton Mifflin.

Sequoia Natural History Association. 1988. Air pollution significant threat. *Seedlings* (newsletter of the Sequoia Natural History Association) 5: Jan.

Stebbins, G. Ledyard. 1948. The chromosomes and relationship of metasequoia and sequoia. *Science* 108: July 30.

Stocking, Stephen K., and Jack A. Rockwell. 1989. *Wildflowers of Sequoia and Kings Canyon National Parks.* Three Rivers, Calif.: Sequoia Natural History Association.

Sumner, Lowell, and Joseph S. Dixon. 1953. *Birds and Mammals of the Sierra Nevada.* Berkeley: University of California Press.

Teale, Edwin Way. 1954. *The Wilderness World of John Muir.* Boston: Houghton Mifflin.

Tweed, William. 1987. Born of fire. *National Parks* 61: Jan.

Waldo, Allen W. 1954. A seldom observed feeding habit of the pileated woodpecker. *Yosemite Nature Notes* 33: May.

Willard, Dwight. 1994. *Giant Sequoia Groves of the Sierra Nevada.* Privately published by Dwight Willard, P.O. Box 7304, Berkeley, CA 94707.

Wood, Richard Coke. 1949. *Tales of Old Calaveras.* Angels Camp, Calif.

Wuerthner, George. 1993. *California's Sierra Nevada.* Helena, Mt.: American and World Geographic Publishing.

4. FIRE ECOLOGY

Anderson, Kat. 1990. California Indian horticulture. *Fremontia* (newsletter of the California Native Plant Society) 18: April.

Babbitt, Bruce. 1995. To take up the torch. *American Forests* 101: July–Aug.

Barbour, Michael, and Valerie Whitworth. 1997. Fire and its role in rejuvenating plant communities. *Fremontia* 25: Oct.

Barrett, S. A., and E. W. Gifford. 1933. *Miwok Material Culture.* Milwaukee Public Museum Bulletin 2: March.

Berrey, Henry. 1987. Burning the sequoias. *Yosemite* 49(3).

Biswell, Harold H. 1961. The big trees and fire. *National Parks Magazine* 35: April.

———. 1959. Man and fire in ponderosa pine in Sierra Nevada of California. *Sierra Club Bulletin* 44: Oct.

———. 1989. *Prescribed Burning in California Wildlands Vegetation Management.* Berkeley: University of California Press.

Biswell, Harold H., Hayle Buchanan, and Robert P. Gibbens. 1966. Ecology of the vegetation of a second-growth sequoia forest. *Ecology* 47: summer.

Burcham, L. T. 1959. *Planned Burning as a Management Practice for California Wild Lands.* Sacramento: California Division of Forestry.

———. 1960. *The Influence of Fire on California's Pristine Vegetation.* Berkeley: University of California Extension Forestry Office, Agricultural Extension Service.

Colby, William E. 1953. Yosemite—then and now. *Yosemite Nature Notes* 32: March.

Conniff, Richard. 1989. Yellowstone's "rebirth" amid the ashes is not neat or simple, but it's real. *Smithsonian* 19: Sept.

Dudley, William R. 1896. Forest reservations: with a report on the Sierra reservation, California. *Sierra Club Bulletin* 1: Jan.

Hallenbeck, Cleve. 1940. *Alvar Nuñez Cabeza de Vaca: The Journey and Route of the First European to Cross the Continent of North America, 1534–1536.* Glendale, Calif.: Arthur H. Clark.

Hartesveldt, Richard J. 1963. Sequoias and human impact. *Sierra Club Bulletin* 48: Dec.

———. 1964. Fire ecology of the giant sequoias. *Natural History* 73: Dec.

King, Clarence. 1935. *Mountaineering in the Sierra Nevada.* New York: Norton (repr.).

Kroeber, Alfred L. 1953. *Handbook of the Indians of California.* Berkeley: California Book Co.

Larson, Geraldine B. 1966. Whitaker's Forest. *American Forests* 72: Sept.

Leopold, A. Starker, Stanley Cain, Clarence Cottam, Ira Gabrielson, and Thomas Kimball. 1963. Wildlife management in the national parks: a report to the secretary of the interior. *Audubon Magazine* 65: May–June.

McLean, Herbert E. 1995. Fighting fire with fire. *American Forests* 101: July–Aug.

Manson, Marsden. 1899. Observations on the denudation of vegetation: a suggested remedy for California. *Sierra Club Bulletin* 2: June.

Muir, John. 1876. God's first temples: how shall we preserve our forests? *Sacramento Record-Union:* Feb. 5.

———. 1901. Hunting big redwoods. *Atlantic Monthly* 88: Sept.

———. 1896. Proceedings of the meeting of the Sierra Club (Nov. 23, 1895). *Sierra Club Bulletin* 1: Jan.

Reynolds, Richard. 1959. Effect upon the forest of natural fire and aboriginal burning in the Sierra Nevada. Master's thesis, University of California, Berkeley.

Sauer, Carl O. 1950. Grassland climax, fire, and man. *Journal of Range Management* 3: Jan.

Weaver, Harold. 1964. Fire and management problems in ponderosa pine. *Proceedings, 3d Tall Timbers Conference.*

Williams, Ted. 1995. Only you can postpone forest fires. *Sierra* 80: July–Aug.

5. RED FIRS AND LODGEPOLES

Arno, Stephen F. 1973. *Discovering Sierra Trees.* Three Rivers, Calif.: Yosemite Natural History Association.

Barbour, Michael G., and Jack Major. 1988. *Terrestrial Vegetation of California.* Expanded ed. Sacramento: California Native Plant Society.

Bull, Evelyn L., and Mark G. Henjum. 1987. The neighborly great gray owl. *Natural History:* Sept.

Crenshaw, Elisabeth C. 1945. Slow freight to Tuolumne. *Yosemite Nature Notes* 24: Oct.

Ingles, Lloyd G. 1952. The ecology of the mountain pocket gopher, *Thomomys monticola. Ecology* 33: Jan.

———. 1958. Mammals of mountain meadows. *Pacific Discovery* 11: Jan./Feb.

———. 1960. A quantitative study on the activity of the dusky shrew. *Ecology* 41: Oct.

Kings River Team and Connie Gill, Pacific Southwest Station. 1997. Kings River sustainable forest ecosystem project. *Forestry Research West:* Sept.

McGinnis, Bridget. 1991. Great, gray, and mysterious. *Yosemite* 53(2).

McKeever, Sturgis. 1964. The biology of the golden-mantled ground squirrel. *Ecological Monographs* 34: autumn.

Orr, Robert T. 1949. *Mammals of Lake Tahoe.* San Francisco: California Academy of Sciences.

Seideman, David. 1997. Whither the spotted owl. *Audubon* 99: March–April.

Spencer, Wayne D., and William J. Zielinski. 1983. Predatory behavior of pine martens. *Journal of Mammalogy* 64(4).

Struble, George R. 1967. Insect enemies in the natural control of the lodgepole needle miner. *Journal of Economic Entomology* 60: Feb.

Sumner, Lowell, and Joseph S. Dixon. 1953. *Birds and Mammals of the Sierra Nevada.* Berkeley: University of California Press.

Telford, Allan D. 1961. Features of the lodgepole needle miner parasite complex in California. *Canadian Entomologist* 93: May.

Telford, Allan D., and Steven G. Herman. 1963. Chickadee helps check insect invasion. *Audubon Magazine* 65: March–April.

Tevis, Lloyd P., Jr. 1953. Stomach contents of chipmunks and mantled squirrels in northeastern California. *Journal of Mammalogy* 34: Aug.

Todd, Paul. 1989. In search of the elusive Sierra mountain beaver. *Yosemite* 51(3).

Weeden, Norman F. 1996. *A Sierra Nevada Flora.* Berkeley: Wilderness Press.

Wentz, Charles M. 1950. Experimenting with a coral king snake. *Yosemite Nature Notes* 29: Aug.

Zielinski, William J., and Connie Gill, Pacific Southwest Station. 1997. A sensitive measure of forest ecosystem health. *Forestry Research West:* July.

6. TREE LINE AND BEYOND

Ahern, Julie. 1996. Amphibians under siege. *Yosemite* 58: spring.

Bartholomew, Orland. 1930. A winter in the high Sierra. *Sierra Club Bulletin* 15: Feb.

Broadbooks, Harold E. 1965. Ecology and distribution of the pikas of Washington and Alaska. *American Mid-Land Naturalist* 73: April.

Clausen, Jens. 1965. Population studies of alpine and subalpine races of conifers and willows in the California high Sierra Nevada. *Evolution* 19: April.

Edgar, Blake. 1996. Silent nights in Yosemite. *Pacific Discovery* 49: fall.

Flynn, John. 1991. Forest without trees. *Amicus Journal* 13: winter.

Forstenzer, Martin. 1994. Ozone damage to forests. *Audubon* 96: July–Aug.

Fry, Walter. 1930. The wolverine and the badger. *Sierra Club Bulletin* 15: Feb.

Gaines, David. 1988. *Birds of Yosemite and the East Slope.* Lee Vining, Calif.: Artemesia Press.

Garth, John S., and J. W. Tilden. 1986. *California Butterflies*. Berkeley: University of California Press.

Grinnell, Joseph, Joseph S. Dixon, and Jean M. Linsdale. 1937. *Fur-bearing Mammals of California*. 2 vols. Berkeley: University of California Press.

Henson, Ryan. 1997. Sequoia National Forest takes small steps to improve grazing practices. *Wilderness Record* 22: July.

Hill, Mary. 1975. *Geology of the Sierra Nevada*. Berkeley: University of California Press.

Hubbs, Carl L., and Orthello L. Wallis. 1948. The native fish fauna of Yosemite National Park and its preservation. *Yosemite Nature Notes* 27: Dec.

Ingles, Lloyd G. 1965. *Mammals of the Pacific States*. Stanford: Stanford University Press.

Jameson, E. W., Jr., and Hans J. Peeters. 1988. *California Mammals*. Berkeley: University of California Press.

Johnston, Verna R. 1994. *California Forests and Woodlands: A Natural History*. Berkeley: University of California Press.

Karlstrom, Ernest L. 1962. *The Toad Genus Bufo in the Sierra Nevada of California*. University of California Publications in Zoology 62, No. 1.

Kendeigh, S. Charles. 1961. *Animal Ecology*. New York: Prentice-Hall.

Klikoff, Lionel G. 1965. Microenvironmental influence on vegetational pattern near timberline in the central Sierra Nevada. *Ecological Monographs* 35: spring.

Lanner, Ronald M. 1996. *Made for Each Other: A Symbiosis of Birds and Pines*. New York: Oxford University Press.

Luoma, Jon R. 1997. Vanishing frogs. *Audubon* 99: June.

Lynch, Colum. 1996. Global warming. *Amicus Journal* 18: spring.

Ochsner, David C. 1952. A badger secures his meal. *Yosemite Nature Notes* 31: Aug.

Rauber, Paul. 1997. Heat wave. *Sierra* 82: Oct.

Schneegas, Edward R., et al. 1965. Habitat management plan for native golden trout waters, Inyo National Forest. Mimeographed. U.S. Forest Service, Bishop, Calif.

Schneider, Stephen H. 1997. *Laboratory Earth: The Planetary Gamble We Can't Afford to Lose*. New York: Basic Books.

Sharsmith, Carl W. 1940. A contribution to the history of the alpine flora of the Sierra Nevada. Ph.D. diss., University of California, Berkeley.

Sumner, Lowell, and Joseph S. Dixon. 1953. *Birds and Mammals of the Sierra Nevada*. Berkeley: University of California Press.

Teale, Edwin Way. 1954. *The Wilderness World of John Muir*. Boston: Houghton Mifflin.

Trefil, James. 1997. Nitrogen. *Smithsonian* 28: Oct.

Wales, J. H. 1957. *Trout of California*. Sacramento: California Department Fish and Game.

Zwinger, Ann H., and Beatrice E. Willard. 1972. *Land Above the Trees: A Guide to American Alpine Tundra*. New York: Harper and Row.

Barraclough, Mary Edith. 1951. A trip to Mono Lake and the Mono Craters. *Yosemite Nature Notes* 30: Aug.

Brennan, Kathleen. 1996. Plummeting bighorn sheep populations prompt concern. *Yosemite* 58: summer.

Brewer, William H. 1949. *Up and Down California.* Berkeley: University of California Press.

Calhoun, Alex. 1967. Research dividends at Lake Tahoe. *Outdoor California* 28: May–June.

Christensen, Jon. 1997. The greening of gambling's golden boy. *New York Times,* July 6.

Christenson, Daniel P. 1994. Golden trout of the little Kern River. *Outdoor California* 55: July–Aug.

Cordone, Almo J., and Ted C. Frantz. 1968. An evaluation of trout planting in Lake Tahoe. *California Fish and Game* 54: April.

Dasmann, William P. 1958. *Big Game of California.* Sacramento: California Department of Fish and Game.

Downs, James F. 1966. *The Two Worlds of the Washo.* New York: Holt, Rinehart.

Fischer, Jon K. 1994. Future bright for California elk. *Outdoor California* 55: June.

Forstenzer, Martin. 1997. What's wrong in the Sierra. *Audubon* 99: March–April.

Frantz, Ted C., and Almo J. Cordone. 1967. Observations on deepwater plants in Lake Tahoe, California and Nevada. *Ecology* 48: late summer.

Goldman, Charles R. 1967. The bad news from Lake Tahoe. *Cry California* 3: winter.

———. 1993. Lake Tahoe: a microcosm for the study of the impact of urbanization on fragile ecosystems. In R. H. Platt et al., eds., *The Ecological City: Preserving and Restoring Urban Biodiversity.* Amherst: University of Massachusetts Press.

Harper, Harold T., Beverly H. Harry, and William D. Bailey. 1958. The chukar partridge in California. *California Fish and Game* 44: Jan.

Hart, John. 1996. *Storm Over Mono: The Mono Lake Battle and the California Water Future.* Berkeley: University of California Press.

Hinkle, George H., and Bliss M. Hinkle. 1949. *Sierra Nevada Lakes.* New York: Bobbs Merrill.

Jameson, E. W., Jr., and Hans J. Peeters. 1988. *California Mammals.* Berkeley: University of California Press.

Johnsgard, Paul A. 1967. Dawn rendezvous on the lek. *Natural History* 76: March.

Lanner, Ronald M. 1981. *The Piñon Pine.* Reno: University of Nevada Press.

———. 1984. *Trees of the Great Basin: A Natural History.* Reno: University of Nevada Press.

Lee, W. Storrs. 1962. *The Sierra.* New York: Putnam.

McCullough, Dale R., and Edward R. Schneegas. 1966. Winter observations on the Sierra Nevada bighorn sheep. *California Fish and Game* 52: April.

McLean, Donald D. 1958. *Upland Game of California.* Sacramento: California Department of Fish and Game.

Manson, Marsden. 1899. Observations on the denudation of vegetation—a suggested remedy for California. *Sierra Club Bulletin* 2: June.

Nord, Eamor C. 1965. Autecology of bitterbrush in California. *Ecological Monographs* 35: summer.

Ryser, Fred A., Jr. 1985. *Birds of the Great Basin: A Natural History.* Reno: University of Nevada Press.

Scott, John W. 1942. Mating behavior of the sage grouse. *Auk* (journal of the American Ornithologists Union) 59: Oct.

Seymour, George. 1960. *Furbearers of California.* Sacramento: California Department of Fish and Game.

Sierra Nevada Ecosystem Project [SNEP] Report. 1996. Davis: Centers for Water and Wildland Resources, University of California, Davis.

Storer, Tracy I., and Robert L. Usinger. 1964. *Sierra Nevada Natural History.* Berkeley: University of California Press.

Wales, J. H. 1957. *Trout of California.* Sacramento: California Department of Fish and Game.

Wehausen, John. 1997. The future of bighorn sheep. *Mono Lake Newsletter* 20: summer.

Wells, Philip V., and Rainer Berger. 1967. Late Pleistocene history of coniferous woodland in the Mohave Desert. *Science* 155: March 31.

INDEX

Duckweed (*Lemna minor*), 166
Dudley, William, 78

Eagle, golden (*Aquila chysaetos*), 130
Eastern slope: birds of, 152–53, 166–69; Jeffrey pine forest of, 148–49; mining and logging on, 160–62; Mono Lake region of, 149–50; native species of, 167–72; nonnative species of, 165–67; pinyon pine forests of, 150–53; plant communities of, 146, 147, 169–70; red fir forests of, 147–48; Washo valley of, 157–58. *See also* Washo Indians
Eisen, Gustav, 33, 57
Endemics (localized species): of alpine Sierra, 128–29; of western foothills, 31–33
Endlicher, Stephan, 55
Environmental impact: of acid precipitation, 140–41; of air pollution, 58–59; of disturbed food chain, 173–74; of fire/fire suppression, 77–81, 83; of global warming, 141; of logging, 48, 78–79, 162–64; of sheep/cattle overgrazing, 9–10, 141–42, 168–69; SNEP study of, 48, 175; of urbanization, 165; of water diversion, 149–50
Ermine (*Mustela erminea*), 93. *See also* Weasel
Eschscholtz, Johann Friedrich, 181–82n3
Evermann, Barton, 143
Evolution: of foothill woodland, 13–15; of golden trout coloration, 143; mountaintop investigation of, 122–23; shrew survival and, 107–8; of Yosemite toad, 139–40

Fages, Pedro, 181n1
Feeding habits. *See* Foraging/feeding habits; Hunting/feeding habits
Filaree (*Erodium*), 9, 10, 11, 30
Finch: Cassin's (*Carpodacus cassinii*), 114, 115, 118; gray-crowned rosy (*Leucosticte arctoa*), 129–30, 132
Fir: red (*Abies magnifica*), 48, 86–87, 147; white (*A. concolor*), 36, 47, 48, 83, 147. *See also* Douglas fir
Fire: chaparral's adaptation to, 30–31; drill's production of, 71–72; Indians' use of, 47, 72–74; lightning, 74–76; logging, 78–79; as prescribed burns, 81–82, 84–85; results of suppression of, 80–81, 83; set by shepherds, 77–78
Fire drill, 71–72
Fish: bluegill (*Lepomis macrochirus*), 144; California roach (*Hesperoleucus symmetricus*), 142; hardhead (*Mylopharodon conocephalus*), 142; minnow, 142, 159; mountain whitefish (*Prosopium williamsoni*), 158, 163–64; Piute sculpin (*Cottus beldingi*), 164; riffle sculpin (*Cottus gulosus*), 142; Sacramento squawfish (*Ptychocheilus grandis*), 142; Sacramento sucker (*Catostomus occidentalis*), 142; Tahoe sucker (*Catostomus tahoensis*), 158, 164; Tui chub (*Gila bicolor*), 164. *See also* Salmon; Trout
Fisher (*Martes pennanti*), 96–98
Flycatcher, olive-sided (*Contopus borealis*), 111, 114, 115, 116
Flying squirrel, northern (*Glaucomys sabrinus*), 45–46. *See also* Squirrel, ground
Font, Pedro, 1, 181n1
Foothill woodland: grasses of, 6–9, 10; pine and oak of, 15–16; tarweeds of, 10–11; Tertiary evolution of, 13–15; wildflowers of, 11–13
Foraging/feeding habits: of acorn woodpecker, 42–43; of Belding's ground squirrel, 134; of blue grouse, 113; of California ground squirrel, 114; of California quail, 24; of chickaree, 45, 65–66, 67 fig.; of chipmunk, 90–91, 92–93; of chukar, 167; of Clark's nutcracker, 130, 131 fig., 132; of deer mouse, 68; of flying squirrel, 45–46; of golden-mantled ground squirrel, 91–93; of mountain beaver, 105–6; of mule deer, 170; of pika, 125; of pileated woodpecker, 63–64; of pinyon jay, 153; of pocket gopher, 102; of porcupine, 99–100; of rosy finch, 129–30; of shrew, 106–7; of western gray squirrel, 45; of white-headed woodpecker, 64; of woodrat, 27, 151. *See also* Hunting/feeding habits
Forbs (broad-leaved herbs), 7, 10

Ripgut grass (*Bromus rigidus*), 9, 10
Ritter, William, 42, 43
Roach, California (*Hesperoleucus symmetricus*), 142
Rockefeller, John D., Jr., 58
Rock rabbit (pika), 124–26, 127
Rockrose (*Helianthemum suffrutescens*), 31
Rocky Mountains, 2, 14, 29, 84, 114, 116, 128
Roosevelt, Theodore, 143
Root-rot fungus (*Heterobasidion annosum*), 47
Rose, mountain (*Rosa*), 167
Roughing It (Twain), 79
Rushes, 166
Rust, white pine blister (*Cronartium ribicola*), 47–48

Sacramento *Record-Union*, 78
Sagebrush (*Artemisia*), 146, 167, 169; big (*A. tridentata*), 146
Salamanders: acid precipitation and, 140–41; arboreal (*Aneides lugubris*), 17–18; California slender (*Batrachoseps attenuatus*), 18; limestone (*Hydromantes brunus*), 140; lungless, 18; Mount Lyell (*Hydromantes platycephalus*), 140; Sierra Nevada (*Ensatina eschscholtzi platensis*), 17, 181–82n3; tiger (*Ambystoma tigrinum*), 140
Salmon, 163; kokanee (*Oncorhynchus nerka*), 144, 164
Saltbush (*Atriplex*), 160
Sandpiper, spotted (*Actitis macularia*), 142
San Joaquin River, 33
Sapsucker, Williamson's (*Sphyrapicus thyroideus*), 116
Sauer, Carl, 73
Save-the-Redwoods League, 58
Scorpion (*Vejovis*), 40
Sculpin: Piute (*Cottus beldingi*), 164; riffle (*C. gulosus*), 142
Sedge (*Carex*), 127, 166
Self-cutting ability: of lizards, 39–40
Senecio, 116, 129
Sentinel Dome, 112

Sequoia (*Sequoia gigantea, Sequoiadendron giganteum*): birds of, 62–65; Boole, 57, 60; federal conservation of, 58–59; fire scars on, 83–84; fire suppression's impact on, 80–81, 83; General Grant, 60, 61; General Sherman, 59–60, 61; global planting of, 182n3; Grizzly Giant, 61, 75; Haverford, 84; lightning strikes on, 75–76; location of, 56–57, 173; logging exploitation of, 57–58; McKinley, 60; mammals of, 65–66, 68; naming of, 54–55; prescribed burning of, 81–82, 84–85; rubber boa of, 69; seed dissemination of, 65–66, 67 fig.; size/longevity of, 59, 60–62; Stump, 60–61; tannin protection of, 65; Telescope, 75, 84
Sequoia National Park, 29, 81, 141, 170; Giant Forest of, 57–58, 59–60
Serra, Junípero, 7
Serviceberry (*Amelanchier*), 112
Seton, Ernest Thompson, 66
Sheep: bighorn (*Ovis canadensis californiana*), 171–72; grazing pressure of, 9–10, 77–78, 141–42, 168–69, 174; post–Civil War increase of, 76–77
Shellhammer, Howard, 61
Shield leaf (*Streptanthus tortuosus*), 89
Shinleaf (*Pyrola secunda*), 88, 89
Shooting star (*Dodecatheon*), 106, 116; alpine (*D. alpinum*), 129
Shrew (*Sorex*), 106–8, 118
Shrimp, brine (*Artemia monica*), 150
Side-blotched lizard (*Uta stansburiana*), 40
Sierra Club, 5, 58, 144
Sierra Forest Preserve, 79
Sierra Madre Occidental of Mexico, 14
Sierra Nevada: age of, 3–4; closed food chain of, 174; duration of droughts in, 50; glacial history of, 119–21, 128; length/heights of, 3; localized species of, 31–33; as middle mountain barrier, 2–3; naming of, 1, 181n1; parks/monument/forests of, 5; road maps of, 177–80; Tertiary changes in, 13–15. *See also* Eastern slope; High Sierra; Midmountain forests; Red fir forest; Western foothills

Toyon berry (*Heteromeles arbutifolia*), 22

Treefrog, Pacific (*Hyla regilla*), 138

Trout: cutthroat (*Oncorhynchus clarki*), 142–43; golden (*O. aguabonita*), 142, 143, 163; Lahontan cutthroat (*O. clarki henshawi*), 158, 162–63; rainbow (*O. mykiss*), 142–44, 163. *See also* Brook trout; Brown trout; Lake trout

Truckee River, 142, 159, 161, 163

Truffles, 92

Tule elk (*Cervus elaphus nannodes*), 170–71

Tule Elk Refuge, 170–71

Tuolumne Meadows, 116–17, 133–34, 135, 177

Twain, Mark, 79, 149

U.S. Forest Service, 48, 58, 141

U.S. National Park Service. *See* National Park Service

Vetch (*Vicia*), 106

Vireo, Hutton's (*Vireo huttoni*), 41

Virginia City, 160, 161

Visalia Weekly Delta, 58

Vole (*Microtus montanus;* meadow mouse), 104–5

Wake, David, 141

Waldo, Allen, 63–64

Walker, Frank, 58

Walker, Joseph Reddeford, 55

Walker River, 142, 157

Warblers: black-throated gray (*Dendroica nigrescens*), 41; hermit (*Dendroica occidentalis*), 41, 115; MacGillivray's (*Oporornis tolmiei*), 41; Nashville's (*Vermivora ruficapilla*), 41, 115; orange-crowned (*Vermivora celata*), 41, 115; Wilson's (*Wilsonia pusilla*), 41, 108, 115; yellow (*Dendroica petechia*), 41; yellow-rumped (*Dendroica coronata*), 41, 109, 114

Washo Indians, 47, 154; food gathering by, 159–60; game hunting by, 155–57; gold discovery's impact on, 160; Lake Tahoe and, 158–59, 165

Wasp, parasitic, 118

Weasel: hunting/feeding habits of, 93–95, 109; long-tailed (*Mustela frenata*), 93; protective traits of, 95; short-tailed (*M. erminea*), 93

Weaver, Harold, 82

Wellingtonia gigantea, 55. *See also* Sequoia

Wentz, Charles, 113

Western fence lizard (*Sceloporus*), 39

Western foothills: chaparral wildlife of, 22–25, 27–29; climate of, 6, 7, 10–11; grasses of, 6–10; localized species of, 31–33; marginal zone of, 16–19; plant communities of, 6; tarweeds of, 10–11; Tertiary changes in, 13–15; wildflowers of, 11–13. *See also* Chaparral; Foothill woodland

Western juniper. *See* Juniper, Sierra

Whitaker's Forest, 68, 82

Whitefish, mountain (*Prosopium williamsoni*), 158, 163–64

Whitethorn, mountain (*Ceanothus cordulatus*), 89, 112

White-Inyo Mountains, 151

Whitney, Mount, 3, 128, 147

Whitney Allotment, 142

Wildflowers: John Woodhouse Audubon on, 12–13; of high Sierra, 127, 128–29; of red fir forest, 87–89; of western foothills, 11–13

Wild oat (*Avena*), 9, 10

Willow, snow (*Salix nivalis*), 128

Wolverine (*Gulo gulo*), 136–38

Woodpecker, 118; acorn (*Melanerpes formicivorus*), 42–44; pileated (*Dryocopus pileatus*), 63–64; white-headed (*Picoides albolarvatus*), 64, 115

Wood-pewee (*Contopus sordidulus*), 111, 114, 115, 116

Woodrat: bushytail (*Neotoma cinerea*), 25–27; dusky-footed (*N. fuscipes*), 25, 27; foraging habits of, 27, 151; trading technique of, 25–27

Woolyleaf ceanothus (*Ceanothus tomentosus*), 31

Wren, canyon (*Catherpes mexicanus*), 40

Wrentit (*Chamaea fasciata*), 23–24

Yaqui Basin (Sonora, Mexico), 29
Yerba santa (*Eriodictyon*), 33
Yosemite National Park, 58, 141, 170, 177
Yosemite Valley, 51, 144; canyon live oak of, 38; fire dangers to, 78, 80–81; glacial history of, 120; Indians' management of, 74; koo-chah-bee delicacy of, 150; needle miner outbreaks in, 117–18; state protection of, 58
Young, Stanley, 53

Compositor:	Impressions Book and Journal Services, Inc.
Text:	12/14.5 Adobe Garamond
Display:	Perpetua and Adobe Garamond
Printer:	Edwards Brothers, Inc.
Binder:	Edwards Brothers, Inc.